Planned Purity®

for parents

*Creating an Environment for Responsible Sexuality,
Starting with the Heart*

*Based on the Planned Purity seminar
presented by* PurityWorks®

by Jennie Bishop
author of the best-selling children's book
The Princess and the Kiss

Xulon PRESS

To all the readers of
The Princess and the Kiss
whose passion to save the kiss
inspired *Planned Purity*

CONTENTS

ACKNOWLEDGMENTS

I am continually flabbergasted by the number of people it takes to get a book into print and beyond, not to mention the cheerleaders of every sort who have encouraged me to finish this very "serious" book without pictures (from a children's author).

I'm grateful for the faithfulness and generosity of PurityWorks friends Kirk and Michelle Solberg, David and Sharon Deetz, Edgerton Christian Church, George Fender, Rich Milam, Gil and Jan Diaz, Larry and June Vollmer, Tim and Kim Wright, Mark and Wendy Nation and others who have kept the office up and running and provided for this project in so many ways.

Thanks to the readers who made wonderful notes on my first draft. You helped transform this book into something really usable. I'm grateful for your open eyes and open hearts, your honesty and grace. I am indebted to you, Jan Bangle, Dawn Fox, Margi McCombs, Rich Milam, Rob and Amy Beckman, Laurie Copeland, Sharon Mitchell, Shelly Shafer, Beth Lemmon, Jan Diaz, Julie Campbell, Robin Fogle, Kathy Pedersen, Janet Surette and Betty Steele Everett.

Thanks to Xulon for my first foray into self-publishing. You've made the publishing process relatively simple, and I know that's not easy.

Thanks to Robin Stanley, who devoted hours of work to proposals and forced me to write outlines. Your heart is behind all this work. I'm so grateful to have you as a friend, always.

Thanks to Debbie Poulalion, an excellent, humble, and personally invested editor.

Thanks to Ginger Schmaus, another gifted editor and last-minute treasure.

Thanks to Shavanna Pinder and Anthony Ganus for cranking out artwork on a crazy schedule.

Thanks to my daughters, who have lived with the pressure of being the children of both a pastor and a "purity queen." You've turned out beautifully, and I wouldn't trade you.

Thanks to Randy, who has always believed in me and put up with anxiety, whining, breakdowns, rush edits, and all kinds of ridiculous shenanigans. I would rather have survived these things with you than anyone else on earth.

Finally, thanks to Mom and Dad, my biggest fans in heaven and on the farm.

And also, to any I may have missed, thank you for remembering that the house is surrounded by grace.

INTRODUCTION

"Mom, all my girlfriends have boyfriends. I need a boyfriend. Someone already stole somebody else's boyfriend!"

In 1999 our family lived in the sleepy city of Anderson, Indiana, where I worked as an editor at a little publishing house while my husband, Randy, took on the role of stay-home dad for our two little girls. The oldest made this urgent declaration after school one day. She was in kindergarten.

As parents we were trying very hard to be intentional about raising our daughters. We wanted them to be comfortable with their sexuality in appropriate ways as they grew. But we hadn't expected to deal with boyfriends in kindergarten!

That night as our little girls, ages three and six, snuggled in their beds, I prayed. I had painted a bright jungle fantasy on their violet bedroom walls to wrap them in beautiful dreams as they slept. But I was anxious about them being caught off-guard in a jungle of real-life risks. How could Randy and I teach them now about the importance of friendship over romantic relationships? Was it even realistic, with these kinds of early influences, to expect them to "save themselves" for marriage?

Little did I know that the plan set in motion that night would contribute to addressing the concerns of parents all over the world.

The first answer came in the form of a children's story I wrote, titled *The Princess and the Kiss*. The picture book featured a princess saving her "kiss" (portrayed as a ball of light) for a prince.

What does it mean to "save a kiss"? This ongoing conversation is one of my favorite discussions, one I carry on through written resources and talks with boys, girls, children and adults all over the world. More than 350,000 books later, I am still wrestling with that question.

Though I love the thought of saving one's first kiss for the commitment of marriage and have been present at such beautiful events, the "kiss" in my children's book symbolizes so much more than lips touching. In giving over their kisses, the Princess and her husband are surrendering themselves to each other, body and soul. This concept goes far deeper than a simple kiss (although I'd love to see the practice of kissing be returned to its status as a sign of commitment and not just a recreational pursuit or casual exchange).

The pursuit of sexual abstinence is vital, but must be precluded by the development of a good heart.

My hope is to broaden this discussion of the kiss, of purity, and of abstinence through this book. *The pursuit of sexual abstinence for a season and honorable purpose is viable and even vital, but must be precluded by instruction and the development of a good (others-centered)heart.*

Included here is a concept for the development of families and children of integrity and respect who honor the sexes and their differences deeply, deeply enough to question present practices of dating, casual sex and even emotional intimacy.

I am not writing this book to convert you, if you are not a Christian. Though biblical concepts are presented here and of course I care about spiritual wellness, I have no wish to present this message to a Christian community alone. I believe it is suitable for people of many faiths.

I am not in this for the money. (I wish!) I am a child of Midwestern farm life, and being a traveling speaker is not necessarily what I envisioned for my life. On many days I would be glad to sit on my back porch and watch flowers bloom.

But now I've seen too much, read too much, lived through too much. I really can't stay on that porch anymore, and in spirit I have left it for good.

I have seen teens of my friends with babies of their own. I've seen Ukrainian orphans who have been bartered for sexual favors. I've seen AIDS rampant in Africa and across the globe. I've seen pornography creep over the world like a cancer and infect my own life and the lives of my family.

But I've also seen the difference that a good heart AND responsible abstinence can make, in my life and in others'. I've seen couples at the altar share their first kiss (and report incredible married sex lives). I've seen orphan girls in North Ukraine freed from fear because someone explained to them what happened during menstruation and how babies were made. I've seen African college students ignited by a desire to be free of immorality and AIDS. And I've seen restoration from pornographic habits and histories of immorality in our own family.

I believe that men and women with good hearts can change the world. I believe good hearts are the answer to personal problems, social problems and global problems like the AIDS crisis. I believe that *a good heart is the critical foundation for sexual abstinence outside marriage,* and that any parent can train their children to guard their hearts and bodies.

My children are older now and our home is in a metropolitan area instead of a cornfield. But in both the girls' rooms there is a bell jar with a glowing "kiss" inside (a hidden light bulb), fashioned by their father and reminiscent of the kiss in *The Princess and the Kiss.* These kisses are a constant reminder of how our family's hearts have been changed and how others' hearts are being changed all over the world.

A good heart is the critical foundation for sexual abstinence outside marriage.

The pursuit of a good heart is a path available to all of us. May these concepts lead you and others to freedom and peace, and may all "kisses" be spent well and wisely.

Jennie Bishop

Part 1

The Ground—Preparing to Build

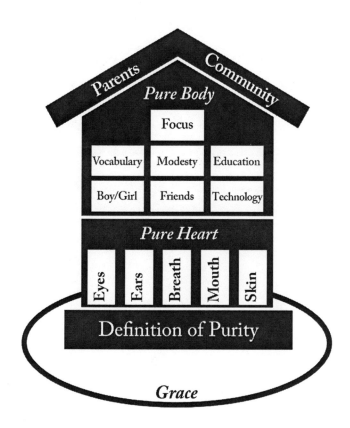

Chapter 1

Planned Purity

M ost of the world seems to plan for sexual *activity*, not for sexual *responsibility*. Condoms are becoming more available for middle and high school students. Entertainment shows young children involved in romantic relationships. Parents give sexual advice saying, "when you're ready," rather than, "when you're married." Many take their daughters to doctors for birth-control pills.

The definition of *responsibility* includes being obligated and/or willing to give account. Responsibility includes the consideration of the well-being of a member of the opposite sex that one truly cares for. With the variety of sexual diseases transmitted simply by touch, the deep emotional problems that can result (especially in women) from "hook-ups," the now-proven dangerous effects of pornography (brought starkly into light in the book *Pornified* by Pamela Paul) and the obvious opportunity for an unexpected pregnancy and the resulting impact on the child's life, it should be obvious that casual sex is irresponsible, even in the extreme. But American culture (and others) has decided to ignore statistics that favor long-term responsibility in favor of immediate personal gratification. This is an indication of a disorder of our hearts.

Many experts accept sexual activity as a fact of life. For example, a mom who suspected that her daughter was engaged in sexual activity asked for advice from a well-known expert on teen behavior. The expert responded: "To forbid your daughter to have sex or to deny her contraception is naïve….Telling a sexually interested or active teenager to not engage in sexual activity is like shoveling sand against the adolescent tide."[1]

In other words, the expert said, "Give up! It's impossible for teens to follow a standard of purity."

I believe as parents we can push *against* those norms. Parents are capable of planning for responsible abstinence—rather than promiscuity—for their children. That's why this program has been presented under the title of Planned Purity and not Planned Parenthood.

Sexual abstinence for teens is a hot issue for concerned parents. Consider these statistics from the National Campaign to Prevent Teen Pregnancy:

- Nearly one in five adolescents has had intercourse before his or her fifteenth birthday (this does not include figures for other kinds of sexual activity). At age twelve, 4 to 5 percent have had sex, increasing to 10 percent at age thirteen, and 18 to19 percent at age fourteen.

- Approximately one in seven sexually experienced fourteen-year-old girls report having been pregnant.

- Parents tend to be unaware of what their children are actually doing sexually—only about a third of parents of sexually experienced fourteen-year-olds knew that their child had sex.

- Dating in general (defined as an unsupervised social outing) and dating someone older, in particular, greatly increases the chances of having sex. [2]

Fear and a desperate desire to keep kids sexually innocent have resulted in a variety of teen abstinence programs, focusing on the age when sexual issues begin to obviously appear.

Programs for teens are excellent and necessary. They sometimes make the difference in motivating a teen to abstain from sex until marriage. But abstinence training for teens may not be as effective as hoped. Statistics show that an "abstinence pledge" alone only delays sex for about eighteen months, with 88 percent of pledge makers eventually choosing otherwise.[3]

Abstinence training in the teen years, important as it is, is not the whole answer. First of all, heart formation needs to begin in the younger years as a foundation for the embrace of true sexual responsibility. In addition, emphasis on teen abstinence has overshadowed the need for continued integrity and abstinence *after* high school, during college and into single or married adulthood. It isn't enough to be "pure" *until* marriage—*a good heart and responsibly abstinent body is important in every age and stage of life!*

Before your child's teen years arrive, much information is available to help you guide him or her on a path of sexual responsibility for a lifetime, not just upon entrance to high school. That is real, transformational purity: a lifetime pursuit, starting with the shaping of the heart.

Now—if you're the parent of a teen, don't lose hope because you feel as though you missed training in the younger years. It's never too late to start, even if virginity has been lost. Picture your situation this way: your child has a boat that will carry them through the waters of life. Training during the younger years mostly consists of fortifying the boat so it can be sent into adolescence watertight. If training begins during the teen years, you will need to repair some leaks in the boat (misunder-

Abstinence training in the teen years is not the whole answer to sexual purity.

standings about responsible sexuality or early forays into sexual activity). The job can be done either way, but different tools are needed. The good news is: it absolutely can be done.

Visualize the Goal

The first step toward training your child is to visualize your goal, which is to build a household of purity for you and your family. Remember that a key part of the training will be implementation of the strategies for yourself as well as for your children.

This book will show you how to build this structure from foundation to roof. You'll find tools for training young children and also ways to add missing "bricks" if you begin training in later years. You will be equipped to make the pursuit of a good heart and sexual responsibility a daily exercise rather than a one-shot experience that may or may not result in a lasting impact.

To help you visualize this process, the book is organized according to the Planned Purity diagram that you see at the beginning of this chapter. At the beginning of each section, a certain area of this diagram will be highlighted, reminding you of which part of the "house" we're working on at the time. Once you've been through this training, you'll easily be able to use the diagram to explain it to your family and others.

Here is a brief description of what you'll gain from each part.

Part 1: The Ground—Preparing to Build

No developer builds a house without preparing the plot of ground. This section introduces intentional planning, healthy relationships and an awareness of the inner life. It describes the relational "site preparation" necessary for building effectively.

Part 2: The Foundation—Understanding Purity

The foundation for Planned Purity is having an accurate definition of *purity*. It's so much more than choices about sexuality!

Part 3: The First Floor—Five Doors

The first floor shows the formation of a good heart through guarding input from the Five Doors (senses). The Five Doors concept is the most basic and vital element of Planned Purity training, and easy enough for a very young child to understand. At the end of each door lesson, you'll get specific action steps for making it real in your household.

Part 4: The Second Floor—Seven Windows

The second floor discusses practical standards relating to sexual responsibility. These may be implemented after purity of heart is understood, and even during its pursuit. The boundaries described in the second floor need the support of the first floor to be effective. At the end of each window lesson, you'll get a list of specific opportunities for taking action on the lesson.

Part 5: The Roof—Accountability

A roof provides protection for the entire house. In our model, the roof represents the protective role of parent and community in providing authentic modeling, accountability, mentoring and evaluation of resources.

Part 6: The Fence—Security in Grace

Finally, like a white picket fence, grace surrounds the entire house. Mistakes made inside the fence of grace can always be opportunities to learn something new.

Part 7: Starting Construction—Practical Steps

Starting Construction will explain how to implement what we've learned from our completed diagram. The appendices, or Toolbox, will provide a host of resources to do so.

At the end of key chapters, you will find a list of Building Materials that point you to the exact resources from the Toolbox that you need for that lesson. (Some are designated with stars because I personally recommend them.) You can also scan the Toolbox at any time to find books, web sites, key Scripture references, scripts for challenging conversations, object lessons and more.

You'll also notice that many areas of the book prompt you to journal about your specific situation. When ideas come to mind, write them down! These will create your family's personal strategies for building a unique strategy for the pursuit of purity in your household. I probably do not know you or your family, but you are the expert. You are the most qualified to create your own solution!

The goal of this book is to equip you to build intentionally.

The goal of this book is to equip you to build *intentionally. You are starting a journey that will produce terrific rewards.*

Let's get started!

Chapter 2

Loving Relationships

Let me ask a question, not about your child, but about you. What is the condition of your relationship with your child? The state of your relationship is priority number one because this is the ground upon which your household's strategies for purity will be built.

Good ground is required for plants and flowers to grow. That fertile soil is like the loving interaction that we must provide for training in purity to be effective.

We must assess our ability to communicate and maintain healthy, loving relationships with our kids before we start to build. The process includes *modeling* the behaviors that we so want to see in our kids.

My Story

I am not a model of parenting perfection. I'm still growing in my ability to implement the concepts of this chapter.

For example, I remember a season when my children were both preschool age, and my husband was staying home with them while I worked. I would often come home tired and just want some peace and quiet. I would wonder, "Who can we get to keep the kids for awhile?" even though I already saw so little of them each day!

Loving interaction must be provided for training in purity to be effective.

The situation got worse and worse. The less time I spent with my children, the less I wanted to be with them. I wasn't investing time in really engaging with them and addressing specific problems. (I had plenty of my own.) So the problems worsened instead of getting better.

My husband did all he could and was a great stay-at-home dad, but I wasn't helping. Then my situation changed. Randy got a job, and I stayed home. Wake-up call! I learned that the more time I spent with my children, understanding them and working out issues, the more I liked them—and the more time I wanted to spend with them!

When I was living at an emotional distance from my children, the ground where we were trying to build our "house" of purity was rocky with neglected issues. As I returned home, I began to remove those obstacles, leveling the plot so it could better receive a foundation.

Interaction and Interest

We live in a world of incredible, frenetic busy-ness. With all the opportunities available to us, we can lose sight of relationships with our children. *Real* relationships with our kids and *true* parenting is absolutely vital to making authentic purity work.

What does it mean to have a *real* relationship or to *truly* parent? Well, first of all, *our kids aren't barn animals.* We don't provide food, shelter, and material needs for them and let them go on as they please. That's raising livestock—*not* parenting.

Our children need interaction and interest. They need affection and affirmation. They need listening ears *We aren't raising chickens;* and eyes that are on them instead of dis-*we're raising children.* tracted by a computer, TV, or hand-held electronic organizer. They need more personal time with parents and family and fewer planned activities.

How many hours a day are we spending in actual communication with our children? During a regular day, there are so many opportunities! We may talk in the car together, write an email, put a note in a lunch box, catch up after school, talk together at supper, play a game together in the evening, read a story or spend some quiet time reading or praying before bed. Ask yourself:

- Do we *take* the opportunities that arise, and also *make* opportunities wherever we can?

- When a crisis arises, do we intensify our efforts and cancel our appointments to meet the need?

- Do we make birthdays and other milestones a family priority?

- Do our children know by the way we spend our time that they are treasured?

We have a lot of information to pass on before our children leave our homes. It's not up to the church or school to provide this teaching, although these institutions are *Nothing matches the impact of a* helpful. We are first and foremost *healthy relationship between* responsible for preparing our kids *parents and children.* for life, and research shows that children learn life skills (or the lack thereof) from parents more than any other source.[1]

Nothing matches the impact of a healthy relationship between parents and children, no matter what we're teaching. That doesn't mean there is never a disagreement. But it does mean there is always room for discussion and a warmth and desire to help. Children in such a supportive environment will be more open to hearing us on really important matters.

The ideal hierarchy of relationships in our lives should look like this:

1. Relationship with God (begin by at least admitting a need for a higher power than ourselves)

2. Relationship with our spouse (if married)

3. Relationships with our children

Using this hierarchy, *we love our kids to purity.* The word *love* is absolutely essential. Other motivations (and there are many) will sabotage the construction of the house in the Planned Purity diagram. We must be sure our motivations do not rest on protecting our reputation and convenience, or avoiding an obligation to raise grandchildren born to a single parent.

Loving our children involves being truly interested in doing what's best for them, training them as best we can, and receiving the gift of their presence with joy. We "made 'em so we train 'em."

Not Just Rules

Some of us grew up in homes where we were simply expected to follow the rules, spoken or unspoken. Our parents may have been physically present, but heart-to-heart talks were rare. We may have grown up not really being known or understood, though certain boundaries for safety existed.

On the flip side, today fewer parents stay together or marry at all. Rules for children can be completely overlooked in the complexity of separate families. I recently heard of a sixteen-year-old in counseling for depression who was working a job, going to school, involved in sexual relationships with two of her managers, and thought she might be pregnant. The girl could stay out all night if she liked and report her whereabouts to no one. Her household was without rules, and her divorced father *still* thought she would turn out all right.

Good parenting involves relationship and rules.

A balance between these two worlds—a million rules or no rules at all—does exist. Parenting is not about rules alone, and parenting does not leave a child (no, not even a high schooler) to himself to "figure it out." *Good parenting involves relationship* and *rules.* Healthy relationships make the rules meaningful and more likely to be received as protection instead of fun spoilers.

Too many early high school kids are treated as adults when they are still developing biologically and emotionally. New hormones bring on feelings that need explanation and management. In addition, high school students are in desperate need of purpose (sometimes even the simple purpose of physical work can be the answer).

High school is no time to disengage from relationship and standards with our children. While offering new freedom and responsibility, we should continue to give guidance and support.

Don't forget that as teens our ancestors were being married, holding down jobs, and raising families. Our teens need both our anchors of guidance and our firm insistence to progress into adulthood. We can protect them from becoming irresponsible, immature adults and show them the joys of giving and living by standards.

When it comes to sexual responsibility for teens, we cannot default to churches or schools to do the training. This is our job. We must model abstinence outside marriage and joyful affection within marriage to train young children in preparation for the teen years.

Personal Ownership

When I talk about teaching children to embrace the pursuit of a good heart, I am speaking very strongly of *ownership on the part of the child*. The goal is for the child to *personally desire and choose to act out practices of purity*. This goal cannot be accomplished by a set of rules. Instead, the Planned Purity house is modeled authentically while being articulated through ongoing communication.

There is perhaps a time when a "big talk" is appropriate in relation to sexuality, but it is completely unrealistic to think that one talk can cover all the aspects of integrity, relationship and sexuality. Instead, the continued conversation of ongoing engagement will help lead your children to choose goodness for themselves. You cannot choose it for them. In these days when blended families are common, grandparents and parents may not share value systems you are teaching in your home. In that case, your children need to be able to say *no* for themselves, sometimes at a very early age.

A young child must take personal ownership of his purity, speaking out and guarding his heart for himself, not just because his parents told him to.

For instance, if a child is taught that certain situations on TV or in a movie are inappropriate and to steer clear of them, he will be better able to speak for himself outside the home. If a child spends time at Grandma's house or an ex-wife or husband's home, the adult will be more likely to respond to the child's unwillingness to watch than to the parent's insistence that the child not watch. This is the helpful result of *teaching a young child to speak out and guard his heart for himself.* This ability will play an even more crucial role in his standing firm during the teen years.

Modeling

Because integrity and sexual responsibility (and most other subjects) is caught rather than taught, your children will be watching you closely. Do your language, dress, entertainment, and relationships look like these things are important to you? A child who sees, "Do as I say, not as I do," most likely will not! Therefore, it's wise to read this book not only in view of your child's needs, but also your own.

A study from the *Journal of Applied Developmental Psychology* explains the importance of both doing and explaining when it comes to influencing our children toward our values. The author of the study, Lynn Okagaki, reported that children are more likely to adopt their parents' beliefs when they have a clear understanding of exactly what the parents believe and value. [2]

Live what you teach to the best of your ability. This is some of the most important training you can give your child when it comes to a life of integrity.

Once we have a handle on these relational issues, we're better equipped to dig into the practical matters of what we're pursuing. The word *purity* has been a popular term when speaking of abstinence, but that usage in itself is limiting, as we'll see in the next chapter. The word *purity* evokes some strong images, but are they accurate? Let's find out.

Part 2

The Foundation—
Understanding Purity

Definition of Purity

Chapter 3

Purity Defined

When you're making cement, a certain mix is crucial. If you don't add the right elements in the right proportions, you get a watery mess or something too thick to pour. In the same way, to create a strong foundation in our planned purity, we need the right mix of ingredients as we define our goal. In this book, I'll be using the word *purity* to define this goal of integrity (a good heart) and responsible abstinence.

Let's begin by clearing up two common misunderstandings.

The first misunderstanding is that purity is about sex. It isn't. Purity is about the condition of the heart or inner person. Without a pure heart, sexual responsibility and abstinence outside marriage are desperately difficult to embrace.

Second, purity applies to every person at every age. When the word *purity* is mentioned, we tend to think of teenagers. However, the practice of pure living applies effectively to little ones, teens, and adults. In fact, marital sex is a celebration of sexual purity.

To restate, the two defining points of purity are as follows:

1. **Purity refers to both sexuality *and* the condition of the heart.**
2. **Purity is a continuing journey in every age and stage.**

Now let's see how the development of a good heart and sexual responsibility work together.

A Good Heart

Training in sexual responsibility is vitally important, but the key to this responsibility is to understand and pursue a good heart *first*. This is the distinguishing element of Planned Purity training—starting with the heart.

This concept is based on a passage in the book of Proverbs that says the heart is the "wellspring of life," so it must be guarded above all else.[1]

Purity is about the condition of the heart more than sexuality, and is important at every age.

Imagine a spring-fed well that overflows with life so that lush, beautiful plants grow around it. In the same way, our hearts are like springs that affect others around us, especially our family and close friends.

In ancient times, a spring was the center of a city's resources. An entire city could be conquered by cutting off access to its spring. Today some of those ancient springs are clogged with centuries of dirt. They were neglected and now they are useless because water can't flow from them. Our hearts are similar. We choose to keep them clean, or we allow them to become clogged.

Clean Inside and Out

A person can be sexually inactive and still be impure. Jesus made a strong statement to the leaders of his day who were supposed to be pure in their hearts and bodies, as keepers of the Law. He told them that they still were not clean—that they had to clean the *inside* of the cup before the *outside* could be clean as well.[2]

That's a good way to look at purity. Imagine a big, white cappuccino cup as a model of our lives. Our goal is to keep our cups clean inside and out—that's purity. Most of us keep the outsides of our cups looking pretty good, while the insides of our cups are stained brown. The stains on the inside will eventually show up on the outside, moving from our thought lives into our actions. That's often what happens when rules are given for actions but the heart has never been formed.

Purity of heart (our character and thought life) is like the inside of the cup; sexual (physical) purity is an outer expression, part of the outside of the cup. If we don't understand or intend to practice purity of heart, then we'll have a hard time with sexual responsibility.

When we began house shopping in Florida a couple of years ago, we saw a particular house that impressed us in a small neighborhood north of Orlando. The lady of the house had beautiful taste and had painted some walls of the main room a striking burgundy. Freestanding walls featured gorgeous floral arrangements, and matching window treatments tied everything together. There was a roomy master bath and even a room that would work as an office for me to write in.

Being Midwesterners, it was a big deal to consider a house with a pool, and we were told this home had one. We couldn't wait to look out back! Surely with such a beautiful home, the pool would be sparkling and inviting as well.

Sadly, it wasn't true. The deck around the pool was partially finished and the yard was full of weeds. Even worse, the cleaning system wasn't working, and the water was literally black. It ruined our impression of the property. Ick!

A heart that isn't pure is like that. No matter how good things look on the inside, the outside is certain to expose itself sooner or later. How many times have we seen beautiful girls full of hatred and selfishness and meanness towards others? How many times has a handsome man had no respect for the women he could attract? The heart makes the difference, no matter what's portrayed on the outside. Without a good heart, the entire house crumbles.

You can also compare purity to an iceberg. The tip of the iceberg is all that's exposed. But the part of the iceberg beneath the water is huge—big enough to sink a ship.

Purity of heart is like the hidden part of the iceberg. When the battleships of irresponsibility are in the ocean, we need the bottom of that iceberg to sink them.

In most of the Bible's Old Testament, the word *pure* was used almost exclusively in regards to the sacrifices that God demanded. The gold for the place of worship, the incense burned in offerings—everything that was offered was pure according to God's requirements.[3]

But in the Psalms, we see the word *pure* being often used as a descriptor of something other than sacrifices—the human heart!

Because *pure* is used to describe God's desire for sacrifice *and* the condition of the heart, it makes sense to believe this quality is of extreme value. A good heart willing to make sacrifices on behalf of others means that life-changing love can flow from the inside out, through attitudes and actions, like a clean, gushing spring.

A Responsibly Managed Body

Many people think the definition of sexual purity is self-evident—not having sex! But as explained earlier, sexual purity includes much more than not having intercourse before marriage. It also includes refraining from sexual acts that don't meet the definition of "intercourse."

When a person understands purity solely as restraint from intercourse, they can hurt others, even unintentionally, in numerous physical and emotional ways. When a selfish heart is left to itself, it will take advantage of others and put itself first.

My personal story is that I experienced *everything but* sexual intercourse before I was married. The scars from that type of involvement with a number of partners have caused years of pain and confusion in my sexual relationship with my husband.

Growing up in a small Midwestern town, I was sheltered from many of the cultural influences that are unavoidable for city children. My parents seemed nervous about discussing sexuality, and so the subject was never approached. The bits of information I did find were learned from friends, television, and popular music.

When I left home for college (to pursue a degree in musical theater), I entered an entirely different world. On the secular college campus, I was exposed to everything from drinking to gay friends to coed dorms.

Being as naïve as I was, and having a heart that really did have a bent toward God, I got involved in a church group, hung out at theater parties (carrying my own brown bag with non-alcoholic grape juice inside), and looked for romantic relationships to fulfill my need to be loved.

My view of purity was ineffective. I would tell my boyfriends I could only "go so far" because I was a Christian. This made everything short of sexual intercourse OK for me, and everything else is what I did.

My junior year I transferred to a Bible college, but I still poisoned others and myself, wrecking emotions and lives, by becoming too physically involved. When I finally did marry a wonderful Christian man, I struggled with intimacy—sexual and otherwise—because I didn't understand abstinence *or* sexuality. I was lost.

An Ongoing Pursuit

Our kids must understand that any type of sexual touching, activity, or intense sexual conversation can be ruinous to their hearts and bodies. A study in the journal *Pediatrics* stated, "Sex of any kind can harm teens emotionally" [4] (not to mention younger children).

But who will tell our kids which types of touching and interaction are inappropriate, and when? By the time the hormones come into play, it will be much more difficult to introduce these ideas. Instead, we need to explain specific sexual boundaries to our kids as they grow, in age-appropriate ways. We also must show that the pursuit of a good heart is the foundational requirement for healthy, honorable sexuality, continuing into the adult years.

The pursuit of a good heart is the foundational requirement for healthy, honorable sexuality.

This kind of training does not have to be stressful and unnatural, especially because you do it over time rather than cramming it into one "big talk." In fact, all your conversations about purity and sexually responsible behavior will deepen your relationship with your kids and give more opportunities for sharing good information.

A Definition of Purity that Works

Dictionaries define the word *purity* with phrases like "free from what weakens or pollutes" and "containing nothing that does not properly belong." These definitions are closely tied to a spiritual meaning.

All of us know what it is like to have too much clutter in our houses or garages. Spiritually, we need to remove the clutter—those things that do not properly belong.

To summarize what we've learned so far, *purity* can be defined this way:

Purity is a lifestyle of inner housekeeping

that is taught and practiced over a lifetime,

beginning with a good heart

and working its way from the mind and thoughts

into the life and actions.

In this definition, sexual purity is definitely a part of but not the crux of the matter. A good heart is the foundation for all purity, sexual and otherwise.

The journey toward this kind of purity includes many conversations, successes and failures, all viewed as learning opportunities. The heart is "dirtied" by unwanted material or selfish actions, intentionally or not. Humility, focus, time and surrender are necessary to recover that innocence.

A good heart is the foundation for all purity, sexual and otherwise.

But new habits *can* be formed. Healthy, honorable sexuality is a part of this pursuit.

Has this new definition challenged some of your old reactions to the word *purity*? I hope so. Keep these new concepts in mind as we look at the timeline on which purity of heart and body develop.

Chapter 4

The Purity Continuum

A grandmother I know read my book *The Princess and the Kiss* to her four-year-old grandson. This children's picture book features a princess who saves her "kiss" for the young man who is chosen to be her husband. He's recognized as the one for her because of the fact that he has also saved his kiss for his future wife.

This preschooler came home one day from a playgroup to tell his grandma that a little girl on the playground had asked him for a kiss.

"Did you give her one?" the grandmother asked.

Hands on hips, the boy replied, "No, Mawmaw! I don't want to marry her!"

I'm always delighted by the ability of children to quickly grasp concepts about intimacy. Because they have spent less time exposed to our relativistic culture, children can immediately assimilate a behavioral standard (especially through story) and put it into practice.

I spend a good deal of time trying to catch up with parents who run past my book table with the words, "Well, we're not quite ready for that yet." Little do they know that even preschoolers are ready to pursue a good heart if given the tools and the chance. This heart condition leads to integrity and sexual responsibility as it's modeled, taught, and formed over a lifetime.

Preschoolers are ready to pursue a good heart if given the tools and the chance.

The Purity Continuum will give us a better picture of how lifetime purity of heart and body is ideally pursued throughout life. The word *continuum* simply means that purity develops in a continuing cycle, not just at one point in a life.

Ideally, parents can begin thinking about responsible sexuality training for their children even before the children are born. At this writing, however, few of us realize the opportunities so early on. So start from where you are right now and fill in the missing pieces as you discover them. Your efforts will be rewarded!

Ten Stages of Purity Development

Let's take a look at how we can teach integrity and sexual responsibility in different stages of development. As you read, refer back to the continuum (see below) and the Planned Purity diagram at the head of chapter 1. Think about ways that an understanding of a good heart and responsible sexual behavior *Purity in your children is very much about purity in you.* was (or wasn't) imparted to you as you were growing up. Consider those missing "bricks" and how you'd like to replace them in your own life, or provide them for your children. And don't forget: Purity in your children is very much about purity in you.

The Purity Continuum

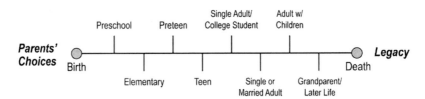

Stage 1: Pre-Conception/Conception/Birth

Children are impacted by the experiences parents have before the child is born. For example, a parent who associates shame or guilt with sexuality because of childhood abuse or poor decisions in the teen/adult years will harbor a tainted view of what purity means, which will in turn affect the child.

Some of us were raised in homes where any discussion of sex was taboo, or no model of integrity, respect, and honor was provided. As a result, we may have little understanding or desire to embrace purity, and we may not even see the value of marriage.

In my case, my husband and I came into our marriage with plenty of misunderstandings about good hearts, sex, and children, but we did understand marriage to be a lifetime commitment. We did a lot of redesigning with our purity blueprint and are still making renovations to the shaky areas of our diagram. But we have been able to pass on new ways of thinking and practicing purity to our children, which is indescribably rewarding after previously living selfishly, with little understanding. I believe our children helped us discover a good deal of the selflessness we needed. Maybe yours did, too.

A man and woman who have maturity and real commitment to each other can provide a positive, stable environment for a baby to be born. Single parents using wisdom and sensitivity can also find creative ways to meet a child's needs—but it will take finding extra support besides the parent alone. Parenting in general takes more resources than any of us can provide on our own!

Stage 2: Preschooler

Even at the preschool age, a child's growing understanding of love and purity is influenced by their environment. Choices of music, entertainment, and types of interaction all make an impact. In our home, we played recordings of biblical passages under the children's beds as they slept. We prayed for them, and many others prayed for them as well. We played together and considered the images they viewed if we watched a movie. We played tender lullabies for them. All of this was an effort to create a sweet environment where unconditional love and good hearts could grow.

The biggest influences in an American home are the screens of televisions and computers. Make intentional choices in these areas to guard your child's innocence. Experts now recommend that a child not even be exposed to material on screen until after the age of two, as early viewing prevents healthy development. A heavy diet of television after two, even "good" programs, will affect a child's ability to learn normally and to lead an active, physically engaged, real life versus a passive, "virtual" life.[1]

A heavy diet of screen entertainment will affect a child's ability to learn normally.

Helping even a young child to recognize that too much or certain types of TV/computer/entertainment choices aren't approved lets them begin to grasp the concept that culture will require evaluation throughout life. Screens are not trustworthy friends. For this reason and others, our quantity of time with our children personally should always be overwhelmingly more than any time before a screen.

Reading is a wonderful way to spend time with a child. Choose stories that exemplify goodness and demonstrate how to serve instead of being served. You will be especially glad for this foundation during the hormone-laden teen years.

Stage 3: Elementary School Student

Any time children are with other children, they will be influenced by their peers. The purity of heart they've been taught and had modeled at home will be the filter through which they understand what they hear. The parent needs to interact with the child before and after school days (cookies and milk are a great help in the afternoons). Show an interest in the goings-on at school, help the child understand the interaction he/she is experiencing, and give the child permission to say *no* to inappropriate actions.

For example, we know of an instance where a child in kindergarten was taught to masturbate under the lunch table by a friend of the same sex. The parents were able to find out about the incident and manage it because they had been talking with the child every day. Once the situation was understood and they got over the shock, the parents could give the child all the counsel needed.

How different it would have been if the child and parent were not interacting openly and the child experienced shame or developed an unhealthy, guilty habit out of a fear and lack of understanding, hiding the truth and suffering for it.

Another friend's son discovered pornography in second grade via the Internet and a friend in a Christian school. The parent was immediately able to speak to the boy about his curiosity in a calm way and to explain why further viewing must be prevented.

Our own child came to us in kindergarten saying that she needed a boyfriend. We made some decisions about our stance on friendship versus dating shortly thereafter.

Teachable moments arise all the time, whether a little boy wants to know why girls don't stand up to use the toilet or a little girl learns to keep her dress over her legs instead of over her head.

At this stage, all entertainment should be previewed for appropriateness. In addition, children can be taught to recognize inappropriate images and song lyrics and turn them off or turn away—even when parents aren't around. (The how-tos of "turn off/turn away" training will be covered in Part 3, The First Floor.) When technology is introduced, guidelines for use must be very clear.

Stage 4: Preteen

Preteens, called "tweens" or "tweeners," are often described as ages eight to twelve. Because they have matured in their ability to learn, they can benefit from exploring answers to questions such as:

- How should young men and women treat, respect, and protect each other?

- How do we evaluate what we see and hear and the effect it has on our hearts?

- How do we value others' lives, not just our own?

- How do we speak in such a way as to encourage and not discourage?

- How do we find the affection that is necessary for our emotions to be healthy?

- How do we continue to practice modesty and self-respect?

It's vital that these important questions are answered before the teen years, when the onset of hormonal activity makes it harder for teens to listen and learn. For example, tell your children your position on dating as early as you can. Prior to the teen years explain when they might be able to date (along with a very specific definition of dating and its purpose), or explain that you prefer them to focus on friendship over dating.

Tell your child your position on dating as early as you can.

41

This is a key developmental period when children can begin to embrace aspects of sexual responsibility based on their commitment to a good heart.

All these things are taught through modeling and talking, which means it's vital for the family to have time together. Don't let TV or computers rob your family of "talk time" and "down time." Virtual reality is not reality at all. Your child needs relationship away from technology to live a full, rich, complete life. Enjoy each other's company during relaxed and casual conversation, discuss a helpful booklet, pursue a hobby, or take a walk or bike ride.

Kids may be more likely to become addicted to "screen time" at this stage. They are also likely to be exposed to pornography because it pops up when they aren't expecting it. One of our girls was looking up seemingly safe material when she encountered an explicit introductory clip to a video on YouTube. This kind of accident can happen with any child who knows how to use the Internet. Many researchers are trying to identify the typical age at which American children are exposed to porn and may begin addictive viewing. Conservative researchers tend toward the age of fourteen,[2] while others report eleven and even seven, in some cases.[3]

The "tweener" years are a perfect time to involve kids in church youth groups or other groups with strong values.

During the preteen years, appropriate and inappropriate TV, movies, Internet use, gaming, and phone use can be delineated. Clear boundaries now can make the teen years easier for both parent and child.

The "tweener" years are also a perfect time to involve kids in church youth groups or other groups with strong values. Provide a positive environment where they enjoy hanging out with friends of integrity now, before they're distracted by driving, dating, heavily competitive sports, and other pressures of teen years.

Stage 5: Adolescent/Teenager

Application of principles comes to the forefront in the teen years. Our goal is for our youth to understand how to guard their hearts so that they are less likely to put themselves in situations of risk. The girl who understands the impact of her beauty on a young man will understand how to protect him through innocent conversation and modest dress instead of flirting and physical display. The young man who values a young woman's life and future will be more likely to protect that future by saying, "I care about you, so I'm limiting how I interact physically," instead of, "If you love me, you'll let me." He will not inflame a girl's emotions because he knows he can hurt her deeply if the relationship ends.

Dating and illicit relationships surround our children. We can help them understand the incredible power of beauty and desire and how to prevent it arousing or "awakening" in a way that is destructive or risky. [4] And we still need to give them appropriate physical affection at home to keep them "fed" and healthy.

During the teen years, parents are tempted to pull out of kids' lives, talking and interacting less. But our teens need continued family involvement and lots of conversation. Statistics clearly show that teens would rather learn about sexuality from loving parents than any other way. [5]

Our youth need some freedom but not abandonment. It can seem like a daily raft ride on unpredictable rapids as we deal with the ups and downs of the teenage years. But our kids need us to fight hard to stay in the boat with them, sometimes with long talks way after (our) bedtime.

Many well-meaning parents struggle with over-scheduling. There is no harm in reducing a student's schedule to one or two necessary extracurricular activities. Parents may also need to cut back on their own extra pursuits during the teen years. Anything that takes away from healthy relationships at home must be evaluated.

The lasting bonds of a healthy family are the best preparation for marriage and also for healthy friendships. Don't cheat your child out of family time in the teen years. They're about to leave your house. If not now, when will you teach them what they need to know?

This concept was brought home to me recently by my teen's questions about a bank account, college, and homemaking. I am seeing the need to set aside time to share with her "everything she needs to know before she lives on her own." The list of topics includes everything from car management to being a good wife to managing her own apartment. She still has so much to learn, and we hope to guide her even beyond her high

Don't cheat your child out of family time in the teen years.

school years. I certainly found my parents' advice valuable after I left high school—and still do today.

Accountability and mentoring through youth leaders or other parents is also very helpful. For example, my oldest daughter has two mentors. These are adults we trust deeply who check in with her regularly and keep confidences unless she is in danger. They are powerful voices in times when my daughter feels misunderstood or needs another perspective on our standards.

Stage 6: Single Adult/College Student

When our children are in college or part of the work force, they apply what they know and make mistakes. They seek out their own continuing training, set up their own accountability, and make new friends. But they don't have to do it alone.

No matter the choices they make, we keep ourselves available for our children to come to us when they need us. We guard against falling out of relationship by staying in communication by phone, email or visit. Our children should be included in family plans whenever possible, making sure they know that they are welcome to be part of the family activities at any time.

Family standards should be clearly stated in the home, but more discussion will take place as the child makes choices that might not be what we expect. Whether they live in or out of our homes, they still need love. They still need us to be their cheerleaders as they navigate a more independent life.

And of course, we pray because our children will be making their way through all kinds of new situations, but we put our trust in God because we've done and still do all we can.

Stage 7: Married or Single Adult

Our children may enjoy the precious lifetime relationship of a spouse or the equal joy of being set apart for singleness. We hope our children have embraced purity, received all its rewards, and now spend time with a network of those who operate with the same values,

Show up whenever you're invited into your adult children's lives.

but maybe they aren't there yet. Their choices to responsibly abstain or treat intimacy casually will have a deep impact on their marriage relationship or their single lifestyle.

As parents, we recognize the child's independence, but also maintain a healthy openness and interest in our children and their expanding worlds. We celebrate, we pray, we love. We show up whenever invited. The "training video" of our lives is still being watched, though perhaps not as consistently.

Our children and their spouses will need our ongoing support as they work through life issues we've already experienced. Without taking sides, we can offer advice *if it is requested* and encourage professional counseling if it seems helpful. Most successful singles and couples benefit from some type of counsel during their lives; there is no shame at all in seeking it.

Stage 8: Adult with Children

If our children raise children, our kids will become the examples for their own little ones. We can walk alongside and provide invaluable support as they train their children through the same stages that we trained our own.

We can assist in training our grandchildren in direct or indirect ways. We can share our stories and support the standards by which we raised our own children. Some grandparents arrange getaways for extended families or grandchildren.

If our own children are no longer following that example, or never have, our voice will be even more important to our grandchildren. We can write letters, record Bible passages, study together, send emails or gifts, or visit often. Our good heart and our relationship with our spouse will be vital for our grandchildren.

Stage 9: Later Life

Our example continues as we watch our families grow, as we serve each other through difficulty, and as we pray for those who struggle.

As we attend christening ceremonies, weddings, reunions, and other family gatherings, we can write notes, give gifts, and make a personal and lasting impact on each occasion, having moved into position as elders in the family. Our contentment in our marriages or singleness will reflect our satisfaction with a life where purity has become central and challenges are clearly recognized as learning opportunities. Our continued pursuit of a good heart and responsible sexuality will play a role in whether we will be honored as time passes.

Stage 10: Legacy

After we die, our legacy of a good heart and life will continue. What will our families remember about us? What will they tell their children and grandchildren? What did we teach—not just with our mouths, but with our lives? My grandparents on both sides were married for life, and so were my parents and my husband's parents. These rare examples have certainly affected our desire to model committed faithfulness to our children and grandchildren as well. Attributes of thrift, good planning, hard work, thoroughness and love of beauty have also been passed on to us.

What will our families remember about us?

I remember my mother especially for her willingness to serve, and my father for his resourcefulness and financial honesty. Both my parents were models of a terrific work ethic. How do you want to be remembered? How will this reflect your pursuit of a pure heart and body today?

Foundational Understanding

- **Evaluating heart and body.** How successfully do you think you and your family have pursued good hearts and sexual responsibility up to this point? Which pieces of the definition of purity might be missing or weak?

- **Consider the continuum.** Which of the ten stages are particularly meaningful to you right now? Which ideas are new to you? Highlight them in your book.

- _____

  _____

  _____

Building Materials

Truths to Memorize
See Appendix B for complete texts.
Wellspring of Life (1)
Pure from Contamination (32)

Object Lessons
See Appendix E for more details.
Clean Cups, Dirty Dishes (1)

Chapter 5

Emotions and Thought Life

Astory was told to me of a father who, during the Christmas season, noticed a certain area on a wall of his home that seemed hot. Because he was unable to trace the heat to any particular source, he shrugged it off, and the family went about their holiday business. Sometime during the night while they slept, all the outer walls of the house burst into flames. The problem had traveled through the wiring of the house, erupting everywhere at once. The man made it out of the house, but his wife and son died in the fire.

The thought life feeds emotions and leads to action.

Just as hidden electrical problems can destroy a house, so hidden thought problems can destroy our lives from the inside out. *The thought life feeds emotions and leads to action.* Right thoughts and managed emotions will power us with strength and light a path to do what's right, but more volatile feelings and out-of-control emotions can plunge us into paralysis and darkness.

The inner life is the "wiring" of a person. Unseen, but full of power, adults may write off signs of "heat" as "kid stuff" or "teenage stuff." But flare-ups may also be warning signs that the entire life is getting ready to erupt into an inferno, destroying a good heart and the pursuit of a pure life.

Just as a street lamp's glow proves its connection to a power source, a child's actions will reveal the emotions and thoughts that are hidden in his inner person. It will take *intentionality* for us to be aware of what is happening in our child's inner life.

Recently there was a report in our city of a seventeen-year-old young man who hanged himself. He was an honor student, came from a religious family, and seemed to have everything going for him. But his girlfriend broke up with him, and the emotional explosion plunged him into a rash decision. His parents did not realize how deeply the young man was affected by his emotions—deeply enough to take his own life.

The unseen thought life and emotions in his heart were key to this young man's living or dying. His story certainly gives us the kind of initiative we need to commit ourselves to caring for our children's thought lives and emotional needs.

Let's evaluate our attentiveness to our child's unseen life. How do we teach discipline of the thought life to protect the heart (even as we struggle with the same issue)? And what are those crazy emotions for, anyway? How do we lead our children in managing these unseen elements of their lives?

Think About What You're Thinking About

Here is the single most important concept we can teach our children about their thought lives: *We can control what we think about!* If thoughts are undisciplined, negative emotional flare-ups will follow, leading to destructive actions. Many people, adults included, do not recognize how wrong thinking leads to the loss of life's power and light. We *must* control what we are thinking about if we want to pursue good hearts and responsible sexuality.

For the best instruction on managing the thought life, read Joyce Meyer's *Battlefield of the Mind* (also available in a format for youth). This book is marvelous in its explanation of managing the thought life. After we understand that we can actually discipline our thoughts, how can we teach our children to do it?

First, they need a strategy for handling thoughts that don't belong. For instance, if a child has negative thoughts, try to help him or her recognize and define those thoughts. Then replace the negative thoughts with a positive truth. Author and teacher Beth Moore calls it "changing wallpaper."[1] When my youngest daughter was afraid at night and thought of nothing but monsters, we used strategies like prayer, soothing music, and a night-light. We also encouraged her to change her mental wallpaper. When she thought of monsters, we suggested she replace those creatures with puppies or mermaids or dancing pink cows (her personal favorite).

This same daughter struggled with anxiety the night before her first day of middle school. She had a vague but troubling feeling that her day wouldn't go well. We talked about thinking of those negative, lying thoughts as little flies that we could flick away. She ended up laughing as I asked her to picture herself and God lying in bed and flicking flies. Other creative ideas will come to all of us parents when we are listening.

We can control what we think about!

Controlling a thought life isn't neat and easy. It takes a good bit of practice. I personally didn't realize how undisciplined my thought life was until my late thirties. It took repeated replacing to change thoughts that have been shaping me for years. That's why it's best to teach children how to manage their thoughts when they're young and their thought habits are still being shaped. Remember to be patient with them during the learning process (and with yourself!).

For a preteen or teen, a disciplined mind is an invaluable tool for dealing with sexual thoughts, urges, and curiosities. The child should feel comfortable describing those thoughts to a parent who has already demonstrated sensitive listening. In response, the parent can offer a verse, image, or action to help the child redirect thoughts to a healthier direction before the fires of emotions burn out of control.

With help and practice, our children will learn to control their thoughts. Teaching our children to manage them is well worth our time.

Managing Emotions

I used to love my emotions so much that I used them as the basis for all my actions. If I was excited about something, I did it. If I wasn't, I put it off until it got me into trouble. If my feelings changed, so did my response. Consistency was not my strong suit!

Actions must be based on truth and a sense of honor or responsibility, not how we feel. Otherwise, the laundry would never get done and no one would pay bills. Yet, without spontaneity, how boring life would be!

Emotions require management for life to be balanced with fullness of feeling and a determination to do what's right and necessary. It is vital to teach your child that *emotions alone are not trustworthy in making lifelong decisions.*

A middle schooler or teen, especially one who is feeling less-than-connected to parents, can be swept away by feelings like abandonment, hopelessness or infatuation. During the teen years when the hormones arrive and the brain develops further, emotions become unexpectedly strong.[2] Our children desperately need to know the purpose of emotions and how to manage them.

Emotions alone are not trustworthy in making lifelong decisions.

First, we can help our children understand that when feelings happen, they aren't wrong—they just are. Emotions are part of how we are beautifully designed, for our enjoyment and as red flags that make us aware of our needs. Trying to force emotions into a "flat line" is dangerous and unhealthy. Emotions enhance every day's existence. What would life be without the awe we feel when we look at a new baby, the joy of friendship, or the thrill of attraction?

Emotions were meant to enjoy, but when they push us to destructive choices we must be equipped to focus elsewhere. As parents, we want to validate our children's emotions while correcting their actions as needed and helping them to be driven by truth instead of feelings. The keys are to listen, remind them of what's true and right in a level manner, and talk through the situation and feelings without judgment.

You can begin to help your child handle emotional flare-ups in their young years. For example, after your little child experiences anger, take time to discuss what the anger is about and teach him how to handle it. This will empower the child to manage his anger as he grows. Slamming a door is not acceptable, but the anger that makes your child want to slam the door needs to be explored.

Also, when your child feels attraction to the opposite sex for the first time, it's crucial for him or her to talk to an adult about those feelings. The adult can help the child sort out feelings from facts by talking about the person's character and future possibilities. This kind of talk will help engage the intellect alongside the feelings. Emotions tend to shut off the brain, so train your child to turn the brain back on.

If your child is still a preteen, watch for opportunities to prepare them for the normal feelings that may be ahead (example: feeling like their parents don't understand), and tell them that you will be there to talk about them.

Some children (especially tweens) deal with strong emotions of inferiority and self-doubt on a daily basis. They wonder if they fit in. They don't feel good enough. Remember the awkwardness you experienced at that age—the fear of being "last one chosen"? Those crushing, painful memories remind us how much our children need our care when they experience hurtful feelings. They need to know we will protect their hearts.

An open, fear-free, communicative environment is the best setting in which emotions can function in tandem with a good heart and even enhance it. As a parent, watch for opportunities to talk at all times of the day or night.

For great insight on protecting and teaching your children, read Brienne Murk's *Eyes Wide Open: Avoiding the Heartbreak of Emotional Promiscuity.* Another good resource is the book *Before You Meet Prince Charming* by Sarah Mally.

Listen—and Listen—and Listen

How do we know what our children are thinking about and feeling? There is only one way—by listening and being interested. Even the finest families can become too busy and take emotional stability for granted. Parents too involved with work or too tired to talk will miss deep pain—and joy—in their children's inner lives.

We can be tempted to think a child's thoughts and feelings aren't that important—that they're just a part of growing up. This is irresponsible. Children may actually be more in touch with their feelings than we are! The loss of a pet can be devastating for a child. A doubt about physical attractiveness can be earth-shattering. The thrill of a "first love" can block out everything else.

We must feed our children emotionally with praise, affirmation, affection, and loving attention. We must engage with them and celebrate each unique, amazing person we're so privileged to have in our family. Too often these efforts are left off our to-do lists, and our tasks become more important than the people we love. This tendency must be avoided! The house may be dirty, the lawn may need mowing, but those things disappear in light of the priority we have in tending to our children's emotional needs. Kids need to be heard, not ignored.

As hormones come into play, our kids can be embarrassed about their feelings, and they will only talk with us if we have already nurtured open discussion about emotions in prior years. As parents, we need to be established as a reliable source of information and a place where the child is accepted with risk of ridicule. Otherwise, our children will learn from questionable sources.

Many children who have their emotional needs neglected will eventually end up in uncommitted sexual relationships. They aren't sure why they feel empty, but they use attention from the opposite sex as a comfort that makes everything seem better, at least for a while. Filling their emotional "tanks" with the love of parents and families will do much to help prevent them from seeking unhealthy attention elsewhere.

Of course, there is balance involved. We should not try to control our children or know every thought or ransack their rooms looking for secret diaries. At the same time, guarding their emotional health may mean setting standards to know when privacy is appropriate and when disclosure is better.

As emotionally loaded issues are intentionally observed, discussed and managed, great benefits result. We can be empowered to understand our children better and work with them more effectively, especially at times when their hearts are most vulnerable.

Seeing the Unseen

As you parent, you are most likely to be aware of experiences that may trigger strong emotions in your child. Have they experienced emotional stress like bullying, the death of a loved one or the trauma of divorce? Help them grieve as needed and work through feelings of anger or helplessness. Validate their emotions. Help them move forward.

Do they seem "stuck" and in need of further assistance? Look into professional counseling and don't feel any sense of guilt or failure for using a counselor. A greater failure is not to get the help the child needs!

As a parent, I hope you're encouraged to be aware of "hot spots" and take the time to investigate them, no matter your child's age. Find the source of the heat, whether it's a one-time or ongoing issue. And remember, hormones are just like gas added to a fire. If your child is still young, then take the opportunity to check the wiring way before the teen years. If you're in the midst of adolescence, be prepared to let your words and interaction be a source of cooling assurance. With intentionality, you can build a home that supports inner lives of beautifully managed power and light.

Now that the "wiring" in our house has been addressed, we can move to the construction of the first floor. This floor features the Five Doors of the Heart, which are perfect for building a good heart, even in a very young child.

Relationship Evaluation

- **Are you really listening?** Honestly evaluate your relationship with your child(ren). Are you truly interested in them, no matter their age? Consider beginning a weekly one-on-one just to get to know them better. Ask them to share of themselves, but also be sure to set the example by sharing of yourself as well.

- **Rules AND relationship** are vital to a child's growth. Too many rules can easily lead to rebellion. If you feel stressed, you may be trying to control too much. Relax and watch, and consider less intervention.

- **Consider the thought life and emotions.** Have you and your child ever discussed how to manage thoughts, or how to make decisions because of facts, not because of feelings? Read *Battlefield of the Mind* yourself, and consider the younger versions for your family.

- _____

  _____

  _____

Building Materials

Books and Web Sites
See Appendix A for more details.
★*Eyes Wide Open: Avoiding the Heartbreak of Emotional Promiscuity*, Brienne Murk (25)
Emotional Purity: An Affair of the Heart, Heather Arnel Paulsen (26)
Also see appendix A, numbers 11, 18, 22, 37, 41, 43

Truths to Memorize
See Appendix B for complete texts.
Pleasing Thoughts (21)
Right Thoughts (28)
Avoid Evil (41)

Scripts
See Appendix D for complete texts.
Social Networking Chats (11)
Maintaining Cell Phone Boundaries (12)

Object Lessons
See Appendix E for complete texts.
Clean Cups, Dirty Dishes (1)
Text the Love (12)
Loving Listening (16)
Cell Phone 101 (17)

Contracts
See Appendix F for complete texts.
Contract B: The Bishop Family's House Rules

Part 3

The First Floor—Five Doors

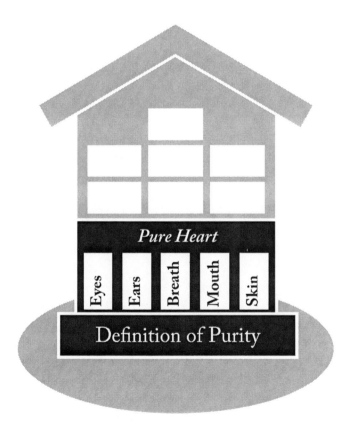

Chapter 6

The Inner Person—A Pure Heart

Our senses are incredible tools that enable us to experience the world around us. But our senses also reveal spiritual doors of the heart. The material we bring in through these doors must be chosen and evaluated to guard our hearts spiritually and keep them clean. That's why the first floor of the Planned Purity diagram focuses on guarding the five senses.

The wisdom of guarding the five senses is taken directly from a passage in the book of Proverbs where a father is giving his son advice for living a successful life. Read this paragraph and circle the words that relate to the five senses.

"My son, pay attention to what I say; listen closely to my words. Do not let them out of your sight, keep them within your heart; for they are life to those who find them and health to a man's whole body....Put away perversity from your mouth; keep corrupt talk far from your lips. Let your eyes look straight ahead, fix your gaze directly before you. Make level paths for your feet and take only ways that are firm. Do not swerve to the right or the left; keep your foot from evil."

Proverbs 4:20-22, 24-27

Here are the five references to the senses:

1. "Let your eyes look straight ahead." (Eyes)

2. "Listen closely to my words." (Ears)

3. "[My words]...are life to those who find them." (Breath, referred to as "life" and connected with the physical sense of smell)

4. "Put away perversity from your mouth." (Mouth, connected with the physical sense of taste)

5. "Make level paths for your feet and take only ways that are firm." (Skin, referred to as "feet" and connected with the physical sense of touch)

What comes through the five doors of our senses makes a huge difference in our understanding and pursuit of a good heart. As parents, we want to continually evaluate our children's cultural influences (not to mention our own). We also want to train our children to choose positive influences and avoid negative ones. Even the youngest children can understand that their hearts can be "dirtied," that they can choose to keep them "clean," and that they can start again when they fail.

What comes in through the five doors of our senses makes a huge difference in our pursuit of a good heart.

The Doorkeeper

Whatever is true, whatever is noble, whatever is right, whatever is pure, whatever is lovely, whatever is admirable—if anything is excellent or praiseworthy—think about such things.[1]

This verse lets us know exactly how we should be "loading our children up." Everything that's good and right should be coming in through these Five Doors.

Remember, purity is about everything we experience and think about. Sexual sin can make us dirty, but sexual sin isn't how we get dirty in the first place. We get dirty because we don't carefully choose what we allow through our doors, sexual or otherwise.

When I wrote my book, *The Squire and the Scroll*, I felt strongly that that story needed to explain the Five Doors of the Heart. In the story, the squire has to successfully complete five quests, based on the doors of the heart, to retrieve the Lantern of Purest Light for his kingdom. I wanted parents to have a tool to use with boys or girls to introduce the idea of using the Five Doors to keep their hearts clean.

In the following chapters, we'll look at each door of the heart in detail. The Upgrading sections at the end of each chapter will provide suggestions on ways to open the heart to good input. Downsizing sections will suggest ways of limiting negative input to the heart.

You'll also find space provided for you to record ways that you can downsize or upgrade in your own family. You know your family best, so please write down the ideas that come to your mind because they will be even better and more personal than what I can provide here. Now let's get started by looking at the first door, the door of the eyes.

Building Materials

Books and Web Sites
See Appendix A for more details.
The Squire and the Scroll, Jennie Bishop (5)
A Child's Book of Virtues, William Bennett (7)
Preschool Purity of Heart, Jennie Bishop (3)
Life Lessons from The Squire and the Scroll, Jennie Bishop (13)
Life Lessons from The Princess and the Kiss, Jennie Bishop (17)

Truths to Memorize
See Appendix B for complete texts.
The Five Senses of Purity (2)
Eyes (3)
Ears (4)
Breath (5)
Mouth (6)
Skin (7)
See also General Purity Verses, numbers 18-33.

Object Lessons
See Appendix E for complete texts.
Clean Cups, Dirty Dishes (1)
Pick Your Poison (2)
Be Good to Your Boat (3)
Pure Premium (4)

Door 1

The Eyes

During a trip to Tanzania, Africa, on a drive to the Kenyan coast, our family circled stunning Mt. Kilimanjaro. We couldn't stop looking; our eyes were glued to the magnificent mountain. Photographing it from every side, jockeying for positions at the window, we feasted our eyes.

In a museum at the Lavra Monastery in Kiev, Ukraine, we viewed works of art that were only observable through a microscope. The tiny details of the designs in these pieces were as breathtaking as the mammoth, breathtaking thousand-year-old architecture of the monastery itself—all of it enjoyed through the miracle of sight.

Back home on the farm, I love the skies and the acres of wheat waving in the wind. That's one of my favorite sights of all—next to the faces of my family.

Think of how Adam felt when he first looked at Eve, or how you feel when your child or spouse looks especially beautiful to you. What an incredible gift God gave us when he made us to see!

Our eyes can never be full of looking, looking, looking. Unfortunately, not everything set before us contributes to a good heart and a clean mind. It's important to recognize that the things we view again and again can mold us to think and then behave in certain ways.

We want to help our children guard themselves from what could enter through the eyes to pollute their hearts.

Turning the Eyes Away

Especially in the case of our young men, we must teach the art of "turning our eyes away." (*Every Young Man's Battle*, authored by Stephen Arterburn and Fred Stoeker, [Waterbrook Press], includes excellent instruction in "bouncing" the eyes.) Degrading images that we never dreamed would be displayed in public are now brazenly tacked onto billboards and pasted in mall windows. We have seen so many of them that we barely notice, but that very familiarity is what drags our country into moral decay. How can we regain our innocence and guard our children's innocence as well?

Our family has had several discussions about the way our minds keep a catalog of images. Intense, fearful, or graphic images can remain in a viewer's memory for a long, long time, creating fear or unhealthy fantasy, tipping behavior toward violence, or tempting a married person to compare a spouse's performance to the one they saw on-screen.

Virtual Reality

We all know that technology is fun, helpful, and a great danger at the same time. Let's figure out how to get the benefits and avoid the problems.

The first consideration is time. The time spent focused on technology can make us less interactive and separate us from those we love and those we have the responsibility to help. Whether it's television, games, or the Internet, on-screen pursuits can easily snatch hours away from us—hours that could be spent living our own lives instead of living them vicariously through characters on a screen or in a virtual world. Too much time in front of a screen will sap our energy to share what only we have to offer in person, and that is a terrible tragedy.

It isn't fair to say "I have no time" when we are spending hours on the Internet. And it isn't beneficial to a child to be allowed to spend hours in front of a screen and become inept at conversation, or too technologically entranced to read, play a board game, take a walk or ride a bike. Too much technology can ruin a good heart.

Television

Consider this quote from author John Piper, an expert in priorities that lead to personal satisfaction:

TV still reigns as the great life-waster. The main problem with TV is not how much smut is available, though that is a problem. Just the ads are enough to sow fertile seeds of greed and lust, no matter what program you're watching. The greater problem is banality. A mind fed daily on TV diminishes... The content is so trivial and so shallow that the capacity of the mind to think worthy thoughts withers, and the capacity of the heart to feel deep emotions shrivels...[2]

A good warning. Not only is television a time-waster; most of it is mind-numbingly trivial and shallow.

The solution is to evaluate television the same way you evaluate your diet. Are you watching what contributes to your family's health, or are you wasting hours ingesting junk food?

Previewing takes time, but its payoffs are huge. Watch before your children watch (or at least watch with them), and don't forget to evaluate your own viewing as well. Evaluate the

Watch before your children watch, and evaluate your own viewing as well.

practices, attitudes, and situations for whether they will reinforce positive or negative growth. Use movie review sites to check out movies before you watch them if you can't view them in entirety. (Good sites include www. pluggedinonline.org and www.dove.org.)

Television has some good to offer, and educators agree that a well-produced children's program can develop a child's learning abilities. But even neutral programs should not be daily fare. Seemingly innocent children's programs often foster disrespect, commercials breed materialism, and all this contributes to a muddied heart.

A good friend of mine plopped her preschool son down in front of the TV long enough for her to take a shower. When she returned she was shocked to find him in front of a sexy Britney Spears soft drink commercial. We can't take a chance with TV babysitting!

During the younger years, watch what they're watching. Show them how to use the "off" button. As children get older, facilitate deeper discussion. When you watch a movie or show together, talk about what's happening. Ask if they approve or disapprove, and why.

Set family standards early and teach your children to use online reviews for guidance. One great device we have used is the TV Guardian, which can be set to blank out obscenities. This won't catch everything, but it can be a good start in protecting your children's innocence if the material has merit without the profanity.

Pornography

Pornography is legally defined as "the representation in books, magazines, photographs, films, and other media of scenes of sexual behavior that are erotic or lewd and are designed to arouse sexual interest."[3]

A Canadian study shows that one out of three boys thirteen and fourteen struggles with a developing addiction to pornography.[4] Seventy percent of eigh- *Pornography has moved to* teen- to twenty-four-year-old men in the U.S. *the mainstream* visit pornographic sites online in a typical *of our lives.* month. Imagine—only 30 percent of these men choose *not* to do so. This statistic alone proves that pornography has moved to the mainstream of our lives.

When men are in their twenties and thirties, the percentage who report being regular users of pornography remains almost as high (66 percent).[5] Most of these users continue to view porn as they grow older. Forty million U.S. adult viewers (72 percent male, 28 percent female) are regularly looking at online pornography.[6]

Even what society defines as pornography has changed greatly since I was young. In my growing up years, today's ads for women's underwear would have been completely inappropriate. Now those images are enlarged and plastered in store windows and on billboards for everyone to see—child and adult alike.

John Adams, our second president, made this troubling observation about women and modesty. As you read it, think about how it applies to our society.

From all that I have read of history and government and human life and manners, I have drawn this conclusion: that the manners of women were the most infallible barometer to ascertain the degree of morality and virtue of a nation. The Jews, the

Greeks, the Romans, the Swiss, the Dutch, all lost their public spirit and their republican forms of government when they lost the modesty and domestic virtues of their women.[7]

Judging by John Adam's quote, our country is in big trouble. Because we see so much pornography in so many mediums, we must protect and educate our children in matters of human value, modesty, integrity, and honor. When our children do view something inappropriate, we need to take the opportunity to educate, not overreact.

Let me give you a personal example. Some time ago, while I was away, my daughters saw the movie *The Phantom of the Opera*. I had not previewed it. They were so excited about the movie that they asked me to watch it with them.

The movie was stunning, in music, in sets, in performances, and costumes. But as I watched the scene with the famous song "The Music of the Night," my heart began to pound. This was a scene of seduction, with the female lead character wearing sensual nightclothes and the Phantom touching her intimately. One of my daughters exclaimed, "Oh, Mom, this is my favorite scene!"

I had to leave the room to check my emotions. By now, I was speaking regularly on guarding the heart from such intimate displays of sexuality. For years I had tried to instill these concepts in my daughters, and was brokenhearted by my young girl's inability to see through the beautiful music and sets to the inappropriateness of the scene for viewing in our home. I paced for hours, so angry I could barely speak or pray. What would I do? I wanted to yell—at my kids, at the person who had shown them the movie, at God. Instead, I recognized an opportunity.

That night the girls and I had a talk. We defined words like *pornography*, *obsession*, and *lust*. We talked about whether or not we should allow anyone to touch us like that. And I printed out the words to "The Music of the Night." Here's just a sample:

Touch me, trust me, savor each sensation.
Let the dream begin,
Let your darker side give in,
To the power of the music that I write,
The power of the music of the night![8]

What a perfect lesson of how we are coaxed to let down the guard around our hearts! My girls and I talked about the beauty and popularity of the song and the scene, but how its message might influence someone to do something they regretted later. We talked about the beauty of a marriage bed and the fact that the Phantom was placing Christine on his bed to lead her into an act of immorality. That night was an amazing learning opportunity.

Now, *Phantom* is not a movie that I want my children to watch over and over, even with edits, or one that I would show to guests. But its intrusion into our lives gave me an opportunity to teach in a moment I did not expect.

Acting Out

As a past student of musical theater, I understand that some scenes may be portrayed somewhat graphically to be true to the subject matter. I also understand nudity in classical art. But I believe our society has gone too far with actresses and actors performing more and more sexual acts for the public to view. This kind of acting out is not artistic but immoral.

It used to be that sexual portrayals of this type would be limited to showings in seedy houses of erotica. But now even more explicit scenes are available for showing in the privacy of our homes.

Please hear me: if someone were doing those things in front of you or your family live, would you allow it? I doubt it. But because the acts are in a movie, we tolerate them and sometimes say, "It's just a movie."

If your child actually views such a scene, please do not ignore what happened. Explain that it is never appropriate for actors and actresses to act out sex or sexual acts for others to watch. Those who do so will leave destruction in their wake, affecting children, marriages, families and general moral character. Such acting degrades the viewers and actors in the process. Set your family's boundaries accordingly. Discuss the fact that actors are paid to entertain, and their roles do not necessarily reflect truth, goodness or beauty, sexually or otherwise.

Don't say, "It's just a movie." Sexual acts portrayed for public viewing are immoral.

Video Games

Similar dangers exist in the world of video gaming. What games are our children playing? Have you actually watched while they play? If not, you may be in for some unpleasant surprises.

First, games often feature scantily clad female characters (sometimes for the purpose of virtual prostitution), which can lead to the objectification of real women. Second, the high level of violence numbs players toward violence, objectifies people in general, and lowers the understanding of the value of life.

Many games speak of success in terms of the number of "kills." Preserving other humans' lives is the most basic level of morality, but our games give us the opportunity to practice murder. Yes, it's just a game; but when the game numbs our perception of the seriousness of injury and death to human beings in real life, it becomes dangerous, as was the case with Devin Thompson. This sixteen-year-old from Alabama copied actions he saw in a video shooter game to kill two police officers and a dispatcher.[9]

First-person shooter games mimic military combat exercises without the context or safeguards of specialized military training.

Devin's heart was definitely affected and resulted in murderous behavior.

Most normal human brains are hardwired against killing their own species. In the military, soldiers are desensitized to this aversion through a monitored process. In many ways, first-person shooter video games mimic the process used by the military. The problem is that our teens play these games without the context, safeguards, or discipline of specialized military training.[10]

Evaluate the games your children play. Are they exceptionally violent? Are the characters immodestly dressed? Is evil celebrated? Set boundaries intentionally so that your children will learn how to set boundaries for themselves and how to be intentional in their own choices.

Play or watch video games with your children so you're aware of exactly what they're seeing and what other information is on the game DVDs. If you don't enjoy these games, you may find it painful (I can relate), but participation will reveal negative aspects of some games, often hidden in the extras or in higher levels. You may be able to get some information about games from the Internet, but engaging with your child through video games is a more beneficial path to ongoing communication.

Are there benefits to playing games of gratuitous violence and blood? I have trouble answering that question in the affirmative. If you decide that these games will not be played in your home, be prepared to back your reasons up with truth and explain them to your family. As with all technology, remember to set time limits for the video games that you choose to allow. Your child is meant for so much more than a virtual experience.

The Internet

Just as television has great advantages and great pitfalls, so does the Internet. A child (or a writer like me) can accomplish a load of research and finish a project just by surfing online. We can check weather, stay in touch by email, and find all kinds of creative, educational materials.

On the other hand, the Internet makes pornography rampant and accessible to everyone. And the Internet creates a way for relationships to be built on nothing but cyber conversation, sometimes with disastrous results. You wouldn't allow a stranger to walk in your front door, go into your child's room, shut the door, and have a long conversation. In the same way, you have a right to restrict who your child communicates with online.

Social networking (Facebook is popular at this writing) can be extremely dangerous for youth. Online predators are adept at building friendships and luring young women into meeting them. For example, a sixteen-year-old from Michigan named Katherine Lester met a young Palestinian man online, built a secret relationship, bought a plane ticket to the Middle East, and was on her way to Tel Aviv before her parents figured out what was going on.[11] Katherine was intercepted at the airport, but other young women have managed to secretly meet online "friends" who had sex with them and dumped them or held them captive for sex trafficking. Therefore,

Restrict who your child communicates with online just as you restrict who comes in your front door.

online relationships must be understood, monitored, and limited to guard our children's hearts and even their lives.

Keep the family computers in an open, common area and limit time spent "surfing." Require that sites are approved by a parent before they're visited. Outlaw interaction online with anyone the child does not know. Set boundaries before the technology enters the house if you can. (See appendix F for a sample family technology contract.) I will say much more about technology in a later chapter.

Reading Material

Reading has somewhat fallen out of favor with our modern world, but youth are still the target markets for a lot of literature. Be aware of what your child reads and load them up with good books and classic literature. But recognize that even when you

Parents choose if, when and how their school-aged children will be exposed to new information.

try to make good choices, not everything in a book may reflect your values. Help the child understand story lines through the filter of your values and the pursuit of a good heart. Read what your children read when you can, and be open to any communication on subject matter. Ask questions about books that are read as requirements for school. Many classics have disturbing sections that might need explanation for your child at his or her age. As a parent, you choose when and how your school-aged child will be exposed to such information, if at all.

Ask what your child likes to read, and buy books for them. Be interested. When your child is young enough to be read to, choose books with great messages and talk about what the story teaches, or just read for fun. Reading is the best way to be well-rounded in our education, and it's a relaxed way to spend time together.

Again, check your own reading material. How do the stories you enjoy contribute to a lively, virtuous imagination in your own life? What magazines do your read? Load up on the good stuff, limit or toss away the negative influences. Read a lot, but also evaluate how reading material is affecting you and your kids.

Summary

Remember: Proverbs says, "Let your eyes look straight ahead,"[12] implying that we should be intentional about material we focus on visually. We want to avoid being distracted by visual images that will contaminate our hearts and lead our minds into dangerous places.

At the same time, we want to constantly learn how to focus the door of our eyes on good things, loading the heart with good input as we share a sunset, a meaningful film, or a conversation with a hurting friend via the Internet. This is one very important and practical way we and our children develop and maintain pure hearts.

At the end of this chapter, I offer you ideas for downsizing less beneficial material and upgrading the good input. These ideas are intended to inspire you to write your own ideas, either in this book or a separate notebook. After you've got the creative juices flowing for ideas about the door of the eyes, you'll be ready for the next chapter as we similarly discuss the door of the ears.

Downsizing

- **Limit nightly TV.** Interrupt the habit of sitting around the TV. Set aside at least one night a week for family time without a video screen. Instead, do an object lesson devotional, work on memorizing verses or fun poetry, or just play board games. The key is to engage as a family, to talk, and to have fun. Make snacks together. Go bowling. Walk or ride bikes. Live out the answer to the question, "What did we do before television?"

- **Cut back computer screen time.** Talk with your spouse about what you think is enough screen time per day. Encourage the kids to use the screen time they are given wisely. Always be cheerful and offer options. "Okay, screen time is up! I've got two choices for supper. Want to help decide?"

- **Take a break.** Agree to go cold turkey from TV, the Internet, and video games for a time. Let everyone buy new books or visit the library and take the time to read instead. Before bed, gather as a family to give everyone a minute or so to talk about what he or she read. Offer to get more new books if your child liked the one he or she read.

* _____

   _____

   _____

Upgrading

* **Read together.** Read silly poems to each other. Take turns reading chapters of a book like *The Tale of Despereaux* or one of the hilarious Judy Moody stories. Make up character voices. Fun for all ages!

* **Host a game night.** Let the kids teach you their favorite computer or video game. Take the time to understand how to play and give it your best shot. Caution: you might have fun! Really listen to your child's reasons for enjoying the game, and offer to play it with them again at another time.

* **Surf the Internet together.** Choose a subject you want to know more about, or look up a local restaurant to check it out, and then go there for supper. Use these opportunities to talk about safety online and to learn more about your child's interests.

* _____

   _____

   _____

Building Materials

Books and Web Sites
See Appendix A for more details.
Preschool Purity of Heart, Jennie Bishop (3)
The Squire and the Scroll/Life Lessons from The Squire and the Scroll, Jennie Bishop (13)
Life Lessons from The Princess and the Kiss, Jennie Bishop (17)
★www.icarecoalition.org/icare.asp (63)
www.defenderministries.com (64)
★www.cpyu.org, Center for Parent/Youth Understanding (44)
★www.pluggedinonline.org, movie/music review site (59)
www.dove.org, movie/music review site (60)

Truths to Memorize
See Appendix B for complete texts.
The Five Senses of Purity (2)
Eyes (3)

Scripts
See Appendix D for complete texts.
Explaining Pornography: Son (5)
Explaining Pornography: Daughter (6)
Making Movie Choices (7)
Editing Inappropriate Movie Scenes (8)
Social Networking Modesty (10)
Social Networking Chats (11)

Object Lessons
See Appendix E for complete texts.
Dark Inside (9)
Real or Not? (Movies) (10)
Real or Not? (Games) (11)
Text the Love (12)
Online Study (13)
Screen Time Log (14)
Pioneer Night (15)

Cell Phone 101 (17)

Contracts
See Appendix F for complete texts.
Contract C: Technology Agreement

Door 2

The Ears

Think of the many joys of hearing. Beautiful music, the sound of a loved one's voice or a baby's coo, birdsongs, the rushing wind, water lapping against the sand—all of these are gifts. Because hearing is so important, we guard our ears physically. For example, we may steer clear of extreme noise. I recently accompanied a friend to an MRI test and was handed earplugs to cut down on the jackhammer-like sounds of the machine. And I can't count the number of times my mother reminded me, "Don't stick that Q-tip in there too far—you could hurt your eardrum!"

The importance of our sense of hearing is made evident simply by the number of times the word *listen* and its derivatives are used in the Bible—more than five hundred! When Jesus wanted to underscore a vital lesson, he often said: "He who has ears, let him hear!"[13]

On the other hand, hearing isn't only about the sounds we experience. An ability to be comfortable with quiet is also important for each of us, especially in our media-saturated country. Leaving the TV or radio on as constant companions is not beneficial, even if the programming is good. Bob Smithouser of *Plugged In* magazine asks, "How can we expect to hear his 'still, small voice' amid the cacophony of culture? The din has become…an obstacle."[14] Limitations on listening time and devoting certain hours at home to quietness will help the whole family value their listening ability. It will also improve the likelihood of developing a sensitivity in listening to others or in prayer.

Consider the following opportunities to keep our hearts pure through the door of our ears.

The Influence of Music

When I was a teen, I remember vehemently defending one particular album to my mother. On the cover, the artist was depicted as a prostitute, but I was so drawn to the music that I didn't care. Music has a powerful ability to evoke and connect with feelings. As such, it prepares the heart for transformation—either toward goodness *or* toward moral decay.

Musical styles are not necessarily a gauge of the "goodness" of music. Lyrics, however, often leave little doubt as to musician's intent. In Christian music the desire to reflect faith is most often obvious, but today's secular music sends all kinds of messages, many of which can be incredibly violent, hateful or explicit.

Some people argue that music lyrics do not influence behavior, but plenty of truth exists to the contrary. Jingles are used in advertising because they cement a brand name into a listener's memory and therefore increase sales. Who could forget "Plop, plop, fizz, fizz, oh, what a relief it is" (Alka-Seltzer) or the completely cat-performed Meow Mix theme? For the same reason, churches set biblical concepts and verses to music to make them easy to memorize. However, on a darker note, negative messages set to music have been associated with depression, suicides, murders, and many losses of sexual innocence.

Music powerfully evokes and connects with feelings, preparing the heart for transformation—good or bad.

Artists are given a cultural power in America that is too powerful and dangerous to ignore. If we guard our children's ears when they are young and teach them to evaluate music for themselves, they will learn to steer clear of subjects incongruent with goodness. However, if we are uninvolved in the musical fabric of our children's lives, their values, our relationships, and their futures may all erode.

Actively Listening to Music

We trained our daughters to evaluate music lyrics when they were very young. One day in a retail store, one of my daughters came to me with her hands over her ears.

"What's the matter, honey?" I asked.

"Mom, don't you hear those words?" she said. "I don't want to listen to that!"

She had been listening actively to the background music in the store, although it had gone right over my head. Recognizing the song as one we had pointed out as inappropriate, she took the initiative to guard her ears on her own.

As we train our children to listen actively, we must also evaluate our own listening habits as well. How do we as parents allow ourselves to be influenced? Have we allowed questionable listening material to wash over ourselves and our families, naively believing that its message has no power?

When children are young and as they grow, have conversations about lyrics and the power of the music behind them. Use these times to build an appreciation for different musical preferences. Distancing ourselves from youthful music as we grow older seems natural but leaves our children to fend for themselves against the dangers of the modern music soundscape. Our children need us to be familiar with present media trends so we can relate to them—otherwise those trends will very likely divide us.

An appreciation of diversity in musical styles is helpful in parenting and all our relationships.

This is what often happens with music in families—differing tastes in styles can build walls of separation. But this is unnecessary. Adult snobbery toward musical styles only pushes our children away. An appreciation of diversity and personalities is helpful in parenting and in all our relationships. For updates on music and other key elements of teen culture, visit cpyu.org (Center for Parent-Youth Understanding).

I live in a musical household. My husband is a composer, and my daughters enjoy ballet and opera. We also appreciate pop music, jazz, classical, rock, and musical styles from all over the world. Sometimes we listen to songs by Sting or Johnny Cash or Paul McCartney or Paul Simon. Our younger daughter may be cranking up an inspirational station in her bedroom or listening to piano concertos. Our older daughter appreciates a lot of guitar, but at our house she is usually the one hollering for Dad to turn down the volume on his guitar. The key is that we stay mindful of how the musical input is affecting us. Too many empty, negative, or inappropriate lyrics are to the heart like too much candy to the body: they can eventually cause a sickness that draws us into a world of emptiness and untruths.

A special area of which to be aware is the "romantic song." Yes, there are plenty of great love songs out there, and many are simply sweet. But a preteen or teenager who is spending too much time listening to songs that constantly focus on falling in love can easily be distracted from a pursuit of a balanced life and a good heart. She may become crippled emotionally in her thought life.

The rest of our culture is convinced that romance is the apex of existence. Lasting love between a man and woman is precious and wonderful, but not to the exclusion of all other experiences and pursuits. To help guard the emotional purity we discussed in "Emotions and Thought Life," our children will need instruction to develop discipline in listening habits.

In conclusion, remember that you don't want to create arguments about music during the preteen and teen years or outlaw music without showing your child that you have made an effort to understand it. Listen, discuss, and seek truth together instead of making legalistic rules and overreacting. You will build relationship with your preteens and teens and help them develop their own consideration of music that contributes to the development of a good heart.

Seeing + Hearing = Powerful Impact

The power of television is in the combination of seeing and hearing. Be intentional about what your family hears through the television. Protect your family's innocence by purchasing a device to "bleep" profanities, being careful to pay attention to reviews and ratings (although ratings do not always accurately reflect what we consider offensive content).

When unexpected speech or situations do arise, it's important to talk about them instead of ignoring them. Saying nothing can make our child think the language or situation is acceptable.

Music videos feature some of the most explicit aural and visual material on TV today. An artist can easily introduce a song with innocent lyrics and then produce a filthy video to go along with that song, making explicit images available to anyone online. MTV (and shows like it)

Saying nothing about language or inappropriate viewing material may lead your child to believe you condone it.

wants to own our children through addictive, offensive lyrics and images.[15]

These types of entertainment should never be "just part of growing up." They are dangerous and damaging to our children. They destroy their understanding and practice of goodness. They encourage immodesty, promiscuity, and violent, selfish behavior. It's as simple as that. Never underestimate the power of eyes and ears being engaged simultaneously.

Profanity

Sooner or later, your children will hear someone in the community use profanity of some kind, and will look to you for explanation. This is a golden teaching opportunity. After the first day at public school, our teenager's first observation at the dinner table was this: "I've never heard the f-word so many times!"

Our sixth grader asked, "What's the f-word?" Good question! Right there at the dinner table, we took the time to actually identify the word, to discuss where it came from, to talk about how the word cheapens the beautiful gift of sex God gave us, and to show how people who use the word feel powerful for awhile but end up just having a terrible attitude and not looking very smart.

If we don't explain what these words mean, someone else will. Or if the word is heard and not explained, it may be thought of as no big deal, just another acceptable way of speaking. Communicating without coarse talk is beneficial spiritually, intellectually and relationally, no matter what the norm on the street seems to be.

Respectful Speech

At the same time we talk about words to avoid, we also want to talk about words to encourage in our families' conversations. The words we hear daily at home have the power to refresh, recreate and encourage us, or to discourage, disempower, and destroy. The "thank you" and "I love you" that seem optional are actually prerequisites for healthy growth in a child, and we as parents should certainly foster such speech and practice.

Summary

Proverbs says, "Listen closely to my words."[16] This particular verse comes from a father instructing his son in matters of a good heart. The number of choices and sources in listening material today is astonishing, and we are responsible for the choices we make in guarding our hearts via the door of the ears.

Modern music plays a strong role in forming our hearts and the hearts of our children. Choosing listening material wisely will not only make us more successful in a pursuit of integrity and responsible relationships, but will also draw us together as we share what affects us emotionally without judging.

If we don't explain explicit language to our children, someone else will.

Following are ways to downsize and upgrade when it comes to the heart and the door of the ears. Please add your own ideas. In the next section we'll explore a very unique door of the heart—the door of the breath.

Downsizing

- **Limit secular music.** Begin to find ways to bulk up on music and songs that inspire and skim off songs without positive content. Think of music as a kind of pyramid, just as we think of the food pyramid. Music not directly contributing to growth in goodness may not be harmful, but it still can be junk food compared to music that is directly intended to inspire, reflect, or celebrate. Challenge your kids to maintain a balanced musical diet.

- **Outlaw cutting comments.** Really listen to the conversation that goes on at home. Would you say such things to friends or business associates? Would you allow your children to speak in such ways outside the home? Open lines of communication to allow each other to say, "That hurt!" and seek to strike hurtful comments from the family vocabulary. Load each other up with compliments and encouragement instead.

* _____

  _____

  _____

Upgrading

* **Enjoy music together.** Whether it's during a family devotional time, or a ride in the car, or a time when you're just celebrating in an uninhibited, even silly way, play and/or sing music as a family. The more you do it, the more natural it becomes.

* **Listen together.** Teach your children to appreciate style differences and to evaluate lyrics critically. Use any inappropriate lyrics as opportunities to talk about how some speech or ideas are dishonorable.

* **Buy music.** Make positive music a priority in your family budget; see it as an investment in your family's heart health! Offer to buy your child CDs or songs that are consistent with family guidelines for purity, your child's age, and style preferences. When you buy music for them promptly, you become an ally on the music front instead of an enemy.

* **Require respect.** Restore the old-fashioned manners that give others value, especially at home. Greet one another in the morning. Make the words "please," "thank you," "excuse me," and "I'm sorry" requirements of family life. Before you tell other family members to use their manners, make sure you are using yours as well!

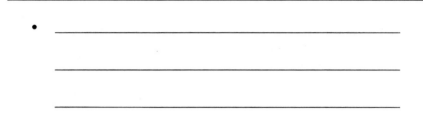

Building Materials

Books and Web Sites
See Appendix A for more details.
Preschool Purity of Heart, Jennie Bishop (3)
Life Lessons from The Princess and the Kiss, Jennie Bishop (17)
Life Lessons from The Squire and the Scroll, Jennie Bishop (13)
★www.cpyu.org, Center for Parent/Youth Understanding (44)
★www.pluggedinonline.org (59)

Truths to Memorize
See Appendix B for complete texts.
The Five Senses of Purity (2)
Ears (4)

Scripts
See Appendix D for complete texts.
Speaking to a Host Parent About Media (9)
Maintaining Cell Phone Boundaries (12)
Responding to Unwanted Phone Calls (13)
Making Music Choices (14)
Online Bullying (17)
Sexual Bullying (18)

Object Lessons
See Appendix E for complete texts.
Loving Listening (16)
Cell Phone 101 (17)
Plug Your Ears (18)
CD Frenzy (19)

Door 3

The Breath

None of us knows exactly how we came into being. But we know that when we left the womb we had to breathe air, or we wouldn't have survived. With our first coughing, gasping or crying breaths, we inherited the magnificent gift of life.

What is the purpose of the breath we're given? Without clean air, living things wither and die—and without purpose, breathing becomes a desperately empty affair, perhaps even a despairing process that we seek to end.

We guard our physical breath by avoiding dangerous inhalants, drugs, and cigarettes, and teaching our children to do the same, even in the early years. But how do we guard against the poisonous attitudes that corrupt a good heart and devalue human life?

Job uses the phrase "the breath of God" being in him in his well-known biblical account.[17] The very breath we breathe is a gift, and the life we give, share, respect and protect is a treasure.

Celebration and Thanksgiving

Our first response to the breath of life should be employing it in celebration and thanksgiving. Recognizing the great privilege of being alive leads us to honor the one who made us and loves us, and this worship is the energy that makes life worth living. We were made to reflect and radiate the same care for everyone in all we do.

Sadly, the definition of *worship* is often limited to "the music people do in church" just as *purity* is defined only as "sexual abstinence." A more accurate definition says that we worship when we do our jobs cheerfully and well. We can worship as we care for our families with gratitude for the "messiness" of their presence. We can celebrate with each word, each action, each loving and grateful expression of the sacred life we enjoy. We can constantly express thankfulness, even (and perhaps especially) when times are hard. Our trials prove we are alive, and give us new opportunities to develop good hearts as we choose to approach trouble or inconvenience with optimism and hope instead of complaining.

This broader definition makes the importance of the breath paramount as a door to the heart. Without the breath we would have neither life nor purpose. What an incredible gift, a gift to celebrate hour by hour, even when our lives are imperfect!

In Need of Purpose

At the time of this writing, I have an aunt I love dearly who is ninety years old. She has lived a private life in her later years. She has lost both breasts due to cancer, her memory fails daily, and she has broken a hip, thus others must assist to move her from a bed to a chair. Sadly, she has turned to alcohol to bury the loneliness and despair she can't seem to admit.

My aunt used to attend church regularly. She has many dear friends who love her and visit her regularly. She used to enjoy an active social life. But at our last visit, she told us repeatedly, "I keep asking God to take me!" Sadly, she seemed to take no joy in anything.

Now consider our other friend, a neighbor who has endured suffering beyond what I could ever imagine. During a normal delivery of her second son, she was somehow infected with a fast-spreading virus. She was taken to surgery, and when she awoke she discovered that doctors had found it necessary to amputate both of her arms at the elbows and both her legs at the knees.

If I were this woman, I would have given up entirely. Lawsuits ensued and recovery and therapy began. A caregiver was hired to help with her children every day. Yet every time I see this wife and mother, she is smiling and happy to see me. I hug her and shake her elbow as her electric wheelchair purrs beneath her on her way to the mailbox with a caregiver. She has offered to help my daughter with her Spanish.

"There is still a lot I can do," she says enthusiastically. And, indeed, she has made trips to speak to other amputees and share her story. I imagine her talks are wildly successful. She is so excited about the "bionic legs" she will soon receive and can't wait to try them out. She answers the phone, holds her little son, and encourages everyone she sees.

That is a woman who guards the door of the breath. She has hung a sign on the door that says, "No whining—I am alive!" Her heart shimmers, and despair shivers when it passes by the house of life she has built.

When we stand guard at the door of our breath, we protect it by refusing to allow despair in, or allowing others to lose hope. We guard it by believing that we have a purpose in existing. We guard it by refusing to take lightly or complain about the gift of our lives. We let joy in!

Valuing Human Life

Seeing the purpose in our lives leads us to value all life. Where do we stand on the issue of the unborn or euthanasia? These are matters of the breath. When we devalue life and breath, we dishonor ourselves and dirty our hearts in the very deepest way. We ignore the gift of our precious, possible seventy-plus years, and those years that others have been given.

To go a step further, are we willing to give care for those in crisis pregnancy situations and support adoptive parents as well as single moms who choose to value life? Do we stand by the side of the elderly or handicapped, helping bear the challenges that complicate their gift of existence? Do our children know about people in these situations, or have we avoided opportunities to value life and breath by blessing those who are in difficult situations?

When we devalue life and breath, we dishonor ourselves and dirty our hearts in the very deepest way.

Helping those in other cultures through humanitarian efforts is also a wonderful way to value life. When we help with needs outside our cultural bubble, we learn to value our own lives more deeply.

Even simple acts of kindness toward those in thankless jobs in the service industry are deeply meaningful. Do we treat cashiers and waitresses as people of great value, or do we look down upon them or treat them as less than ourselves? We can call them by name. We can encourage them on a hard day. We can be the one person who values their lives, and we will be developing a good, pure heart as we do.

Respect for the Earth and Creation

Valuing life leads us to value the earth and to be thoughtful about how we treat the creatures that live on earth with us. Earth is an amazing place to live, and our responsibility to care for. Without the planet we would perish. Below are some easy ways we can be responsible in caring for our home.

- Teaching our children to care for the earth by recycling and disposing of trash responsibly

- Modeling good stewardship of what we have, and avoiding unnecessarily throwing things away and acquiring more stuff

- Teaching a balanced approach that values all life, but doesn't favor animals over humans

- Voting for policies locally and nationally that will positively affect standards of living here and elsewhere

As Americans, we live in one of the richest countries in the world, and our responsibility is to be aware of conveniences we may be enjoying at the expense of others in the world, whether it is a child laboring in a sweat shop or a village that is sick because of industrial refuse from factories created to serve our consumer desires.

Our treatment of animals also says much about how we value life. Those who want to do what's right care for their animals' needs.[18]

Though animals are not human, the spark of life in them is just as unexplainable and amazing.

When Native Americans hunted for food and made a kill, they would often say words of honor and thankfulness over the animal that gave its life. They didn't kill for sport. Even if we don't adhere to their particular religious beliefs, we need to be mindful when a life is taken and value that sacrifice.

Growing up on a farm in Ohio, I saw life come and go in many ways. I saw insects sprayed for the benefit of growing crops. I saw injured animals quickly and humanely killed to relieve them of misery. My grandfather raised beef cattle and butchered them himself; this was our way of feeding ourselves and other families. My grandfather also told us a story about killing an angry bull with a pitchfork to save his own life.

We need to be mindful when any life is taken or lost, and value that sacrifice.

On the other hand, I knew people who killed animals for no reason at all except that it was fun to operate a gun or impressive to hang a head on a wall. I saw animals treated poorly for entertainment, and did some of that in younger years myself. It's strange how I look back on that now and my heart hurts. But I'm grateful that I feel something.

The divine spark of life is in all creatures. One day a redheaded woodpecker broke his neck by flying into our sliding door. My daughter and I found his crumpled body on the grass and looked at his beautiful colors, his beak and his curved claws, designed to help him climb trees and find food. We mourned, and I validated my daughter's emotions for the bird instead of saying, "It's just a dead bird." When the family goldfish died (who had been with us for eight years), we all said a word around the toilet before he was flushed away. We told stories about the long life of that goldfish, which included miraculous "resurrections" and a trip from state to state in a pizza sauce jar full of green water. With laughter, we were grateful for the enjoyment even this tiny penny goldfish's life brought to our family.

At my house, we frown on needless killing of any kind because we want life to be valued in our household. One day my children will have the opportunity to protect the rights of the unborn—theirs or someone else's—and they will be making choices in the treatment of the elderly, the handicapped, and those different from themselves. If they see or participate in a movie or video game that devalues life or portrays senseless killing, I hope they will be more likely to turn away because they have already been taught to value the incredible gift of life.

Serving Others

When we take time to help others, we are valuing life and guarding ourselves against the tendency to "hoard" our breath for selfish purposes. As Americans especially, we must constantly work against the belief system that life is all *about* and *for* me.

It's easy to encourage a child to take some cookies next door to an elderly neighbor, or to hand a bottle of water through the window to a homeless person. We can take these kinds of opportunities often. We can visit the local mission, take clothes to a center for the needy, or bring non-perishables or diapers to a food or crisis pregnancy drive. We can volunteer as a family to help meet the needs around us.

Children love to serve. They have been known to start their own ministries when given the chance. A group of children I know organized a garage sale, asking for kids from church to donate their toys. The whole effort was based on the initiative of a group of children twelve and under who managed to raise $150 for a local orphanage.

At age two, one of our daughters had seen us pray for people's healing and also wanted to "pay fo da boo-boo." We were thrilled! As she grew, when we drove by a car accident, she would say, "We should pray for them," and we encouraged her to do so. In church, if she saw an adult friend praying at the altar, she would ask if she could kneel with them. We would say, "Of course!" She was developing a sense of her place in the world as an encourager on a very personal level. She still counsels many of her friends.

What are your child's interests? I know a little girl who bursts into tears when she sees homeless people. Her parents have learned to have something in the car that they can share with a person as they drive by, and this delights the girl, who dreams of owning a kind of chuck wagon in which she can drive to areas where the homeless live and cook for them.

Does your child love animals? Caring for creatures can be a wonderful exercise in opening the door of the breath to take responsibility for life.

For older children, you could use community service, perhaps at a crisis pregnancy center, to open the door to further discussion. Ask a counselor to tell your child one of the client's stories. Find ways to make involvement ongoing and regular. After serving, you and your child may want to have coffee or a soda together to talk about the experience.

Observe where your children love to serve, and let them serve themselves silly!

Observe where your child loves to serve, and let them serve themselves silly! As they grow older, serving will become a natural part of life—and they'll reap the rewards of time spent caring for others instead of entertaining themselves.

Ecclesiastes says there is a time to be born and a time to die. Because we don't choose our time of passing, let's focus on our lives, others' lives, and...living! That's how we honor the gift of breath in all of us. And may others come to recognize in our lives an aroma that draws them to the truth that each one of us is valued and loved.

Summary

The breath is an instrument for celebrating and expressing pure joy in being alive, and a sacred trust as it applies to the lives of others and life around us. As we consider the breath as a door of the heart, we evaluate our attitudes about life. We develop deeper sensitivities. Our joy results in service on behalf of others. We practice good stewardship of the life we have and seek to protect the lives of others.

As you consider these suggestions for downsizing and upgrading, remember to add your own. People in your home or around you need the breath of life!

Downsizing

- **Stop littering.** Make a clear rule that trash is never supposed to go on the ground. Just the simple act of keeping a grocery bag in the car for trash makes a statement about the value of the earth. For extra learning value, have the kids decorate a small trashcan with pictures of nature and slogans like "Keep Our World Clean."

- **End fear of the needy.** Spend time talking about how people may become homeless and how to safely meet their needs. (For example, stock your vehicle with water bottles or non-perishable snacks to hand out the window.) Often our fears of getting involved are grounded in unfamiliarity. Look on the Internet together to read about those who are handicapped. Visit a nursing home and chat with the residents.

- **Discourage cruelty to living things.** Children respond strongly to pets, so use that opportunity to teach them about care for living things who depend upon them. As children get older, this care for animals will carry over into their treatment of humans as we help them make the connection.

- _____

_____

_____

Upgrading

- **Choose a buddy.** Is there any elderly person in your life that you could make a priority? Yes, we're all busy. But loving others should be a priority. Who could you visit regularly with your child? Could you bring flowers or cookies or some regular gift to encourage them? Discuss what is doable and go for it!

- **Volunteer.** Take advantage of whatever opportunities appear; just notice those around you who need your family's help. Sort clothes at a pregnancy center. Serve in a soup kitchen for a meal. Play music or sing songs at a nursing home. Help a single mom with childcare.

- **Recycle and garden.** Kids can take on recycling as their own personal responsibility. Teach them how to sort and let them "police" the family! Use the money from aluminum cans to buy a few flowers or even a small tree for the yard, or a potted herb. Most of us don't get enough opportunities to appreciate growing things.

- **Take on a cause.** Have a child's class or study group choose a cause and raise funds for it, perhaps with a garage sale of their own toys and other donated items. Encourage them to put in some spending money of their own as well.

- _____

_____

_____

Building Materials

Books and Web Sites
See Appendix A for more details.
A Child's Book of Virtues, William Bennett (7)
A Child's Book of Heroes, William Bennett (8)
Preschool Purity of Heart, Jennie Bishop (3)
Life Lessons from The Princess and the Kiss, Jennie Bishop (17)
Life Lessons from The Squire and the Scroll, Jennie Bishop (13)

Truths to Memorize
See Appendix B for complete texts.
The Five Senses of Purity (2)
Breath (5)

Scripts
See Appendix D for complete texts.
Bullying (16)
Online Bullying (17)

Object Lessons
See Appendix E for complete texts.
Tissue Talk (20)
God's Breath (21)
Breath Collage (22)

Contracts
See Appendix F for complete texts.
Contract B: House Rules

Door 4

The Mouth

The mouth and tongue mirror a powerful divine attribute—the ability to create. We carry the responsibility of shaping others, and even the world itself, with our tongues. And tongues can so easily be used for great good or terrible evil!

The door of the mouth is interesting in that it swings both ways. We are affected by what we take in through our mouths, but a person keeps his or her heart clean by monitoring what comes out of the mouth.[19] Guarding the mouth is vitally important in the development of strong, pure hearts.

Words are like toothpaste that's already escaped from the tube—almost impossible to put back after they're spoken. And they can squirt out so quickly! So time is well spent in discussing how we can guard this tricky door of the heart.

Unkind Talk

Kindness and gentle words are not natural for many of us. Maybe we've been raised in a home where yelling or stony silence was the norm. Maybe your family mercilessly teased or practiced sarcasm (which literally means "a tearing of the flesh" in Greek).[20] All of us have experienced the sting of an unkind tongue.

In the home where I was raised, the phrase "I love you" was rarely heard. My childhood trained me to be a "fixer" and only to comment when correction was needed. As a result, my children have sometimes been starved for affirmation. I continue to work on developing more generous habits of loving actions and language. It's a good thing we can change and make new choices if we are intentional.

The door of our mouths ought to be used, first and foremost, to express love. The affection evident among early Christians caused people like Tertullian, an ancient defender of the faith, to write, "See how (these Christians) love one another!"[21] I believe the people he observed used both words and actions to show their love.

Loving language is not a luxury, an interruption, a waste of time, or an expression to be hurried. Loving speech is vital and powerful and nurturing. It makes us grow and become all of what we are made to be. Without love, we wither and die. In our families, we must see this as our central and highest calling: to give and receive love, verbally and otherwise.

Just a few words can affect a life for years or decades to come. During my middle school years, I was in a group that did a "circle of affirmation" exercise. Chairs were arranged in a circle and one chair was placed in the center. Each person took a turn sitting in the center. Then all those in the circle offered one-word descriptions of the person in the middle as a way of affirming them.

Loving speech is vital and powerful and nurturing.

Now, I had never fit in too well in our small farming community. So when I sat in the center of the circle, I didn't find it strange that I waited longer than others for someone to begin. They had to really think. But when someone did finally speak up, the person said thoughtfully, "Odd."

After a moment, the person next to the first agreed, "Yes, that's it. Odd!" There was a general nodding of heads and agreement that I was definitely a weird one.

Funny, but I don't remember any other comments made that day. And because I am a natural optimist, I decided to become the best *odd* I could be. I majored in originality for the rest of my life. However, I was also convinced that I didn't really fit anywhere and struggled desperately with self-worth and issues of belonging well into my forties. My heart was "slimed" for years.

One little word, good or bad, can start it all.

Cursing

Words have power. That's why we choose words that shock or words that are associated with God when want to emphasize what we are saying. I have not yet heard anyone say, "Oh, Theodore!" when they hit themselves on the thumb with a hammer. Hmmm.

What is cursing for you? Everyone draws different lines in the matter of "clean" speech. If *darn* is unproductive to your family, outlaw it. There are many other curses besides an inappropriate use of Jesus' name, and they come from the heart, not just the lips.

Consider those you know who curse casually, using names of God or other vulgar terms. Are they really *One little word, good or bad,* impressive? Do they really seem intelli-*can start it all.* gent? Do you respect them? The person who can make a point without cursing appears more self-possessed. A person can keep his whole body in check if he can control his tongue.[22]

Modern movies base part of their ratings system on the amount and type of language in the production. It's easy to get a viewer's emotional response by peppering a story with obscenities. But even more impressive are movies where the same response is brought on without any such talk. Such productions require even more creativity and artistic expression.

Guard your children's ears and discuss what they hear. Make it clear which types of speech are not acceptable. This safeguards the goodness of their hearts and also benefits their intellect and conversational abilities.

Filthy Talk

In today's society, sexuality is in front of our eyes all the time. Sexual terms and images are used to sell everything from underwear to cars to hamburgers. Very little sexual discussion in the media is based on an understanding of healthy sexuality.

I encourage you to ban talk of any type that cheapens sex and makes it a crude way to be entertained. At the same time, explain and model why we treat sexuality with honor. When your family encounters filthy talk, use that as an opportunity to speak about the preciousness of married sex and the rightness of respecting it instead of giving sex crude names.

That said, we also need to have a sense of humor when it comes to sex. When you're trying to talk about sexuality with a child, enjoy the funny moments because you will have some! If a child accidentally interrupts parental lovemaking, see it as an opportunity to leave a good impression of married sex. Gentle laughter and brief, general words of explanation are more healthy than door slamming.

In educating both girls and boys about sexuality, use the correct terms for body parts and functions. Pair this instruction with explanation about appropriate respect for the body and what conversations or talk to steer clear of in peer groups. If they haven't already heard about sexuality in a healthy way at home, children may be ridiculed or more tempted to participate in vulgar talk among their peers.

When you're trying to talk about sexuality with a child, enjoy the funny moments because you will have some!

Both adolescent girls and boys often struggle with humiliation and vulgarity connected with intimate areas of the body. As a sixth grader, I had a terrible time fitting in with my age group. I hadn't developed as quickly as the other girls, was the last one to get my first bra, and was teased about it. A group of girls invited me to a sleepover where I desperately wanted to fit in. Unfortunately, that night I became a victim of teasing and jokes with sexual connotations that scarred me for years. My lack of knowledge of my own body had made me particularly vulnerable to their taunts.

I remember other times when I was confronted with sexual terms that I didn't know how to handle. Girlfriends showed me books with explicit segments. This and other incidents where sex was described with crude language underscored the lie that sexuality was "dirty" and shameful. These lies would affect my intimacy with my husband years later.

Disrespectful language about sex is always harmful. However, it's OK to enjoy a few laughs about other quirks of the human body. If your child is giggling over a word that describes excrement or the strange things that come out of a nose, set limits, but don't be afraid to giggle along. Some bodily functions are wildly entertaining, and a good heart can have a good laugh over them.

Using Words to Flirt or Tease

In today's highly sexualized world, our children learn early to flirt with captivating looks or sexual words. The intent is to attract or tease a member of the opposite sex in a sexual way.

What standards do you want your child to have in his or her interaction with the opposite sex? What do you consider flirting? What do they think? What do they see at school?

Role-play may help clarify what's expected, and can also relax everyone with humor. Questions like, "What would you do if someone said these words in this way?" may be

Role-playing is helpful in exploring the way words and phrases are voiced and understood.

helpful (be ready for laughter). Use words like "hey, baby" (said as a greeting from Dad to Mom when he gets home, or said by a young man who sidles up to a younger lady in the hallway at school) or "nice jeans" (said by a girlfriends or a guy) or even "I love you" (said by a dad to a daughter, a mother to a father, a boy or girl to someone of the opposite sex they barely know).

If appropriate and useful, demonstrate the physical touch that might accompany the phrases in given situations. The variations on the ways a phrase can be uttered are endless, and the family discussion provoked can be lively, productive, and unlimited. Don't be overly judgmental, but listen and seek to understand. Then set clear standards from there.

Ask what seems to be OK among peers and how it agrees or doesn't agree with your family standards. Be clear about how you believe a young man or woman of integrity and honor must act to avoid leading someone of the opposite sex into foolish or hurtful games of emotions and desire. Encourage your children to keep hearts and intentions good.

A Teaching Tool

We've talked about a lot of negative things the mouth can do. But the mouth can also provide a very effective object lesson for teaching our families about guardianship of the heart.

Explain to your children that our spirits need good food, just as our bodies do—that when we guard the doors of our hearts, we keep our hearts and spirits healthy. Junk TV programs can certainly affect the health of our spirits, just as candy bar binges can make us fat, lazy, and sedentary. A diet of explicit lyrics in music will ruin our innocent hearts. Sex outside marriage will damage our intimate lives and marriage to come.

When we instruct a child in the value of self-control in eating, we also build a bridge toward self-control in sexual desires. Binging is an extreme of healthy eating just as promiscuity is an extreme of healthy sexuality.

Picture a table laden with healthy food like grapes, carrots, juicy chicken, even a cookie or two, and a glass of milk. Then imagine a glass of bleach in amongst it all. The glass of bleach looks innocent enough, and your child is unable to tell what it is by looking. None of us would say to our child, "Pick anything you like from the table."

Self-control in eating is a bridge to understanding sexual restraint.

Of course, we know the bleach could be deadly, so we would never give the child the choice. But many parents allow children to choose spiritual bleach from popular culture. That's why it's so important to educate our children to detect these destructive elements that can enter through their senses.

Summary

What comes *out* of our mouths connects to the heart, and our speech can make us filthy spiritually.[23] Intentionality in speech will guard our hearts, just as intentional good eating will build up our bodies.

Words can destroy or create, and the choice is up to us. When we remember our ability to destroy a person's world with unkindness, we're more likely to choose carefully what words are appropriate and make daily efforts to build others up, especially in our families. When we practice kindness and respect in speech, we keep hearts clean.

Make a special effort as you work through the downsizing and upgrading choices to think of ways that your family can make new efforts toward encouraging, respectful speech. Hold a family meeting to decide how to set a new goal if you can. Or just setting a new goal for yourself right now may be enough.

When you're finished, we'll move on to the last door of the heart, the very sensitive door of touch.

Downsizing

- **Outlaw mean talk.** Yes, kids will tease, but when the teasing crosses to unkindness, draw a line in the sand. Take to heart Ephesians 4:29: "Do not let any unwholesome talk come out of your mouths, but only what is helpful for building others up according to their needs, that it may benefit those who listen." When failures occur, discuss respect and love for one another. Review basic manners and practice them at home, not just in public.

- **Stamp out casual cursing.** It may be as simple as committing to say, "Oh, snap!" instead of something else, but both parent and child must participate. A jar of quarters is helpful where offenders may drop their fines for infringements.

- **Avoid embarrassment—for both you and the kids.** If you're married, lock your door during romantic moments—but also discuss exactly how you would speak if an unexpected interruption takes place. Find a sense of humor about it. Being prepared with some explanatory statements should also help you relax a bit more when those knocks on the door come!

- _____

  _____

  _____

Upgrading

- **Pour on the praise.** Look for new, creative ways to tell each other how much you love and value one another using the door of the mouth. When you greet a child in the morning, say with a hug, "Good morning, honey. I love you so much!" (After a few days, they'll get over the shock.) Add a "thank you for our family" to mealtime prayers. Look for every opportunity to praise. "Thanks for wiping off the table. You're a great helper!"

- **Give blessing instead of cursing.** A good friend of mine uses frustration as a reminder to bless others. When someone crosses her, she responds by saying, "Bless you!" in a cheery voice. Our families can use the same strategy. Voicing a blessing instead of lashing out helps make your heart a nonstick surface for unkindness!

- **Plan a sexuality talk.** No matter your child's age, consider some simple aspect of sexuality that they may not be aware of yet. (For a little one, it might involve the differences in boys and girls. For an older child, you probably have heard a comment recently that would guide you.) Arrange for some quiet time between you and your child where you enjoy an activity together. Then begin with, "Have you noticed…" and move into, "Do you have questions about…?" If the child is completely disinterested, move on, but if the child raises an issue, listen and explain without judging. Ask them what they know (what they *think* they know), and let them lead. While educating, protect their innocence at the same time by not offering more information than they ask for specifically.

- _____

  _____

  _____

Building Materials

Books and Web Sites
See Appendix A for more details.
A Little Hero in the Making (manners for boys), Elizabeth George (10)
Battlefield of the Mind for Kids, Joyce Meyer (11)
Keys to Loving Relationships video series, Gary Smalley (52)
I Want to Teach My Child About Manners, Jennie Bishop (35)
Preschool Purity of Heart, Jennie Bishop (3)
Life Lessons from The Princess and the Kiss, Jennie Bishop (17)
Life Lessons from The Squire and the Scroll, Jennie Bishop (13)

Truths to Memorize
See Appendix B for complete texts.
The Five Senses of Purity (2)
Mouth (6)
Gracious Speech (22)

Object Lessons
See Appendix E for complete texts.
Tie It Up! (23)
Sweet or Sour (24)

Door 5

The Skin

We were made for physical contact. Who could doubt it, when we look at the nature of the human skin and the millions of nerve endings that allow us to feel? The wind on our faces is pleasant, the sun is warm, and so is a spray of cool water on a summer's day. We can tell if something is fuzzy, smooth, sticky, greasy, hot, or cold just by a touch.

Our sense of touch is meant both to protect us and delight. We know that a burner on a stove is too hot to touch when we hold our hand over it. We surrender to our spouse's intimate embrace. We wrap our children in our arms, and joy floods our hearts.

We protect the skin physically with an oven mitt, or with coats and jackets, or sunscreen, but guarding the door of the skin to keep our inner person pure is a little more complicated than guarding skin against injury.

The sense of touch is obviously linked to sexual responsibility. However, limiting touch altogether is not the answer to the issue. Our children are hungry for affectionate touch, and as we fill that need generously, we build a barrier in the inner places of their hearts against trouble later on.

Healthy Touch

Fathers especially play an important role in this aspect of sexual purity, where their daughters are concerned. Girls who do not receive validation, compliments, and affection from their fathers develop a skin hunger that is ferocious and difficult to define or satisfy. This hunger can drive them into the arms of any man too early, too fast. A girl so hungry for contact can even overwhelm the defenses of a young man who is devoted to sexual purity.

Dads, as your daughters develop physically, you may experience an awkwardness that tempts you to opt out on touching altogether. Please don't! The young woman before you is still your little girl, and removing physical affection during these times of difficult emotional and physical development can be devastating. She needs to feel beautiful, loved, and cherished more than ever.

Touch in the family should take place in the form of hugs, silly wrestling matches, kisses, sitting together, and so on, recognizing gender and age differences. For example, older boys might need more arm-around-the-shoulders affection, playful punches, or "tackle hugs." Prayer especially gives a wonderful opportunity to hold hands or gently touch each other. This kind of touch is loaded with the power of caring. As our children learn healthy touch in a family environment, they will be more likely to run away from unhealthy or risky touch in any situation.

Many families today greatly suffer from a lack of time together—and if we're not together, we're not being lovingly touched. If a lack of touch is the result of never being in the house together, find ways to simplify your schedule. Nothing is more important than spending time with your family. It's hard to recognize this during certain seasons of life, but no one wants it suddenly to become clear while lying on a deathbed.

As our children learn healthy touch in a family environment, they are more likely to run away from unhealthy or risky touch in any situation.

Virginia Satir (1916-1988), one of the key figures in the development of family therapy, said that we need four hugs a day to survive, eight to maintain, and twelve to grow.[24] In a two-parent home, that means each parent gives the child at least a hug in the morning, at bedtime, upon arrival at home from school or work and one additional hug at another time. Single parents get to give twice as many hugs—but other mentors and good friends can also be enlisted to help!

Healthy Modeling of Married Life

The best way to teach healthy touch in marriage is to model it with your spouse. Showing tender affection toward your spouse will strongly support your child's positive sexual development and protect his or her good heart. A child should see his parents embracing, holding hands, or kissing discreetly. (Save the passionate stuff for the bedroom, please. Your child needs to see discretion as well.) If you are a single parent, point out examples of positive affection between other married couples. Who hasn't seen an older couple holding hands and felt their heart melt?

Showing tender affection toward your spouse will strongly support your child's positive sexual development and protect his good heart.

Take time for regular dates and retreats with your spouse or alone. Reasonable time away makes better parents and reminds a child that the universe does not revolve around him or her. It also reinforces the fact that Mom and Dad will return, with kisses and hugs (and maybe even a gift) to show that the child is loved, no matter the time apart.

It is certainly appropriate to teach your children that after a prescribed hour, Mom and Dad are unavailable except for emergencies. (Define for your child what an "emergency" is.) A simple explanation that parents need private time together at the end of the day should suffice.

Also, no matter what time of day, children can be taught that parents may lock the door to their room and need to spend time together alone (assuming the child/children feels secure and is old enough to be occupied safely). This is indirect training in married sexuality. Guarding this time is a great way to teach a child about the priority of a marriage relationship and to model indirectly the healthy touch that needs to happen for a marriage to be strong.

As a child grows older and figures out what may go on in secret, good-natured teasing may ensue. Be discreet, but recognize your many opportunities to use your sense of humor in these years—it should be employed without hesitation. Have a good laugh, say, "See you in a little while!" and close the door behind you. Your child needs to see you unashamed and happy in your desire for time with your spouse, sexual or otherwise.

Single parents can also model sexual purity and a good use of the sense of touch through their discretion in relationships with the opposite sex. Restraint and contentment with singleness speaks just as highly of saving intimate touch for marriage and looking to a higher source for fulfillment. Single parents have an important opportunity to show that a spouse is not the only or main source of satisfaction in life.

What We Reach For

What do we lay our hands on? Are we more interested in using our sense of touch to test the quality of our furniture? Or are we more delighted with our spouse's nearness or with the tug of a little guy on our pant leg?

We can gauge the condition of our hearts by what we tend to lay our hands on. Materialism is rampant in American culture. We fight to acquire more material possessions than we can ever use. But every possession comes with a price, and part of that cost may be a heart corrupted by greed. Do you have possessions whose maintenance or cost takes away time that you could spend with your family?

Our sense of touch was meant to support others with physical reassurance, to give a sense of value by our desire to be close, and to help us enjoy the world. It has been said that if we want to know what is important to us, we ought to look at the notes in our checkbooks.

- What do we hold close?

- What do we hesitate to release?

- What do we guard, protect, take delight in?

- What things do we "need" to own or acquire?

Where We Go

In the Proverbs passage that talks about the Five Doors, feet represent the door of touch—so it may be a good idea to consider where we walk. Where we choose to go and spend our time can definitely affect our good hearts. If that means using our feet to walk away from magazines at a gas station, or past a bar, or away from a shop where we know we'll spend our money unwisely, that's what we should do. After all, the feet keep the hands safe from infractions by taking them away from opportunity, not always by walking, but by running!

Summary

Timeless wisdom in the book of Ecclesiastes says there is a time to embrace and a time to refrain from embracing.[25] In a world where pornography runs rampant, desires to touch are fanned into flame in ways that are impossible to ignore. Learning healthy touch can equip us and our children to thrive with pure hearts in a world that celebrates promiscuity. We can guard ourselves and our children from skin hunger and deep hurt as we guard the heart via the door of the skin.

As a door of the heart, touch can hurt deeply or heal completely. Sexual abuse is an obviously widespread evil of our time, but loving, affectionate touch can overcome past hurts and start new habits and memories in new generations. Loving touch will feed the heart and satisfy it in ways selfish touch can never match.

Which suggestions below might apply to you or your household? What new ideas can you think of?

This door of the heart completes the first floor of our Planned Purity diagram. In the next chapter we begin construction on the second floor, where we'll open windows of opportunity to set more physical boundaries in the pursuit of sexual purity. Our pure household is taking shape!

Downsizing

- **Stop physical fighting.** Don't allow anyone in your household to use their hands to hurt. (With boys, there may be a fine line between playfulness and pain!) If you spank, spank infrequently and never in anger. Use a flexible instrument, setting your hand apart for assurance and gentle guidance.

- **No bedtime whining.** Plan for prayers or bedtime routines to begin at hours where you will still have energy left for your spouse, and let the children have quiet reading time if they're not quite sleepy yet. Make it clear that the children will be expected to honor Mom and Dad's time together.

- **Limit shopping trips.** This may be a challenge for some moms, but consider what children may learn from shopping as recreation. Explore activities other than shopping, and respect the family budget. This will help guide your child toward better money management as well.

- _____

  _____

  _____

Upgrading

- **Add more hugging.** What's the affection quotient in your house? Find creative ways to increase it. (We all need more.) Use TV commercials as hug breaks instead of watching the advertising. (It's not that great, anyway.) Use stoplights as a reminder to touch someone in the car and tell them you love them, or say something you love *about* them. Start and end each day with displays of physical affection.

- **Plan a date or retreat.** Get away as soon as possible with your spouse. During your time together, discuss how to have these "Mom and Dad times" regularly. They are not a luxury; loving each other well is the reason we're here. If you're a single parent, plan "off time" for yourself with friends and time alone—you need breaks even more than married parents.

- **Gather.** Have friends over often and visit other families. Spend time at church or community events with others. Give hugs, shake hands, pray together, and pat shoulders. Show your children how to share appropriate, affectionate touch with others.

- _____

  _____

  _____

Building Materials

Books and Web Sites
See Appendix A for more details.
★*Good News About Sex and Marriage*, Christopher West (49)
Every Woman's Marriage, Shannon and Steve Ethridge (50)
Every Man's Marriage, Steve Arterburn and Fred Stoeker (51)
Keys to Loving Relationships video series, Gary Smalley (52)
★Chik-Fil-A's WinShape: www.winshape.org/marriage (marriage retreat) (61)
FamilyLife Weekend to Remember: www.familylife.com (marriage retreat) (62)
Preschool Purity of Heart, Jennie Bishop (3)
Life Lessons from The Princess and the Kiss, Jennie Bishop (17)
Life Lessons from The Squire and the Scroll, Jennie Bishop (13)

Truths to Memorize
See Appendix B for complete texts.
Five Senses of Purity (2)
Skin (7)
Being Separate (24)
Flee Evil (41)

Scripts
See Appendix D for complete texts.
How Children Come Into Being (age seven and under) (1)
How Children Come Into Being (elementary age or older) (2)
Explaining Sex—and More (3)
Explaining Oral Sex (4)
Bullying (16)

Object Lessons
See Appendix E for complete texts.
Hot Potato (25)
Shopping for Love (26)

Part 4

The Second Floor—Seven Windows

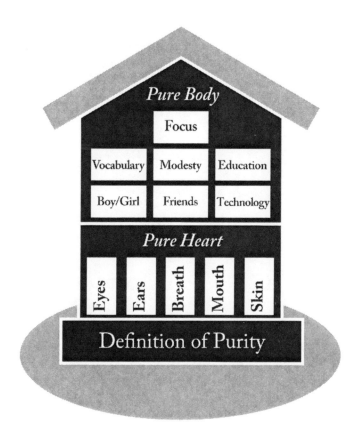

Chapter 7

The Outer Person—An Honorable Life

Wow! We've covered a lot of important material on the first floor of our Planned Purity house. We've learned how to help our children develop a good heart in their youngest years. And that keeps reminding us that our parental hearts have to be pure as well.

Remember, the first floor focuses on the inner person by targeting our attitudes, intentions, and basic personal beliefs—the heart. The key to keeping that inner person pure is to guard the five doors of the heart:

1. Eyes: What we see

2. Ears: What we listen to

3. Breath: How we value life and serve others

4. Mouth: What we say

5. Skin: How we use our hands, feet, and bodies

Guarding the doors of the heart will vitally affect our ability to embrace honorable actions in choices about sexuality, work habits, family issues, and all the other areas of life. When we understand and practice goodness, virtue, integrity, and honor we are much more likely to act out sexual purity, honesty, and all the aspects of selfless, pure living.

With the understanding of the inner person firmly in place, you're now equipped and energized to work on the outer person (purity of body).

When we are intentionally pursuing a good heart inside, then we can begin construction on the second floor of our Planned Purity house. This floor represents a pure body or outer life—a person's actions. On it are seven "windows" of opportunity for setting up standards of behavior.

These categories help us see where we can help our values flow into our actions. We'll find ways to set up guardrails to help define the best behavior and interaction, not just between boys and girls, but between friends, in married relationships, and at any age. Our goal is for our outer-person actions to reflect a good heart and

Guarding the doors of the heart will vitally affect our ability to embrace honorable actions in regards to sexuality, work habits, family issues, and all of life.

attitude that pursues goodness and sexual purity no matter what we face or what environment we're in. Let's quickly preview these seven windows of opportunity:

Window 1: Focus—Living selflessly

Window 2: Vocabulary—Using the right words

Window 3: Modesty—Dressing to honor one's own body and the eyes of others

Window 4: Education—Choosing the right avenues and sources for learning and growing

Window 5: Boy/Girl Interaction—Honoring the opposite sex

Window 6: Friends—Choosing companions carefully

Window 7: Technology—Constantly evaluating modern technology and media

We may monitor these aspects of our children's lives differently depending upon the age of the child involved; however, each aspect is important to develop as our children continue to guard the five doors of the heart and work to let their actions and choices reflect a good heart inside.

Please keep in mind that this list is far from comprehensive. You may come up with other windows as you look for creative ways to guide your children's life habits. Don't hesitate to add them to your book or diagram as you go. This is your family's personal strategy for purity!

Window 1

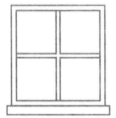

Focus

I n this case, *focus* refers to how we place our attention. It's the difference between a person who sashays into a room and announces, "Well, here I am!" versus one who looks around and greets others with "Ah, there you are."[1] Some people make others' needs a priority, and others choose to present themselves and their desires first.

Popular culture continues to push the "me first" philosophy in every imaginable way. Even the slogans on T-shirts scream selfishness, from the popular motto, "It's all about me," to the brazen, "Hold my purse while I kiss your boyfriend."

Another aspect of this self-centeredness is the obsession with romance that finds its way into entertainment even for the youngest viewers. For example, the Disney version of *The Little Mermaid* falls far from the story Hans Christian Andersen intended, turning Ariel into a rebellious love struck teen and leaving out the sacrifice that the character makes in the original story.

In the Disney movie version of *Bambi*, Bambi's romantic attraction to Faline became a main focus, though the original story was more about Bambi and the stag's relationship, which exemplified mentoring, growth, and passing on a legacy.

Finally, a number of modern animated programs portray children as disrespectful, selfish brats—the perfect method for training a child to be me-centered!

In this foundational window of opportunity, we'll learn how to focus our children on the needs of others first. Selfless serving must be our most basic focus if we want to live a life that naturally pursues honor and sexual purity.

First, we can teach our children to focus their single years on serving others instead of ourselves. Second, we can provide opportunities for service. And third, we can show our children how to defy popular culture by choosing friendships and avoiding pointless pairing.

The Single Years Are for Serving

What is the real purpose of all the years prior to being married (if one chooses to marry at all)? Some would say, "for a person to find out who they are." Others would say these years are for enjoying all the pleasures of life before real commitments spoil everything. Many people act as if the main point of life before marriage is to test drive relationships. Even the youngest children engage in relationship games.

But here's a news flash: The single years aren't for any of those things. *The single years are for learning to serve others in preparation to do what we have been made to do.* No matter

Selfless serving must be our most basic focus if we want to live a life that naturally pursues honor and sexual purity.

what our future holds, we will need to serve. If our future includes a spouse and family, we will need to serve. If it doesn't include being married, we will need to serve. If we become a butcher, a baker, or a banker, we will need to serve!

Through serving, we discover our personal passions and talents, which makes it possible to recognize a spouse with complementary gifts, or to consider a joyful single life. As we develop a service mentality, we prepare to be a sensitive spouse, parent, or single person.

Young men (and women) should enjoy the life they're given, but remember that they will answer for their actions[2] if they think of themselves before others.[3] Being aware that relationships with the opposite sex could lead to marriage is not necessarily negative, but it shouldn't be our single purpose. Our prime-of-life energy can be spent in a desperate search for a marriage partner, or *it can be spent on learning to serve, which prepares us to be persons of value, married or not.*

We are the best we can be when we recognize that all of life, including the life before we marry, must be others-focused.

When we focus on others, we will develop a desire to stand up for what is right and protect those who are weak. Serving others leads us to protect others physically and emotionally instead of selfishly gratifying ourselves.

We can raise men and women who seek to protect each other as people, not to consume each other as products. And in today's sexualized world, that is a high and vital calling that can change everything.

Choose to Serve Together

Serving is a foundational exercise in building up human beings with an others-focused heart. It yields better businessmen, better homemakers, better pastors, and plumbers. Living a life of purpose and value must include more than knowing how to do a job. If we have no idea how to live selflessly, our lives will yield only an empire of dust. All our money and accomplishments are worthless if they don't benefit others and grow healthy relationships. Yet this is what we often see—empires of money and power built to serve a proud and selfish individual.

The single years are for learning to serve, which prepares us to be persons of value, married or not.

Fortunately, some great examples of servant leaders still exist today. Bill Gates is a refreshing, rare example of a wealthy man who has made incredible unselfish efforts that are changing the world.

Mr. Gates rose to the position of "richest man in the world" after his unheard-of success in the computer industry. But he didn't stop there. Since 2000, Gates has given away more than $29 billion to charities and taken an individual interest in eradicating AIDS and other major diseases.[4] Even though I don't support all of his causes, I truly applaud his "interest in the fortunes of others," not just his own.[5]

You may think of examples like Mother Theresa, who lived a life of poverty in service to others, or be familiar with personal examples of those who gave up wealth on behalf of others.

How do we raise children who, wealthy or not, want to do the same? We teach them to serve. Let's tune in to our children, and do an honest evaluation.

- Are our sons and daughters generally selfish, or generally unselfish?

- How can we personally be less self-centered?

- How can we create ways for our children to serve, give, and give away what they have?

Load your kids up with opportunities to serve, and serve as a family. Focus on the adventure of a service effort near home or overseas. Sponsor a child, bake a pie for someone, rake leaves, show kindness.

Service will build healthy bonds within your family. This focus will also prepare your child for loving, honorable, and responsible relationships, making him or her the kind of potential spouse that will protect and serve a mate and others as well.

Young people who love serving others are not distracted by what anyone else likes—they are obsessed with and delighted by what is right and good to do. And as they become a person who values others, they eventually attract a person of the same caliber, if they are to be married. When our children do hard work alongside those of the opposite sex, they will see others' true character traits better than the traditional dating approach where the focus is on appearing and acting attractive. Kids who grow up serving are naturally less impressed by physical traits than character traits. In working hard and getting dirty they find the reward of a job well done and changed lives around them.

Kids who grow up serving are less impressed with physical traits than character traits.

This brings us to our last point in this chapter, which is about how to avoid the pairing off that society pushes on our children.

Choose Friendships Instead of Pointless Pairing

More girls, at younger ages, are becoming "boy crazy." Why is it that little girls are so desperate to be paired with a boy? They may be missing a father, or have a father who is disinterested, doesn't know how to demonstrate love, or is abusive. They may have a mother who encourages her daughter to be boy crazy out of a lack of knowing a better approach exists. They may have been influenced by popular culture.

No matter the reason, a boy or girl who constantly centers life around being paired off will be distracted from some of the once-in-a-lifetime joys of childhood, will be less likely to maintain long-term friendships, and will lack confidence in his or her value as an individual. (Please note that I am talking about an obsession with being paired up, not about simple dreams and desires to be married someday, which are perfectly normal.)

Many youthful years have been wasted by distractions and temptations to behave irresponsibly when "going out" or dating. There is a better way to handle relationships, and that is to focus on friendships.

Friendship is a gift to be cherished, and next to family life, the best way to practice for marriage. In building healthy, strong friendships young people (and adults) can allow a relationship with a future spouse to happen more naturally. Encourage your children to nurture friendships without the distractions of romantic entanglements. It's difficult, but not impossible if we get our heads in the game and manage our emotions well. We can steer our children away from becoming boy or girl crazy and lead them to be others-crazy, and loving to serve.

Family life and committed friendships are the best ways to practice for marriage.

Summary

In summary, the key is our focus—on others, on virtue, on becoming a person worth discovering. That's really what our growing up years are about—learning to love well and recognizing a particular, fantastic plan for our lives. Then we can serve and develop healthy friendships based on character as we become mature enough to handle jobs, children, and the emotional and physical needs of a spouse.

Opportunities for Focus

- Change the focus of your family from inward to outward. Make new efforts toward putting others before yourselves.

- Encourage friendships over romantic pairings. Spend time with boys or girls in service and activity, not in constant movie watching. Choose activities that present good opportunities for communication.

- Build bonds by serving together. Choose a local homeless shelter, crisis pregnancy center, or community service event and attend to help as a family if you can.

- _____

  _____

  _____

Building Materials

Books and Web Sites
See Appendix A for more details.
A Child's Book of Virtues, William Bennett (7)
★*Shepherding a Child's Heart*, Ted Tripp (37)
Growing Kids God's Way—The Child Wise Series, Gary and Anne Marie Ezzo (38)

Truths to Memorize
See Appendix B for complete texts.
Focus (9)
Known by Actions (40)

Object Lessons
See Appendix E for complete texts.
Service! (27)

Window 2

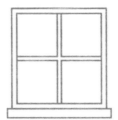

Vocabulary

Think about the words that children and teenagers use to talk about their relationships. What is a *boyfriend* or *girlfriend* to a kindergartener? Middle schooler? High school senior?

What does it mean when kids say someone of the opposite sex is *cute* or *hot*?

Do your kids define *dating* or *going out* the same way that you do?

Words have incredible power to shape our beliefs and feelings about ourselves and others. This window of opportunity will show you how to make conscious word choices that will lead to honorable living.

"Her First Boyfriend!"

Our very young children are often prematurely ushered into the culture of dating by innocent teasing (from adults or children) using the word *boyfriend* or *girlfriend*. These terms are part of our culture, so it's important to consider the effects of their use and our responsibility in defining them.

As a kindergartener, I lived in a rural farming community where mothers carpooled to drive their children to school. A boy named Mark rode with my mom and me. I can still envision him in his plaid shirt and brown corduroy pants the first day his mom dropped him off. Sometimes a pack of Wrigley's or Juicy Fruit gum was in his pocket, and Mark was nice enough to share a stick with me. I remember sitting on the front porch on the swing together one time, chewing our gum together. Mark was my friend.

Much later, maybe during high school, I discovered my "baby book" and noticed a note my mom had written about me around kindergarten time: "Mark rides with us to school and sometimes shares gum with Jennie. Her first boyfriend!"

My first boyfriend? The entry made me giggle because my "boyfriend" was news to me. But that's how my mom saw it. I'm glad I didn't know it then, because the mention of such a word would have certainly confused me.

A child needs to know that he or she is valuable and complete, even if he or she is not paired off. And children must understand that falling in and out of love isn't a game. In biblical language, love should be "awakened" at "the right time."[6] When our children role play adult relationships too early, it sets them up for sexual experimentation as hormonal changes come into play. You may doubt that such innocent teasing could lead to early sex, but don't forget that many brooks of experience pour into the river of choices. Let me share two other examples.

Encouraging youthful pairing through loosely defined "dating language" puts children in an awkward position. I remember having one of those awkward moments while sitting in the dentist's chair, of all places. Although the dentist chair is usually associated with fear and trembling, I happened to be a fortunate child who had a dentist who was gentle and had a wonderful sense of humor. I don't remember discomfort in that chair—except on one occasion.

Encouraging youthful pairing through loosely defined "dating language" puts children in an awkward position.

On this particular day, Dr. Willie asked me (when my mouth was full of instruments, of course), "Do you have a boyfriend?"

I remember squirming and mumbling, "No." I wondered how he could have thought I was old enough for such a question. *Is there something wrong with me because I don't have a boyfriend?* I thought. I guess many of us felt that way at some point in our younger years.

The Princess and the Kiss was written after my daughter came home from kindergarten talking about how she needed a boyfriend because everyone else had one. Since that time, I have talked to mother after mother with similar stories. Children are talking in terms of adult relationships from the time they are small. This can easily set them up for early sexual experimentation in the tween and teen years. We can help retain their innocence just by striking certain comments from our family conversation, and explaining why.

Words that you may want to limit (or save for a much later age, if they're defined clearly) include *girlfriend, boyfriend, going out, hooking up, breaking up, dating,* and others. These terms specifically focus on romantic relationships instead of strong friendships.

Fine-tuning our relational language is a simple way to help preserve our children's innocence, giving young people the freedom to be friends with boys and girls without the distraction of dating games. An understanding of healthy friendship is required and must be practiced for a long while before a young person is ready for greater commitment and responsibility with the romantic heart and feelings of another.

Character over Cuteness

I'm not fond of the word *cute* in describing a young man or woman. Cute is an incredibly nebulous term that reveals very little about a person. At our house, we say, "Puppies are cute. Boys are good-looking." I admit that "good-looking" is only a step away, but it takes just a little more serious consideration.

Teens have also been using the term *hot*. Do they know that the word could be based on the rising body temperature that occurs with sexual arousal? (Insert an "Oh, Mooom!" here.) The term tends to denote outer sexual attractiveness, not inner qualities of virtue. When a teen talks about someone being *hot*, something about their own integrity erodes at the same time. More and more women are voicing their desire to be called *beautiful* again.

Rather than focusing on others' outward appearances by using the words *cute* or *hot*, be intentional in pointing out character qualities. When your first-grade son says, "I like Susie," resist the desire to tease him about having interest in a girl. Instead ask him about her character assets: "What do you like about her? Does she share? Does she make you laugh? Is she nice to other children?" Focus on a friendship rather than a mushy, infatuated feeling, or ending the discussion at, "She's cute!"

Look for ways to celebrate good character. If someone opens the door for you, say to your children, "Wasn't that a kind man?" Point out his politeness and desire to serve. Remind your child that these qualities are extremely valuable.

When your tween or high schooler discovers a romantic interest, listen closely to his or her description of and stories about the person. Use observations of their interaction and gentle questions to draw your child into a thinking process that helps them evaluate the person's virtuous traits (i.e. patience, goodness, kindness, self-control, and so on). If vir-

Be intentional in pointing out character qualities: "What do you like about Susie? Is she kind? Does she share? Is she funny?"

tuous traits are lacking, don't be afraid to gently help your child recognize this problem. Remind them that you think they're smart and responsible, and that you're proud of good choices. (It's best to already have emotional and physical boundaries established. See the window of Boy/Girl Interaction for more information.)

Maybe one day when your little girl sees a "cute guy," she'll also notice whether he is wise or foolish, instead of being blinded by his appearance. Her ability to say *no* to the wrong kind of person may save her a lifetime of suffering.

What Is a Date?

Dating and *going out* are also terms kids use frequently, but what do they really mean? As parents, we first need to seek to understand how our kids define those terms. Then we can define those words for our families and make guidelines for what our children will be permitted to do and at what age.

Right now kids seem to define *dating* as being fond enough of someone to have physical intimacy, which could mean holding hands, kissing, or more involved sexual activity such as fondling or oral sex. In most secular adult circles, intercourse is assumed to be a part of dating. *Going out* is a general phrase for exclusivity between a boy and girl, even if the couple never goes anywhere. Even in elementary school, children talk about going out. When she was little, my daughter pointed out, "Mom, they don't even have cars. Where are they going?" Good point.

At what age (if any) is it appropriate for our children to say they are dating or going out? Many parents are not prepared to answer these questions because they haven't really thought about them until their child asks to go on a date.

We can't wait until the middle school dance to decide what we think. If we don't talk to our children about dating, then they will get their information from the school, a friend, or the media. Remember, it is our responsibility to train our children, not the school's or church's.

When your child is very young, decide what you think about the practice of cultural pairing. If you plan for your child to take part in dating practices, what boundaries will be set? If you choose a courtship route, how will you explain that your family will not be practicing dating but will choose to nurture long-term friendships instead? These questions are vitally important to set your child up for successful relationships as they grow.

What do dating *and* going out *really mean?*

Terms to Define for Your Family

As a parent, you have the power to define the relationship terms that are used in your family. Below is a list of some of the terms that you may want to consider. Start by asking your children how they define the terms if they are already in use. Then decide on the definition that your family will use. Be aware that those outside your family may define the terms differently, so you and your children may need to explain your family definitions to others as needed.

• **Friend:** This word can mean acquaintance or someone you trust with very personal thoughts, depending on the person using the word. However, the introduction of Facebook and *friending* can make a child think of a friend as "anyone who can see my Facebook," which is obviously dangerous. A friend should be a confidante, someone who is known face-to-face and trusted. An acquaintance is not known well. Many, many Facebook "friends" are acquaintances or complete strangers, as we'll discuss in Window 7—Technology.

In terms of a relationship between a boy and girl, friends may be "friends with benefits," which means the couple is engaging in uncommitted sexual activity but remains "friends." A couple may also denote themselves as friends not exclusively interested in each other, making it clear by other words or actions that no sexual activity is taking place.

A good family definition of *friend* may be "someone who is known well face-to-face and has proven their trustworthiness, loyalty, and respect over time."

• **Boyfriend or girlfriend:** In elementary school, it may simply mean that a boy and girl are attracted by outward appearance and decide to be known as a couple. It may also be defined by what they have seen in a movie, so holding hands or kissing may be involved. The "relationship" usually lasts for a very short time. At the preteen or teen age, having a boyfriend or girlfriend denotes exclusivity that may easily include sexual activity beyond kissing. As an adult, the terms usually mean a couple is physically involved at some level.

• **Going out:** *Going out* is used in the same way as *boyfriend* or *girlfriend*.

• **Hooking up:** This term is often used with college students. It denotes a sexual relationship for one-time only, often as a habit, and reveals the dangerous sexual promiscuity that many college students embrace. (For a terrific book that describes the dangers of the college hook-up culture, get *Unprotected* by Miriam Grossman. This book reveals a great deal about the effects of hooking up on young women, and inspires both young men and women to guard their own and others' hearts and bodies.)

• **Dating:** Dating can be defined as going to a movie together at fourteen, going somewhere alone together at sixteen, going somewhere as friends with a group or with parents as chaperones, or spending time alone at a later age with someone who is being formally considered as a possible spouse. It can also mean that a couple is casually dating and having sex. Such varied understandings exist that clarifying definitions is imperative.

• **Courtship:** Though the word can be defined in many ways, *courtship* basically means that a family practices building innocent and discreet friendships between boys and girls with the purpose of maintaining those nonsexual friendships until the later teen years or early twenties, when a young man may ask permission to court a young woman. Courtship is supervised and practiced according to each individual family, but would be similar to dating at a later age, although much more intentional. A courtship makes a couple exclusive, spending time either with or without supervision, with the intent of deciding whether or not the partners are suitable as spouses.

Beware of thinking that any of these terms are innocuous and count for nothing except "growing up." Popular culture and media (which cannot be escaped completely, only managed) have long-term strategies in place to set our children up for heartbreak and devastation. Fortunately, we can respond with long-term exposure to love and truth that will lead to honorable living and sexual purity. Defining vocabulary can be our ally in that important process.

Vocabulary Opportunities

- Steer clear of the terms *boyfriend* or *girlfriend* with little ones, even in a teasing way. Use vocabulary to steer your young child away from romantic role-playing.

- Use words that evaluate people by virtues rather than appearances. Talk about character more than cuteness!

- Define *dating* and *going out*, as well as *friend*, and other terms mentioned in this chapter.

- _____

_____

_____

Building Materials

Books and Web Sites
See Appendix A for more details.
A Little Book of Manners (manners for girls), Elizabeth George (9)
A Little Hero in the Making (manners for boys), Elizabeth George (10)
I Want to Teach My Child About Manners, Jennie Bishop (35)

Truths to Memorize
See Appendix B for complete texts.
Vocabulary (10)
Gracious Speech (22)
Treat Women as Sisters (36)

Scripts
See Appendix D for complete texts.
Social Networking Chats (11)
Maintaining Cell Phone Boundaries (12)

Object Lessons
See Appendix E for complete texts.
What Does It Mean? (28)

Window 3

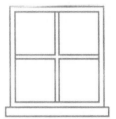

Modesty

At age eleven our daughter was invited to be in charge of the guest book at a friend's wedding. We searched store after store to find a dress that didn't expose her breasts or thighs, or fit like a second skin. After trips to several stores, I was ready to make a concession and sew up a neckline, Dad was adamant that we were not going to buy anything, and my daughter was in tears. More and more parents find themselves in our predicament.

Even little girls' clothes reveal midriffs and are patterned after provocative adult looks. Dolls wear makeup and revealing clothes. Very young girls have makeovers done that make them look years older.

The National Center for Missing and Exploited Children says child exploitation grew from less than thirty-five hundred events in 1998 to over 106,000 events in 2004—a 300 percent increase that continues to rise.[7] More and more children are being seen and used as objects of pleasure. Media images contribute by flaunting provocative dress and "bedroom eyes" instead of femininity and modesty in women.

Our dress reflects something of our inner life, and a pure heart looks better than any sexy advertising.

Boys and men are also pushed toward provocative looks. Male models appear sensual and androgynous in modern-day advertising. Tweens and teens talk about working out to get "buff."

It seems that our society has decided that the purpose of our bodies is to gain sexual attention. But we choose whether to focus attention on our bodies or on greater things like beauty, truth, or goodness. Our dress reflects something of our inner life, and when we have pure hearts, that view is much deeper and better than any sexy advertising.

As our children are growing, we can carefully steer them toward better choices in clothing that will help keep them from being objectified and give them a better chance at healthy friendships over romantically-charged interludes. Let's talk about how, first from the girls' perspective, and then the boys'.

Preserving Girls' Innocence

There is a certain innocence that we should protect in our young women, allowing them to enjoy childhood without being distracted by fashion. Are we steering our little gals to emphasize outer appearances over inner beauty and teaching them to invest too much time in front of the mirror? And when we dress a little girl in a miniskirt, how will we tell her as a preteen that miniskirts are no longer allowed? If we expect our girls to dress modestly in the teen years, then we must help them practice modesty through their growing years.

It's OK to set specific family standards like the following suggested guidelines. Some of these may not be exactly right for your family, but this list should contribute to your own thinking processes.

- Beachwear should reflect modesty to the community and be clearly defined by the family. Cover-ups are a must in shops or on streets.

- Turn off immodest role models in TV, games, and so forth.

- Thong underwear is not practical or healthy (and certainly not that comfortable). Skip it and buy something cute that covers instead.

- Skirts/dresses must be modest enough to bend over without revealing upper thighs.

- Tops should not reveal unnecessary cleavage.

- Jeans or other clothes don't look "painted on" (skin tight). Pants cover the entire behind and underwear when bending over.

- See-through fabric must be layered.

- No sensual words on clothing, such as "sexy" or "hot."

- Nightwear should reflect appropriate modesty. By kindergarten, boys and girls should be covered when in each other's presence. (Mom should keep her special lingerie behind closed bedroom doors.)

- Parents shop with children until the child demonstrates the ability to make modest and financially responsible choices independently.

Clear standards will help your children take a stand against the immodest aspects of modern fashion. Encourage children to find their own style while practicing modesty. For

Encourage children to find their own personal style while practicing modesty and appropriate dress.

example, your daughter may choose a wild-looking top, or crazy jewelry—but if it's modest, it may be best to give a green light. On the other hand, fashionable jeans may not be okay for church, and black, "gothic" type garb isn't appropriate for most situations!

Whether standards reflect modesty or what's appropriate for a particular event or environment, help your child see the advantages of appropriate dress. Teach them how the right clothes at the right time can help others discover your son or daughter's own personal uniqueness and value. Out-of-place clothes, makeup or jewelry can distract or cheat people out of getting to know them and vice versa. Such occurrences are sad and certainly not helpful in friendships *or* job interviews.

Swimwear is a particularly sensitive issue. You wouldn't want your daughter to walk out of her bedroom or along the street in a bra and underwear, but she might be allowed to wear the same amount of fabric (or less) on a public beach. Do you have a good reason why?

Maybe sweatpants aren't practical as beachwear, and pro athletes have a reason to dress in clothing that doesn't inhibit performance. But the fact remains that men are visually stimulated no matter what the reason is for a woman to be scantily clad. A man (of any age) often feels the same thing in *looking* at a woman that a woman feels when a man *touches* her.

Men and women look their best when they honor and protect each other's hearts.

Men and women look their best when they honor and protect each other's hearts as they do brothers and sisters.[8] Women can help protect the men around them from inappropriate thoughts by dressing modestly, and men can help by looking women in the eye instead of "checking them out."

If you and your spouse don't see eye-to-eye on matters of dress, seek a peaceful understanding. Look for honor in the heart and follow it with honorable dress as best you can. Many modes of dress appear "immodest" or "modest" depending entirely on the attitude of the wearer.

Our culture has dishonored men and women as objects in the marketplace. But modesty is a way of regaining that honor and protecting true masculinity and femininity.

Boys Under Fire

In today's society, boys and men are constantly charged with the task of guarding the door of the eyes. Boys are bombarded with sexual images in the media and see many real-life presentations that encourage sexual interest as well. Practical but simple suggestions like "look down," "look away," "turn it off," or "cover your eyes" should be explained and encouraged to guard innocence and foster respect of women.

Boys must be taught to hold to the standard of respecting girls, even when the girls do not dress modestly. A young man needs to know that gazing at exposed parts of a woman's body is a joy to be directed toward his wife someday.

Guarding eyes for a future wife will not be easy when so many women try desperately to draw male eyes to their bodies. Teaching these boundaries in appropriate ways when he is young helps very much (explaining images that he might encounter by chance on billboards, in stores, or on screen). By the time his hormones explode onto the scene, he may already be thinking about the catalog of images he has collected in his head because no one has told him that this is inappropriate. A great resource for this kind of training is *Every Young Man's Battle* by Steven

Gazing at exposed parts of a woman's body is a joy to be directed toward a wife.

Arterburn and Fred Stoeker (WaterBrook Press). Similar studies exist in this series for girls, men, and women (see the list of resources at the end of this chapter).

Standards of modest dress for boys should be set as well. Just because girls aren't as visually stimulated does not mean that boys shouldn't show respect. Covering up boxers in public or removing hats at appropriate times are obvious possibilities.

Body Art

With greater amounts of skin exposed, more men and women than ever are getting tattoos, and sometimes multiple piercings as well. While your child is in your home, you set the limits. Is it appropriate to have a meaningful tattoo? Is it okay to wear a tasteful temporary tattoo?

Does your child know about the scarring and infections that can result from various piercings? How will he be treated at job interviews (for the rest of his life) as a result of his appearance? And will he feel the same about this permanent body art as a father or grandfather (or in a girl's case, a mother or grandmother)? What if he meets a great girl who can't stand tattoos?

Tattoos are permanent, and decisions to get them are often made at an age where a young person still doesn't recognize how that permanent expression will stay with them even as they continue to change. Give your child as much perspective on the progressive and transient nature of life as you can to help them absorb the reality of negative effects that tattoos and piercings may have on their lives and appearances for years to come.

Summary

Modesty is absolutely essential, although what may be right for each family is not the same. Don't hesitate to set and hold to standards in your home as you see fit. Be specific and write them down if you need to. Creative expressions may be handled differently from family to family, but standards should be established because they reveal a pure heart and an honorable young man or woman.

Opportunities for Modesty

- Insist on modest clothing as you shop *with* your children and stick to your guns—even when they are very young. Prepare them for modesty in the future!

- Dress so that outward appearance does not distract from inner character. Choose intentionally and set an example. Moms and dads, don't dress like your teenagers.

- Train boys to protect themselves from society's daily bombardment of sexual images. Read *Every Young Man's Battle* (see below).

- Train girls to show consideration to boys by dressing modestly. Remind them that boys are to be treated as brothers, and it's our responsibility to look out for their best interests.

- Warn of the dangers of tattoos and piercings, and the permanency of body art. Talk about what your child would think about having tattoos as a mother/dad or grandparent. How does he/she think children or other tattoo-free adults in the picture might respond?

- _____

  _____

  _____

Building Materials

Books and Web Sites
See Appendix A for more details.
Secret Keepers, Dannah Gresh (19)
Sexy Girls: How Hot is Too Hot?, Hayley DiMarco (32)

Events and Rites of Passage
See Appendix C for more details.
★*Secret Keepers* date packet, Dannah Gresh (5)
Every Young Man's Battle, Stephen Arterburn (10)
www.purefreedom.org: Dannah Gresh Secret Keepers web site (7)

Truths to Memorize
See Appendix B for complete texts.
Dress (11)
No Hint of Immorality (34)
Treat Women as Sisters (36)

Scripts
See Appendix D for complete texts.
Social Networking Modesty (10)
Diffusing Dress Code Wars (15)

Object Lessons
See Appendix E for complete texts.
Advertising Analysis (29)
Bikini Bare (30)
Fashion Power (31)

Window 4

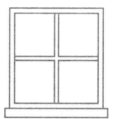

Education

My sexual training when I was growing up consisted of a few disconnected comments and a book about menstruation. When I reached dating age, I don't remember any instruction at all. I made a host of poor choices that left me technically a virgin, but practically—not. I don't blame my parents. They were just nervous about discussing sex, as a lot of parents are, and that contributed to their silence on the issue.

When you feel anxious about educating your child regarding intimate subjects, remember that sexual education is not about one big, nervy talk. We can use a sense of humor and humility to learn and talk together, sometimes through planned activities, but mostly through teachable moments.

Starting when they are very young, your children absorb many lessons by what they see and hear from you. So while your children are at home, make sure you teach them what you want them to know. It's your responsibility, and no one else can do it. Your children are educated by a variety of sources, but consider yourself as a parent Educator-In-Chief!

I hope to encourage you in this chapter by talking about problems being teachable moments in disguise—about training intentionally—about starting early—and, most of all, that parents are the most important educators children will ever have.

So join all the rest of us nervous parents and read along!

Talking About Sex

Although talking about sex can be intimidating, our children want and need to hear the facts from us, whether they are in kindergarten or high school. For example, kids often hear

Our kids want and need to hear the facts from us.

sexual references they don't understand at school or in the neighborhood. Also, the media often impose sexual images or talk when we least expect it (Super Bowl commercials, for example!).

Our job as the main educators of our children is to explain whether materials or actions are inappropriate while recognizing the natural desires of a child to experience things new and exciting. If we shame them, they will take their curiosity elsewhere and get their explanations from magazines, friends, or our unfriendly culture.

When opportunities arise to educate about sexuality, here are some tips for a successful conversation.

1. Start by asking, "What do you know already?" Or, if a child asks for a definition, like "What is sex?" ask, "What do you think it is?" It's important to know where you're starting.

2. For younger children, answer succinctly with only the requested or necessary information. Remember, this is a process, and there will be lots more times to share ahead. You don't have to do it all at once. Keep your child as innocent as possible. For older children, talk about the question for as long as they want.

3. Stress the importance of information being private, between you and the child. Remind the child that each parent has the privilege of teaching their child about these very personal matters, and that it is not appropriate for your child to share what you are talking about with others. Remind them of the right response if a friend asks them a question about private things: "Talk to your parents about that. That's what I do when I have a question." Even in high school, students should be careful of filling friends in with details. Refer children back to parents as often as possible.

Different members of your family will have different comfort levels about discussing sexuality. If one child is shy, you may need to make private appointments to talk about sexual subjects as they get into the eight-to-twelve years, depending on how they develop and what they are exposed to. Other children want to know about sex when they're six years old! These precocious little guys and gals can strike fear into a parent's heart with their early questions!

If you have one of these children with an early hunger for understanding, you may choose an explanation like this: In her autobiography The Hiding Place, Corrie ten Boom recounts an incident from her childhood when she and her father were traveling on a train and she asked a question about sex that her father did not answer. As they prepared to disembark, her father asked Corrie to pick up their heavy suitcase and carry it off the train. Corrie protested that it was too big and she could not lift it. Her father's reply?

"Yes," he said. "And it would be a pretty poor father who would ask his little girl to carry such a load. It's the same way, Corrie, with knowledge. Some knowledge is too heavy for children. When you are older and stronger, you can bear it. For now you must trust me to carry it for you."[9] Beautiful analogy!

Sadly, our world has changed drastically since Corrie's time. In her day, the mother or older aunt filled a bride-to-be in on the details of "birds and bees" a few days before the wedding. Today, the most intimate details are shamelessly, rampantly depicted on-screen and in advertising where little eyes can easily see them. Our children may need more information, earlier, just to keep them safe. But keep in mind that too much information can spoil innocence, even if given with the best intentions. Keep your answers as simple as possible when it comes to your little ones.

Teachable Moments

Teachable moments come in unexpected and sometimes shocking packages. For example, if you discover your young child examining his or her body or another's, or you find your older child looking at an Internet image or reading something explicit, take a deep breath and say to yourself, "This is a teachable moment."

Here's a real-life example of how an unplanned situation resulted in a great opportunity for training. My friend Dawn has two boys, seven and nine years old. On a car trip with them and another boy, Dawn was listening to a "family friendly" comedy radio station when the DJ boasted that his girlfriend had been "all over him" one night. Caught by surprise, Dawn immediately switched off the radio.

Teachable moments often come in shocking packages. Take a deep breath when they happen and remind yourself to take advantage of the opportunity!

Her younger son and his friend were sitting in the backseat, giggling. Her older son sat next to her.

To her credit, Dawn didn't overreact, but sensed a teachable moment. She smiled at the boys in the backseat and said innocently, "You don't even know what he was talking about." The younger boys just kept giggling and then went on to talk about other things.

"I know what they were talking about," said her older son.

"Really?" asked Dawn. "What?"

"Sex."

(More credit to Dawn here.) "Hmmm. And what do you think sex is?"

Her son answered, "It's when a man and a woman are under the covers, rubbing against each other."

"Well, that's part of it," Dawn answered. "We'll talk more about that later."

That night, Dawn enjoyed one of the best talks she's been able to have with her son about his sexuality. She asked where he got his information and encouraged him to ask her and his dad any future questions. Her husband also set aside time later to explain things father-to-son.

I have no doubts that, from here on out, this son will come to his mom and dad for information on touchy subjects. They took time to explain, didn't ridicule him, and set themselves up as the experts who could provide him with accurate information.

Dawn wisely seized the opportunity to inform her older son while sensing that the younger ones weren't ready for information (and that the younger son's friend's parents would be the right ones to answer his questions). Because of these choices, the whole event was a positive experience.

This is what we all want—to respond with levelheadedness to questions and events, maintain good lines of communication, and to grasp teachable moments every day.

You don't have to wait to for a question to arise before you think about an answer. In appendix D of this book, I've provided nineteen scripts that play out conversations about challenging subjects that every parent will need to eventually discuss with a child. Topics include explanations for sex, oral sex, and pornography.

In addition to talking about topics as they present themselves, certain topics will need to be intentionally approached before a problem arises. This can help prepare you to navigate the teen years.

Talk Before the Teen Years

Here is some good news about the teen years: you can help your child put those teen years in perspective before they actually come. One of the most productive educational talks we ever had happened when my eldest was nine or ten (and a few times thereafter). I had just read some advice from Dr. James Dobson about talking to your kids about the teen years before they happened. Dr. Dobson recommended that parents describe for kids the feelings the children might experience as teenagers. I took the advice to heart.

"Honey," I said one day, "when you get older there may be a time when you feel really angry at Dad and me for no real reason. You may feel that we don't understand you, and you may not want to obey us. You may want us to go away."

My adorable, obedient daughter focused her doe eyes on me and raised her chin as she shook her little head back and forth. "Oh, no, Mom, I would never do that."

"Well," I smiled, "it sounds crazy, but it might happen. And if it does, will you remember this talk and know that it's perfectly normal? Will you try to trust that Dad and I love you and are doing what's best for you?"

"Oh, yes, Mom."

During my daughter's preteen and teen years, that talk saved our lives at critical times with just a few words: "Remember that talk? That's what this is."

Her response was often a grimace and, "I know!" but things always went better after the reminder, even if the laughter simply broke the ice!

Conversations with younger children about life ahead are highly productive. Share with each other about the attributes of a spouse, dreams of ministry and occupation, driving, college, marriage, and old age.

All the late nights and "interruptions" are opportunities. These little conversations are the bricks that will build a strong house of the heart and a deeper bond with your child as well.

Not the Church's Job

Let's be honest: it's tempting to relax a little about educating our children if we're taking them to church. But church participation should be a celebration of what we are already teaching at home, not the main source for moral education. In my observations of many families, children who are most powerfully committed to virtue almost always give credit to the training they received at home.

We put unreasonable pressure on youth pastors to nurture children in a group when the issue is about how much one-on-one the youth get at home. Too many youth pastors feel overwhelmed by youth who have received no purity training at home. One such pastor complained to me that he had trouble focusing on his job because of the type of clothing that young women wore to church—an issue which needed to be answered at home.

Children who are most powerfully committed to virtue almost always give credit to the training they received at home.

Not the School's Job Either

Our children's sex education is not the public school's responsibility. We must have our children educated on matters of their sexuality before a school has a chance to present their material. Recent sex education materials in schools have included information that openly champions homosexuality, graphically encourages sexual experimentation, and excludes abstinence as a possibility. Storybooks such as *Heather Has Two Mommies* and *Daddy's Roommate* have become staples in some elementary schools. (Maybe you can donate books like *The Princess and the Kiss* or *The Squire and the Scroll* to your school library as well.)

Opt out of sex education efforts that you find inappropriate, and speak out graciously and clearly. Instead, teach your child about sexuality yourself, in age appropriate ways. The book *Talking with Your Kids about Sex* by Mark Laaser is extremely helpful. (See more resources at the end of this chapter.)

Easy-Access Ideas in This Book

You may have questions about how to go beyond spontaneous, daily teaching to teaching with a little more structure. Don't worry. This book includes a great toolbox in the appendices, including verses to memorize, sample scripts for conversations that may come up, object lessons, family contracts, and more. (For a detailed overview, see chapter 14.)

When you first try a resource, see if your family responds. If they don't, toss it aside and move on to the next idea. Seasons change, and some approaches that work for certain families don't work for others. We've tried methods that didn't go well, or went well for a short time and then flopped, and you will too. But just keep going. The information is getting into your child's head one way or another, if you're choosing to do *something* instead of *nothing*.

Teaching Yourself

With all the misinformation your child may hear about sexuality, one more issue is important to consider. How much do you know about your own body and sexuality?

In my situation, as my girls grew up and needed more information, I realized how little I knew. When I spoke at a Catholic event, I heard a seminar hosted by a scientist/biologist couple, and their knowledge of the body was astounding. I was amazed by what I didn't know, and inspired to understand my own body and sexuality better.

Rampant pornography tempts us to be ashamed about our sexuality, and sometimes churches have made the subject taboo. But we have to learn about our bodies and sexuality because we can't teach what we don't know. Maybe that's why so many of us feel nervous about talking to our children. (Books like *The Sexually Confident Wife* by Shannon Etheridge can help.)

Relax!

Remember, your child is looking to you first for information, and any "failure" or shocking situation can be turned into a teachable moment. So a lot more than you think is working in your favor. Start as early as you can, make yourself the expert that your child can come to safely with any question, and be intentional, taking advantage of all the teachable moments along the way. And breathe!

Many of us know what it's like to grow up with very little guidance regarding our sexuality. Let's make it our business to give our children the right information at the times we choose. Every effort we make is valuable, even when we fumble. Our children need our honest assistance, not an unapproachable perfect example.

One more deep breath. The next chapter is about boy/girl interaction. You can do this!

Educational Opportunities

- Use church participation to celebrate what you teach at home. Take personal responsibility to train your children in healthy sexuality and spirituality.

- Be the primary source of your children's education about sexuality. Carefully evaluate what the school may be teaching and make choices about your child attending specific sex education events. Communicate with your children how the school's views and your family's might differ, and why.

- Browse the back of this book to start considering resources for your family or individual members.

- Talk with your children all the time, throughout life, and definitely before they're teens, if you can. Prepare them constantly with ongoing, age-appropriate information.

- _____

_____

_____

Building Materials

Books and Web Sites
See Appendix A for more details.
Entire section

Truths to Memorize
See Appendix B for complete texts.
Education (12)

Scripts
See Appendix D for complete texts.
Entire section

Object Lessons
See Appendix E for complete texts.
Private Question Journal (32)

Window 5

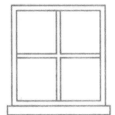

Boy/Girl Interaction

The onset of the dating years can strike fear in a parent's heart, but it's easier when we've prepared our children as they've grown. And this window of opportunity is about more than the rules for dating. It's about honoring others and using that foundation to make good choices about how we treat each other in one-on-one relationships.

Let's talk about what honor looks like, discuss the dangers of "Kleenex dating" and the importance of girls being feminine and boys learning to lead. Then we'll look at two strategies for boy/girl relationships: 1) preparation for courtship or 2) dating with guidelines. If you choose to permit dating (or it's too late to change what you're already doing), some dating guidelines from experts are included. There's even a section exposing one of the most dangerous places for a couple to be during a date. Now you *have* to read on!

Let's start by talking about honor, a concept often sadly absent in popular American culture.

Honoring Others as Precious

Oh, to be back in the days when men threw down their coats for women to walk upon, and women waited for a knight to come and rescue them! Yes, it's a fairy tale of sorts, but in today's world we long for just a little of that chivalry and a touch of that femininity.

Honoring the opposite sex isn't just about rules for dating and romantic relationships. It's about respecting and valuing boys and girls, men and women. Honoring the opposite sex means giving sexuality and physical intimacy a safe place in marriage, honoring others as precious, and remembering the incredible gift of the breath (Door 3).

When honor is absent, the focus becomes physical. The Miss USA pageant (2010) required contestants to pose in lingerie and high heels as part of the competition.[10] This objectification raises a great deal of concern as we consider our culture's attitudes, especially toward women. Objects are to be used. People have feelings, hopes

Honoring the opposite sex means giving sexuality and physical intimacy a safe place in marriage.

and dreams, and are to be treasured. Portraying women as objects of pleasure dishonors and devalues both our women and our nation. Our children need to understand that men and women are not display items in a store window.

How much different things would be if men and women chose to treat each other as brothers and sisters![11] No one would approve of such "use" and devaluation of a person, man or woman. We are not bodies alone, but a complete package—mind, body and soul—worthy of respect and honor. Opportunity to spend time together is a privilege with responsibility.

Help your children to understand what respect and honor look like in their daily lives. Following are four areas where honor makes the difference between building up others or tearing them down.

Courtesy Helps

The principles of good manners are based on honoring those around you. Courteous habits make anyone feel valued. When we say, "please," "thank you," and "I'm sorry," we honor others. When a young man pulls out a chair for a young lady or opens a door for her first, he shows his respect for her. A young lady who allows him such leadership strengthens his role as a man. This behavior starts at home (adults included!), and it's simple to implement. (See the resource list at the end of this chapter for books that offer specific ideas.)

Kleenex Dating

Honoring others means treating them as valuable. That's why I've coined the phrase "Kleenex dating" to describe the practice of choosing boy/girl friends and tossing them away one after another like worthless used tissues. This behavior doesn't show value for others.

Dating and breaking up over and over is good preparation for promiscuity and divorce.

Nothing and no one precious would be treated in such a way. Switching partners on a whim does not teach a young person how to maintain a long-term friendship or a lasting marriage. Dating and breaking up over and over is better preparation for promiscuity or divorce. Lasting friendships and family relationships teach commitment and honor.

Dating games encourage the "here today, gone tomorrow" attitude that hurts and devalues others. No person should be treated as a temporary fling. When one-on-one dating becomes nothing more than a game, we have lost the meaning of the relationship. We become playthings.

Flirting

Flirting is often the lead-in to Kleenex relationships. Women are expressly warned away from captivating with the eyes,[12] body, scents and other flirtations in Proverbs, and men are similarly warned to avoid women who do so.[13] Unnecessary backrubs, winks, and teasing are games that can lead to hurtful misunderstandings and consequences. Are we fanning feelings into flame that we know we will be unable to satisfy?

When women approach men flirtatiously with foolish sexual comments and casual physical contact, they light fires they may not be capable of controlling. This does not respect a man's natural makeup, and puts a woman at risk.

Honor means that girls and boys protect each other's hearts and bodies instead of tempting each other to experiment through flirting, immodesty, and other irresponsible, objectifying behavior.

Girls Pursuing Boys

A final thought about honor addresses a disturbing trend in the way girls treat boys. More and more parents are distressed by young women who pursue boys with phone calls, looks, and immodest dress and actions. These girls are influenced by modern media, and perhaps lack connection with parents, especially dads, and their actions can be very dangerous to young men.

Human physiology shows that men are made to be the initiators because they respond immediately to sight; thus, they initiate relationships. On the other hand, women do not respond immediately to sight, but they must be won over time through an emotional connection.

Girls are more naturally verbal, so they can easily begin a conversation. Boys are not wired the same way. When little girls are carrying on dialogue between their dolls, little boys are making their trucks say, "Vrooom!"

Boys must grow up to be men. As they mature, they learn to be initiators and protectors, and they "catch up" with girls' ability to communicate. Today it's common for young women to pursue boys or make a hobby out of calling them, but this cripples our boys, keeping them from developing as leaders and initiators. They cannot become men unless they struggle with the difficulty of leading, language, and relationship. When a girl initiates, she takes that opportunity away.[14] Thus, our boys lose

Boys grow up to be men by learning to initiate conversation and interaction. Girl initiators rob them of that opportunity.

masculinity, and our girls lose femininity. Roles are garbled, and our children and culture become confused and androgynous.

A special note to parents of boys: If there is a young girl pursuing your young boy, you may need to speak directly to her or her parents about the rules of your household. You may worry about looking overprotective, but take into consideration the growing number of girls without fathers or loving homes who are seeking attention from any man they can approach. In conversations with the girl or her mother, you may be a mentor to help guide her to a new and healthier path. (See the Building Materials at the end of this chapter for a suggested script for responding to unwanted phone calls.)

To Date or Not to Date?

Now that the concept of honor is in place, we should have an easier time sorting out the question of dating. First, let's recognize that *dating* (defined as a boy and girl traveling somewhere alone together for a recreational outing) hasn't been the norm in America for long. Less than a century has passed since the car was invented and a young man could drive up to a house to take a young lady for a ride. Before that, a couple might sit together in a room in the young lady's house with mother and father present. A courting candle may have been lit. The candle going out was a signal that the couple's visit was over, and the young man would go home. (Maybe a courting candle sounds like a good idea to some of us!)

We discussed in the vocabulary chapter how important it is to define what *dating* means in your family. Does it mean that a boy and a girl go out together alone? Or does it denote group dating, where a couple goes out with friends? Or is dating saved as a pre-engagement practice for a more mature/young adult couple ready to consider marriage?

If your child is still younger than nine, or even in the preteen years, how much do they know about what you'll expect in the teen years? How much has your family talked about dating thus far? You can get started by answering the following questions:

- What is your definition of dating?

- Do your kids (of all ages) expect to date in the high school years?

- Where should the couple go on a date? How old should they be?

- As a child matures, how will boundaries be set to prepare for the possibility of a marriage partner, or for a season—temporary or permanent—of single living?

- If dating will not be practiced, what guidelines will apply if a young lady and young man find they have mutual feelings for each other?

- If your child does not date, what options will he or she have when others are dating?

As my husband and I thought about these questions, we realized that we did not want our daughters to participate in dating as defined by culture. But we had to recognize that girls and boys would be attracted to each other, so we needed an alternative. That alternative became *preparation for courtship*. This approach is my first choice, but another option that can be successful is dating with clear boundaries. We'll take a look at both in this next section.

Choice A: Preparation for Courtship

Preparation for courtship is the approach our family has crafted for "more-than-friend" relationships in the high school years. We use the term *preparation* for courtship because the process isn't really courtship due to the fact that neither teen is prepared for marriage—yet.

To be truthful, preparation for courtship was our second choice. We had prepared our girls to have friendships only until they were old enough to consider marriage, but feelings became strong earlier than we planned. Our daughter was passionate about wanting to be a wife and mother, and wanted to feel secure with a single "safe" boy instead of being pursued by many boys. We changed our plan to walk with her through a sort of "supervised exclusivity," mostly because we saw a rebellion starting in our girl that seemed inevitable under our original rules.

Our goal became to keep their friendship healthy until this young couple reached an age where they could consider courtship and marriage (if their commitment to each other lasted that long). We set boundaries to allow friendship but not enough interaction to move beyond that stage.

As they spent time together, we challenged them to grow. Would they be able to:

• *Submit to parental boundaries?* (In marriage, they would have to submit to each other, and, most importantly, to God.)

• *Be honestly accountable with limits on time together,* both online and on the phone?

• *Keep family first?* (Children learn how to be a family through being *with* their families. In the same way, young couples learn how to honor one another through observing examples of their parents.)

• *Keep priorities in order, as far as school, church, and personal goals?* (For our daughter, one personal goal at the time was ballet lessons, while the young man's was baseball.)

Included in this book is a copy of some relational boundaries we set and modified as our children grew into the teen years (See contract A in appendix F). This is part of our family's approach. Yours doesn't have to be the same, because your children are not ours. But you will need some way to manage relationships as they come about. Even if your child isn't drawn into a relationship, he or she will need the same sort of boundaries to prepare for living independently. You are their privileged instructor, and a written set of thoughts will help.

Our Story

As I mentioned earlier, my husband and I planned for our daughters to focus only on friendships through their high school years. That plan worked very well until our oldest daughter, who was sixteen at the time, realized a mutual fondness with a boy from the church youth group. They had developed an interest in each other through youth group and during talks while volunteering at a local bookstore. Our daughter told us about her interest, and my husband met with the young man and his father. We set up guidelines to protect the friendship between our daughter and the boy. Thankfully, both families had some wisdom and a desire to protect our children's friendship. We shared the guidelines with the boy's parents for consistency. They agreed to them as well.

My daughter and her friend had two days a week when they did not interact. They had fifteen minutes to interact (including phone and computer) on school days (they attended different schools). They had half an hour per day on weekends, and they attended the same youth group. They didn't sit together or appear as a couple, but interacted with other friends equally.

We kept our hearts open as we watched their friendship develop. In the end, they couldn't adhere to the boundaries set for them. They found ways to sneak around, and the young man tried to pressure our daughter into deeper involvement. Eventually he broke off the relationship. At this point, our daughter and he do not even consider themselves to be friends.

Our daughter suffered for a while, but it was her choice to begin the relationship; therefore, she learned the pain of ending something deeper than a friendship. She also learned the cost of mistakes she made in becoming too close physically, and decided it wasn't worth it. For the time being, she is choosing to keep her relationships at a friendship level as she waits for the right man for her. She is often impatient, but she is much wiser!

Choice B: Dating with Guidelines

If preparation for courtship is not right for your family, you may choose to allow your child to date with guidelines. If you have someone already dating, it's most likely best to start with boundaries instead of cutting off a relationship entirely and alienating your child. (However, remember that as the parent, your job is not to make your child happy; it is to guide them into being a right person, which will result in more opportunity for happiness.)

Your job is not to make your child happy; it is to guide them into being a right person, which will result in more happiness.

If you allow dating, then your entire family should know the answer to these questions as they are growing up. Write some quick answers right here in the book, or copy this page and take your time writing down the answers.

Dating Guidelines

- At what age will dating begin?

- What kind of young man or woman is a candidate for dating? What kind isn't?

- What age is or isn't appropriate for a dating partner?

- Will you meet the parents prior to the date?

- How long will dates last, and until what hour of the night?

- How often will dates be allowed to occur?

- What places are appropriate?

- What specific behaviors are appropriate or inappropriate during a date?

- How much interaction (phone and computer) will be allowed outside of dates?

Interaction Guidelines

- How should a young man approach a young lady?

- Is flirting OK? What *is* flirting?

- What conversation is appropriate or inappropriate?

Take regular time just to talk with your son or daughter and listen to their feelings and expectations. Then relationally set up the standards of your household in a way that makes your child feel protected and heard, not ignored and trapped.

Dating can be very hurtful for parties involved. Any commitment will end in either marriage or a breakup. At a young age, it will most likely end in a parting of ways. Most importantly, stress to your teen that dating must always honor the two people involved and treat them as precious brothers and sisters. Your teen may be dating someone else's future husband or wife. If so, how would they like someone else to be treating theirs?

Your teen may be dating someone else's future husband or wife. If so, how would they like someone else to be treating theirs?

Although the choice is yours, there are some facts about dating and intimate interaction of which you should be aware for your children's safety. These are listed in no particular order, and there are many more you can consider in many other books on the subject.

- Earlier dating is shown to lead to earlier sexual experimentation.[15]

- Girls often lose their innocence when dating older, more experienced guys.[16]

• Many kids today do not consider oral sex to be "real sex."[17]

• Pam Stenzel, a powerful sexual responsibility speaker, notes that the most dangerous sexually transmitted diseases today can be passed on skin-to-skin, without intercourse. They have no symptoms but may render a woman infertile or cause cancer if undetected.[18]

So, You're Interested in My Daughter...

Let's imagine that you have a teenage daughter showing interest in a boy who returns this interest. You can see that these emotions are not going to fade away. What do you do now? Whether you allow dating or preparation for courtship, here are some observations about the situation to consider:

• Allowing a boy to walk through the difficulty of asking a girl "out" or expressing his interest in her to her dad is helpful in his personal development as a man and head of a household. (Talking to Dad is required of any boy seeking more than friendship with a daughter in our household.)

• When a dad insists on meeting the young man in question, he has the opportunity to say *no* and protect his daughter if she isn't really interested.

• Meeting the parents will reveal a lot about a young man (or woman).

• Emotions can flare very quickly, even (sometimes especially) via technology.

• A guy gets points when he is brave enough to show up for an introductory talk with parents and answer questions.

• Relational boundaries should be clearly designated, openly discussed, written out, and in the possession of all parties involved so expectations are clear.

The Dad's Perspective

If a boy agrees to meet with my husband, Randy has a simple way of explaining his expectations. It goes like this:

I will always protect my daughter fiercely. Therefore, you will commit to the following three conditions:

1. You will protect my daughter from you.
2. You will protect my daughter from herself.
3. You will never, ever try to protect my daughter from me.

Just those few lines, delivered and explained in my husband's authoritative voice, make a deep impression on a young man!

But even before that, as soon as a boy expresses interest in a daughter, we do our research. We check out the parents ourselves and know as much as we can ahead of time. Some interested boys don't even make it into our home or ever hear the three rules.

As you decide what the boundaries look like for your daughters, be intentional and serious, but also have fun putting your list of questions and/or requirements together. This is important, yes, but a little levity can help lighten the air and let us all breathe more freely.

As soon as a boy expresses interest in a daughter, we do our research.

So, You're Interested in My Son...

Now imagine that you have a teenage son who is interested in a young lady. Naturally, you want to make sure that this young lady will behave honorably toward your young man. I asked a number of my girlfriends with sons for advice (so my daughters could take note!), and they came up with the "Big Five" requirements for a young lady:

• The Big #1: Respect. Does the girl respect me as my son's mom (or dad)? Is she willing to talk to me on the phone (if she calls), look me in the eyes, or come in the house to visit? Does she speak respectfully about her own parents? Does she respect my son and herself enough to be interested in his opinions? Does she avoid casual physical contact and flirting?

• The Big #2: Appearance/modesty. Is she more concerned with flaunting a figure than with showing her good character on the inside? (One mom and son agreed that visible cleavage or "skirts that looked more like belts" made a girl undeniably unsuitable!) Body piercings and tattoos immediately evoke suspicion, justified or not.

• The Big #3: Speech. What does she talk about and how? Is she wrapped up in herself and the culture? Does she tear others down with her talk or does she speak of others with honor and respect? Does it sound like she looks for ways to put others first? Profanity or coarse jokes are no-nos.

• The Big #4: Feminine Role. Does she initiate calls and visits constantly, or allow my son to initiate contact and conversation (at least most of the time) so he can develop leadership and manhood?

• The Big #5: Faith and Values. Does she have a faith base/values system that is similar to our family's? What are her family's values?

One mom laughed that they distilled everything down to the funny old rhyme, "We don't smoke and we don't chew, and we don't go with girls who do!" I know her boys are aware of a lot more detail than that, but when she reminds them that this is what the family stands for, they know *exactly* what she's talking about.

Again, every family will have their own set of particular standards. Choose yours intentionally and have a plan in place to prevent unnecessary misunderstandings and relational breakdowns between yourself and your child.

Respecting How the Body Works
Vetting the people our kids take a special interest in is a must, and we should do our best to applaud their wise choices. But if we allow our children to be alone together, it's still difficult not to become physi-

cally involved. When we put two hormonally charged teenagers into a car and send them off on their own, we are ignoring their physiology.

"But I trust my child!" you may say. I trust my children, too. But I also respect the functions of the human body. Males and females are built to be powerfully attracted to each other. Alone together, men and women can easily end up becoming sexually involved or having intercourse.

It's like the ocean. Those of us who live in Florida love to swim, surf, dive, or parasail at the beaches. But we are also very aware of the ocean's power. We avoid specific conditions because we know the ocean could drag us under and take our lives.

The power of sexuality and desire in relationships is the same way. Relationships are a gift of life that we can celebrate. But if we don't understand the power of sexual attraction, an immature relationship can easily lead to pregnancy, emotional devastation, STDs, and even death.

Please bear with me as I share this earthy analogy. If we want two pedigree dogs to mate, we put them in a small, confined space together. For a human being, a car is not

Being alone together is a huge responsibility.

that much different. The sex drive is extremely powerful. Is it really wise to allow our children to be put in a situation of such risk? Why are we surprised when couples go out alone, innocence is lost, and unplanned pregnancies occur?

The difference between a dog's desire to procreate and human sexual drives is that we are smart enough to know how to keep ourselves out of situations where we may fall into unplanned actions. We can consider our future and the future of the other person involved. Our children desperately need this training from us.

Keeping Relationships in Balance

As a final note, let's work hard to help our children keep their relationships in balance. How do we help them maintain relationships in a healthy way? Try discussing the following questions with your child.

- When does interest turn into unhealthy obsession?

- How does a relationship stay balanced instead of exclusive?

- How do hiding, lying, and disobedience to family standards affect the individuals, the relationship, and the families involved? Why should secretiveness always be avoided?

- How do individuals find security and value in themselves apart from any relationship?

The point is not necessarily that there is an exactly right answer, but that the topics are considered intentionally. Keeping relationships in balance is an evolving effort that requires ongoing openness, communication, and flexibility.

Plan, Pray, and Be Creative

Thoughts on dating fill stacks of books. Endless discussion could take place on the subject. Therefore, every parent must educate themselves on the matter and intentionally formulate a plan (though it will most likely evolve) for their child's relational practices between male and female. Preparing the child at a young age will be extremely helpful, but no matter when training begins, the unexpected will happen.

In sixth grade, boys lined up to ask our friendly daughter to "date" them. Aggravated, our girl came up with the idea of a bracelet inscribed with the words, "God is my boyfriend." That way, when someone approached her, she could display her jewelry and end the discussion. (She usually showed the bracelet with her fist in the air, which probably ended the encounter a little more quickly!) The issue quickly cleared up, and some interesting conversations ensued. Her creativity inspired more friendships and less romantic game-playing as she grew.

Pray yourself silly and don't freak out.

We may never entirely understand the mystery of what happens between a man and a woman, but we know that there is a way to make honorable choices in any situation. I encourage you to plan, to be wise, to be patient and involved, to pray yourself silly and *not freak out.* Every misstep is an opportunity to learn and even to laugh. No matter what choices are made, we can always make progress from where we are.

Opportunities for Interaction

- Exemplify value for each other in the home, preparing to value those outside the home as well. What do you do that makes each other feel precious and cherished?

- Teach good manners to encourage respectful relationships between boys and girls.

- Make a list of the pros and cons between preparation for courtship and dating with guidelines. Which do you feel might be best for your family? How might you begin to educate your children about the coming years?

- Answer the key questions about dating and discuss them as spouses or with another parent. Start by defining the word *dating* for your household.

- How are you encouraging the young men in your family to be leaders and heads of households? How are your daughters being encouraged to be confidently feminine and respectful of men?

- _____

  _____

  _____

Building Materials

Books and Web Sites
See Appendix A for more details.
The Princess and the Kiss, Jennie Bishop (4)
The Garden Wall, Jennie Bishop (6)
★*Boys Adrift*, Dr. Leonard Sax (12)
What He Must Be...If He Wants to Marry My Daughter, Voddie Baucham, Jr. (15)
★*Eyes Wide Open: Avoiding the Heartbreak of Emotional Promiscuity*, Brienne Murk (25)
Emotional Purity: An Affair of the Heart, Heather Arnel Paulsen (26)
★*If You Really Loved Me*, Jason Evert (20)
I Kissed Dating Goodbye, Joshua Harris (27)
And the Bride Wore White, Dannah Gresh (31)
www.beforethekiss.com: courtship information (28)
www.stayinthecastle.com: courtship suggestions and creative story resources (30)

Truths to Memorize
See Appendix B for complete texts.
Boy/Girl Interaction (13)
Sincere Faith (29)
No Hint of Immorality (34)
The Marriage Bed (35)
The Sister Attitude (36)
Purpose of the Body (37)
Flee Immorality (38)
Flee Evil Desires (41)
A Good Example When Young (42)

Scripts
See Appendix D for complete texts.
Responding to Unwanted Phone Calls (13)

Object Lessons
See Appendix E for complete texts.
Staying Afloat (33)
Sticking Together (34)
Wild Fire (35)

Contracts
See Appendix F for complete texts.
Contract A: Preparation for Courtship Agreement

Window 6

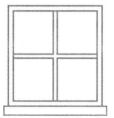

Friends

Guiding our children toward healthy friendships is like a coin's two sides. On one side, we want to protect our children from those who would influence them toward destructive behavior. On the other side, we want our children to be able to speak into the lives of young people who may not have the benefit of moral guidance. How do we do both?

Growing up, I was warned specifically of hanging out with the "wrong crowd." To me, that included beer drinkers, girls who made out with boys, and anybody who took drugs or smoked. I lived in a rural community that covered a lot of ground as far as outward appearances, but it didn't include evaluating the condition of a seemingly good person's heart. It also couldn't cover the many pitfalls of online interaction that we face today.

In today's tech-heavy world, we can still find ways to guard our children *and* allow opportunities for them to impact others. This chapter will discuss the all-important difference between a friend and an acquaintance. We'll also talk about helping our kids navigate the negative influences at school while making a positive impact. And we'll share ways to stay in-the-know as far as where our kids go, physically or online.

Acquaintances vs. Friends

The first step in successful friendships is to make certain that your child —from kindergarten through college—understands the difference between a friend and an acquaintance. Facebook has redefined the word in an unfortunate way, but people of all ages need to remember that a friend can't actually become one at the click of a button. A *friend* is someone who has an ongoing influence in your life—one who has been close for a length of time and shares a special connection with you. A friend is someone you know well and can trust.

An acquaintance is someone you happen to know because you go to the same class or play on the same sports team. But a friend has been with you for enough time to show loyalty and to be trusted with details in your life.

Acquaintances happen casually, often by chance. Friends must be considered and chosen. Someone earns the title. Remember: We have acquaintances by chance, but we should choose friends intentionally, whether the relationship is online or off.

Influences at School

Let's apply this idea of friends and acquaintances to what our kids experience at school. My husband and I have sent our children to a wide variety of schools—home school, public school, and private Christian school. Each type of schooling has its benefits and problems. Many parents evaluate every child's educational approach each year and make changes as necessary or as they are able. A boys' school or a girls' school may be a good choice for some kids, especially when a boy is struggling. (You may want to read more about this in the book *Boys Adrift* by Dr. Leonard Sax.) Possibilities exist for every style of learning and parenting.

We should choose friends intentionally, whether the relationship is online or off.

No matter what situation you are in, you can make your child's learning environment as positive as possible by your involvement. Know your child's friends, classes, teachers and experiences.

For example, my younger daughter went to public school in Orlando in sixth grade, and she told me about kids kissing in the hallways, and bullying. Together we planned ways for her to speak up for her bullied friend, which she did with success. (I'll give some more information about bullying in the next section.)

My older daughter attended ninth grade at a public high school the size of a small city. She saw homosexuality acted out between classes and endured waiting for a bathroom break until she got home because she felt those areas were too dangerous. She also complained that no student really studied in study hall except her, and she was teased mercilessly for her good grades. She had to defend her faith often to a confrontational Latin teacher.

In public school, our daughters had many acquaintances, but they made only a few lasting friends. However, their friends in youth group helped strengthen them.

We ultimately made a decision to send our daughters to private Christian school. The atmosphere was definitely different. But even when most of our children's acquaintances are Christian, the need to evaluate who will be a friend remains essential. Not all Christians act out virtuous behavior. In fact, some non-believers make better friends than some believers. It's healthy to have friends of varying backgrounds as long as the friends have mutual respect for their differences in belief.

It's healthy to have friends of varying backgrounds when there is mutual respect for differences in beliefs.

In fact, respect is at the core of the serious problem of bullying that is affecting so many youth today, whether in person or online.

Bullying

Make sure your children know that you are immediately available if they experience any kind of physical or verbal bullying in person or online. In the case of nasty comments online or the phone, explain that they should leave the device immediately and let you know. If they show a reluctance to go to school, ask whether anyone is making them feel uncomfortable. Many children who are enjoying friendships instead of having a boyfriend or girlfriend are teased as being abnormal, and this is also bullying or harassment.

Reassure your children that if they tell you about a bully, you will not embarrass them or cause a confrontation. Inform school officials immediately of incidents during school events. You can also train your children to stand up against a bully for themselves or a friend (as my daughter did). Explain how to be assertive and not aggressive.

A basic strategy:

1. Avoid the bully, if possible.
2. Speak up for yourself and say "no."
3. Find a friend who can be there when the bully is around.
4. Hold onto your emotions when bullied, but show them later when you report.
5. Don't bully back.
6. Tell an adult.

If your child sees someone else being bullied, the situation could be a way for him to have a positive impact on acquaintances. Students have a much better chance of personally sending a bully packing. Do some role play to teach your child how to be courageous, wise, and safe. Building Materials at the end of this chapter will direct you to a sample script in this book that may help.

Setting Boundaries

We need to know who our children's friends are and what they do when they are together. This is true in preschool, and it's true in high school. When your child is surrounded by friends (or acquaintances), he or she is much more likely to be influenced than to be the influencer. The best way to keep your child safe is to set clear boundaries.

Some boundaries are a matter of common sense. Letting a sixth grade girl go with an eighth grade boy to a movie is a recipe for disaster. Allowing a high schooler to stay out as long as they like any night of the week will most likely result in a host of troubles. Unlimited Internet use leads to problems. But even when a boundary seems obvious, it is wise to make it clear to all parties.

For example, when our sixteen-year-old first got her driver's license, she was elated and decided to stop by a friend's house to give her a ride to church—without asking our permission. We knew the family and the friend well and the church is right down the street, but the issue was that she didn't ask. She just "figured it would be all right." My husband reminded her that using a $20,000 vehicle to do something without the owner's permission as a brand new driver is not all right.

Setting clear boundaries with friends is important because our children do a lot of "figuring it will be all right." Unless we define what is appropriate, we can't expect them to know. And the same is true as we relate to the parents of their friends.

Invitations to any event or time spent away from home should be discussed by the parents first. As your child grows, make it clear that the parents must agree on the event before it is approved and scheduled. This is especially true if the event involves visiting another home or driving others.

Visiting Other Homes

Don't allow your children or teenagers to roam the neighborhood. Know parents before your child is allowed in their household. If you have reservations, don't be afraid to make that household off limits.

In a past community, we had a little girl who wandered from door to door, looking for playmates. We invited her in from time to time, and had to turn her away when our family was otherwise engaged. We limited play to our home because we did not know her parents, and so we could not be sure that her home was safe. Molestation happens every day, and there is no good reason to put a child at risk.

Make room for "wandering children" in your household when you can, but supervise and limit playtime. Note the conversation and positive or negative ways the child interacts with your family members.

If a family invites your young child to their home, but you are unsure, perhaps suggest a time when you and the other parent(s) can share time together in their home while the children play. This way you can get to know the family better and keep an eye on your child at the same time. Always be aware of opportunities to explain the reasons you make the choices you do. You may influence another parent for the better.

Sleepovers

Some parents choose not to allow their children to sleep over, while others are very comfortable with overnight gatherings. Consider your child's age and development, the others attending, supervision and activities before you give permission. If kids do sleep over, ask:

- Will they have access to phones or Internet while the adults are sleeping?

- How will this unsupervised time be managed? Viewings of inappropriate material or irresponsible texting, photos, and emails often happen just because of a lack of good judgment fueled by a lack of sleep.

A number of families are choosing to "check phones and technology at the door" during get-togethers to encourage more attention to the friends present and to control technological interaction. This wise approach protects and deepens friendship between individuals by taking a break from the online community.

A number of families are choosing to check technology at the door during get togethers.

Another approach for elementary-age kids is a "half-sleepover," where kids wear the pajamas, eat the popcorn, participate in the activities, and then come home for bed, maybe a little later than usual. Half-sleepovers involve less unsupervised time and less next-day crankiness, so they make a good in-between option.

Questions to Ask Before a Visit

Never hesitate to ask questions about what will happen while your child is visiting another home. A good household will welcome these questions with ready answers. You may ask:

- How will technology be limited or supervised? (Phones checked at the door? Computer access limited to public space?)

- What movies may be watched? You may offer to have your child bring his own movie if you'd rather. See scripts in appendix D for a sample discussion between parents.)

- What games may be played (particularly video games)?

- What adults will be present? Make it clear to your teen that all drivers and trips anywhere out of the host's home must be approved by you.

(Add your own!)

_____

_____

_____

As always, stay interested, involved, polite, and clear in your setting of boundaries. Consider your child's feelings as they get older, and ask questions outside their hearing to keep them from feeling "babied." You may seem odd to others at first, but those parents may also begin to wonder whether they should begin the same practices themselves.

Remember, this is your child, your jewel. You are responsible for your child's safety and keeping. Don't allow anyone to make you feel embarrassed for taking that responsibility seriously. Your goal is to raise and protect a child who is honorable and responsible. That is a worthy calling.

Opportunities with Friends

- Observe your children's interaction with friends, discussing the difference between friends and acquaintances.

- Continue to stay engaged in daily conversation to hear about friendships at school and how they're going.

- Never be afraid to set standards for behavior/Internet/movies/ music/supervision when your child is invited to an event in another household. Keep your questions brief and gracious, and offer other options or bow out if necessary.

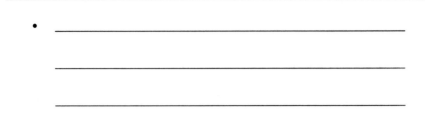

Building Materials

Books and Web Sites
See Appendix A for more details.
The Squire and the Scroll, Jennie Bishop (5)
The Garden Wall, Jennie Bishop (6)
A Child's Book of Virtues, William Bennett (7)

Truths to Memorize
See Appendix B for complete texts.
Friends (14)
Strong Together (16)
Others' Sins (30)

Scripts
See Appendix D for complete texts.
Speaking to a Host Parent About Media (9)
Bullying (16)
Online Bullying (17)
Sexual Bullying (18)

Object Lessons
See Appendix E for complete texts.
Good Friend/Bad Friend (36)
Family Friendship (37)

Window 7

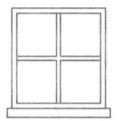

Technology

Media can easily take over the job of instilling values. Do you really want the values of today's media to become your child's values?

When it comes to media influence, many of us are like the proverbial "frog in the pot." We adjust to worse and worse media temperatures until we are boiled in it!

Let's learn some ways to tame the media monster of technology and make him a gentle giant to be used for our benefit and the benefit of others. You'll learn:

- How to tell whether you have a technology addict in your house

- The intensifying effect technology can have on young people's relationships

- How social media can cause dangerous emotion

- Guidelines for phone use and social networking sites

- Good news about some heroes in the media

Let's start by figuring out whether we've crossed the line from *using* technology to being *controlled by it*. How can we tell if we are technology addicts?

Technology Addiction

When technology—more than human interaction and needs—becomes our main means of gaining satisfaction and getting our "orders" for the day, we and our families are in trouble. We can't let our media intake become so pervasive that we sacrifice interaction in our homes. We and our children are at risk of trading in real life for a purposeless, virtual existence.

I don't know about you, but when I'm working on the computer and my husband or a daughter approaches me, I struggle to break eye contact with my computer screen and turn toward my loved one. I'm not sure why the little twist of the head is so hard, but I'm daily learning to do better. Turning away from the computer and toward a spouse or child makes a powerful statement that he or she is more important.

In our present home, we don't have cable and we watch very little TV, but we love watching good movies. Just to make sure our priorities stay in order, from time to time when we are watching a movie, one of us gets in front of the screen and dances around while singing, "I'm more important than the TV!" It's hilarious, a little annoying, and a good reminder of our true priorities.

We can't let our media intake become so pervasive that we sacrifice interaction in our homes.

We are not meant to be isolated consumers of media input. We are meant to enjoy human relationship and the natural world around us. Isolation can be dangerous. On the other hand, technology can lessen isolation and build communities rooted in reality and truth, when used in a balanced way.

Are there technology addicts in your house? Perhaps you, a family member, or the family as a whole is spending too much time "plugged in." Count the hours you or your family spends in front of a screen, how many texts you send in a day, how many times you check email or social networking, and so on. Ask yourself if this expenditure of time is eating up your opportunities to really live. Set your own boundaries.

All of us are struggling with finding new ways to use media sanely. I challenge you to take a few days and turn off technology entirely to make a new start. You'll all survive. Then set guidelines for how technology will be used in your family. (See appendix F, contract C for sample guidelines.)

Technology and Relationships

In a world saturated in technological advances, face-to-face communication is no longer necessary for a relationship to develop. In the past, when the school day ended, the communication between kids ended until the next school day. Now there is no break between interactions. A constant stream

I challenge you to take a few days and turn off technology entirely to make a new start. You'll all survive.

of contact between peers is available, allowing thoughts and emotions to develop with little parental knowledge. At the same time, thoughts and emotions can grow at a dizzying speed. A young man and woman may start by innocently writing notes to each other but end up talking about their feelings and awaken a strong desire to be together—in a very short time.

If we aren't willing to set limits on our children's unsupervised communication, they—and we—could be in deep water fast! We can't underestimate the power of these new communication venues on thought lives and emotions.

Have you seen children or teens "all of a sudden" fall into some moral failure that is a complete surprise to the family or community? Obviously, those choices didn't just happen. They were formed in the mind and emotions before they ever took place in reality.

Let's train our children to understand the need to develop face-to-face relationships and teach them the positive use of technology, setting up filters online and in their own hearts.

The availability of pornography is a prime example of the way technology can pull in a young person quickly and addict them for years. Before there are any problems in your family, explain the addictive qualities of pornography to your children in age-appropriate terms. Require your family to respect all people as human beings and not objects.

Emotional Overload

Drama! What used to be hidden under a mattress in a locked diary is now posted online for everyone to read. The drama that already exists as part of the preteen/teen world is multiplied tenfold, becoming more intense, dangerous, and destructive.

Megan Meier's family is painfully aware of this fact. Their daughter was bullied by a mother, no less, who posed as an online boyfriend and proceeded to torment, harass, humiliate and embarrass the girl, who had supposed the "boy" liked her. After a comment from the "boy" that "the world would be a better place without her," Megan was despondent. She committed suicide.[19]

Make sure your child knows to ask for help when online talk becomes emotionally supercharged for themselves or their friends. Explain the feelings and choices that are red flags for dangerous emotions, like a pounding heart, a feeling that interaction must be hidden from parents, the heaviness of guilt or a feeling of shame. Gently let your child know that they should come to you if any of these uncomfortable "symptoms" occur. Then prepare yourself to understand and to steer clear of harsh judgment.

The drama of the teen world is multiplied by technology.

Phone Guidelines

In the case of a cell phone and any other technology, boundaries should come with the first discussion of bringing the technology into the house. Phones are most often paid for by a parent, and as parents, we are responsible for setting up rules for use. We are also legally responsible if a minor in our care shares sexually explicit material![20]

Here are questions that you can use to help set up phone guidelines for your children.

- Is a phone truly necessary?

- When may a phone be used?

- Is texting necessary?

- What photos are appropriate?

- How long should a conversation be with a friend? A girl or boy friend?

- How does a parent retain access to a child's communications and passwords?

- What are the repercussions of stepping over set boundaries?

- What limitations are the parents setting and keeping as good examples?

If a phone is for emergencies only, we define what an emergency is. We can choose to check in and turn phones off at the door when a child comes home, making it easier for all of us to focus on family when present. We can make it clear that the phone will disappear when boundaries are pressed, and follow through when this happens. We can discuss time limits for conversation and talk about what we think purposeful conversation is. How do we avoid gossip? Are girls allowed to call boys or vice versa? Under what circumstances?

We can check phones at the door, making it easier for all of us to focus on our families at home.

Social Networking

Our household is not lacking in new technologies—far from it. My husband enjoys using new technology and my girls seem to pick up on it just as quickly as he does. As each piece of technology enters the household, from new phones to game systems to networking sites, we have intentional discussions about how they will be used.

Recently we sat down at the family table to discuss new boundaries for Facebook usage. Each one of us enjoy using the social networking, but as in all families, sometimes things go a bit awry—especially when you have two beautiful daughters like ours who love to pose for a camera.

We all agreed that our pages had to reflect our family values. Then we began to discuss the ramifications of being in a social network that sends messages to far more people than you could ever interact with personally. Is a Facebook friend really a friend? How can you be friends with five hundred people? Do you understand that each post you make is like stepping onto a stage and telling five thousand people about your personal life?

Many young people take little time to think about what they share; they take an immodest picture with their phone as a joke, and soon it's posted online for the world to see. (This action now has a name—sexting[21] —and even teens may be legally prosecuted for distributing explicit underage photos this way.)

In our family we realized that practical questions about using a social network site were in order. These questions (using Facebook as an example) can be a starting point for evaluating social networking in your home, too.

- What kind of pictures and albums are OK on your Facebook page? How many?

- What information is appropriate and what information is inappropriate or even dangerous?

- What are new ways we can guard our information? (Facebook now has more privacy options than ever before. Become familiar with Facebook and use them.)

- How do you know when it's necessary to unfriend someone?

- How much time should we spend on Facebook talking to friends (define the word *friends*) or catching up on their news every day?

You can compile the answers to these questions into a family media agreement. Visit www.purehope.net for sample media agreements or see the Bishop family agreement in appendix F.

Media Heroes

Technology has an unnerving way of turning complete strangers into household names. These celebrities are presented as models of perfection that our young people try desperately to emulate.

I applaud actress Jamie Lee Curtis for decrying this false reality. Curtis caused a stir when she posed for the magazine *MORE* in plain white underwear—with no air brushing.[22] Not to advocate underwear photos, but Curtis's point was that she refused to make herself out to be something she was not. She was comfortable being her age and felt that touched-up photographs had gone too far for her and many other well-known media "heroes."

Photo retouching isn't the only way we are fooled by media heroes. The publicity surrounding a celebrity only reveals as much of that person's story and values as they like. Tiger Woods has been a hero of professional golf for some time, but he spent years enmeshed in multiple extramarital affairs without public knowledge.

Many celebrity careers have started with high moral standards and devolved into sexual excess. Singers Miley Cyrus, Janet Jackson, and Britney Spears are good examples. (Britney Spears started her career a Mouseketeer.) As they experienced a growing desire to express sexuality, they brought those expressions to the stage. These girls found that acting out their teen sexual fantasies brought fame and wealth, choosing those rewards over honor and reputation.

Teen idols are just that—idols. Very few people are worthy of the title hero.

The recording artist who willingly makes him or herself a poor example of virtuous living has no regard for the audience's well-being. Often producers, performers, and marketing executives create materials exclusively to make money, dismissive of all other considerations.[23] Our children need to be warned about the greed of the entertainment industry and the unhealthy idol worship it encourages.

Teen idols are just that—idols. There's a reason we use the word. And when our children worship teen idols, we have allowed the influence of popular culture to go too far. No human being has ever existed who deserved to be elevated to an object of worship, and very few people are even worthy of a title like *hero*. It's better to award that title to someone we know well who has had a very personal impact on our lives, such as a parent, grandparent, or mentor.

Media heroes are often not even real people. Sometimes they are the characters in videogames. Why should we celebrate game characters if they are criminal, brutal, or dishonorable? Teach your children to cast a critical eye on all of media's "heroes."

Winding Up "Windows"

Congratulations! As we leave this chapter on technology, we're winding up our section on guidelines for purity that protect the heart and body. Now we can move into Part 5, The Roof, where we'll talk about mentoring and accountability as ways of protecting all these concepts we're working hard to implement with our children. We're well on our way to structural integrity in our household of purity!

Technology Opportunities

- Evaluate your family's screen time, and guard against technology addiction. What are some alternative activities that would give you more relational time together, or more physical activity and exploration, or face-to-face time with friends? Rediscover the delight of reading or reading out loud together.

- Take some time to open and operate a Facebook page or other social networking system. Learn how it works. Relate to your kids through the technology they use. It's next to impossible to set standards for a technology you don't understand. After your children leave home, they will use technology on their own. Teach them standards now, while you have the chance.

- Know your children's media influences. What are they viewing and listening to? Where do they surf on the Internet? Can you operate the same technologies they can? If not, learn how. Have them show you.

- Have a family talk about heroes. Who is worthy of being a hero, and why? Are there any heroes in the media? Why does a person want to be your hero?

- _____

  _____

  _____

Building Materials

Books and Web Sites
See Appendix A for more details.
Life Lessons from The Princess and the Kiss, Jennie Bishop (17)
www.focusonthefamily.com (45)
FamilyLife Weekend to Remember (62)

Truths to Memorize
See Appendix B for complete texts.
Technology (15)
Best Thoughts (28)
Pure from Contamination (32)

Scripts
See Appendix D for complete texts.
Social Networking Modesty (10)
Social Networking Chats (11)
Maintaining Cell Phone Boundaries (12)
Responding to Unwanted Phone Calls (13)

Object Lessons
See Appendix E for complete texts.
Because the TV Said So (38)
Hero or Idol? (39)

Contracts
See Appendix F for complete texts.
Contract B: House Rules
Contract C: Technology Agreement

Part 5

The Roof—Accountability

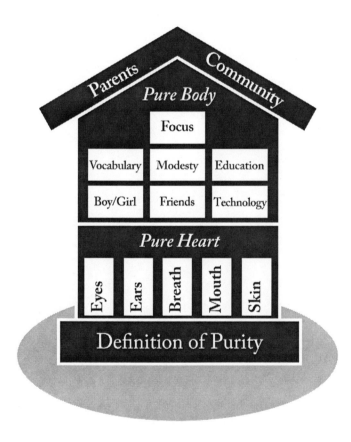

Chapter 8

Wisdom from Mentors

Our pastor often tells stories of when he was young and living in a small town. In that time and setting, every mom and dad in town was allowed to parent him. They could discover him in mischief, take him aside, and say, "Joey, you should know better. Don't let me catch you doing that again!" This may have saved his life. His dad had been an alcoholic, and his mother was a single parent for many of his growing up years. His mentoring community kept a self-acknowledged troublemaker on the straight and narrow by holding him accountable.

Look at the Planned Purity diagram again. The roof is where the words *mentors*, *parents*, and *community* appear. Without the roof of this accountability, the rain will come in and ruin what's been built in our lives.

Let's discuss accountability now because it is often misunderstood. Accountability is not about the more negative idea of catching someone doing something they shouldn't. Accountability is about a positive relationship of prevention, encouragement, and rescue, if needed. If we're doing well, we can celebrate growth. If our roofs are leaky, we can humbly ask for help.

One thing is sure: mentoring ensures greater success. Be willing to be mentored, and give your child the same opportunity.

The next three sections will explain the three key concepts behind the accountability of the roof:

- Mentors—giving personal feedback
- Parents—being authentic
- Community—supporting a good heart

Let's start with mentors.

Mentors are those more mature than ourselves to whom we turn for wisdom and guidance as we grow. A mentoring relationship simply means meeting with a mentor to talk about pertinent issues.

We embark on a new level of interactive adventure when we trust a person to ask difficult questions to help us maintain our integrity or sexual purity. This kind of friend may see us angry or despondent, but we can trust him or her to want what's best for us. How many of us have actually trusted someone with that kind of interaction?

Mentors are those more mature than ourselves to whom we turn for wisdom and guidance as we grow.

Mentoring is a rare pursuit for our individualistic society. We don't like to admit that we could learn from others. But imagine your house without its roof, with all the furnishings ruined by lack of protection. Let your motivation arise from the ensuing wreckage you picture.

Let's look now at how to set up fruitful mentoring relationships in your household.

Mining the Family Wisdom

As parents we have the weighty and somewhat intimidating position of being our children's main mentors, protectors, and accountability relationships. However, we are not meant to be the only mentors in their lives.

The first place you can look for wisdom is from the elders in your family, such as grandparents or other mature relatives. All we need to do is invite them to speak into our children's lives. They may have direct or indirect ways to guide family members toward good decisions, often by telling their own stories.

As a child, I had a nice relationship with my grandparents who lived just down the road, but I wish I had heard more stories of how my grandparents met and married. These "love stories" connect us with our heritage and give us a taste of what our own stories might be like. The simple act of telling the stories communicates the preciousness of the spousal relationship. Encourage your children to ask their mentors to tell these stories.

Some folks will actually sponsor a "grandchild camp" every year. They invite the grandkids to "camp" at their house and give the parents some time off. What wonderful memories! And if Grandma and Grandpa show affection to each other, the children will have a great portrait of what awaits them if they marry and care for each other well.

Elders may be encouraged to journal or just send messages to children from time to time. If they don't write, they could record via video or audio. I know of some grandparents who recorded themselves reading portions of the Bible and gifted the recordings to their grandchildren. What a super legacy!

Mentoring as Children Grow Up

In addition to the wisdom from elders, you may establish mentoring relationships with a variety of other people outside the family who can speak to the different stages of a child's life. Mentors should support the family's standards and give the child new ways to look at things.

A good friend of mine stayed with our family for a number of months. Her presence in our home was an incredible source of encouragement to us and our children when we needed it desperately. She was very wise and gave good counsel to my teenaged daughters, especially during struggles with obedience or relationships. At times the girls plopped on the bed in her room just to talk. We've hand-picked other mentors for our girls who took them out from time to time for discussions, fun and just the presence of a good example.

Mentoring occurs differently at different ages.

When a child is preschool age, mentoring may be accomplished simply by spending time with other families and children who model and strengthen values the child is learning at home.

In elementary school, a child may benefit from having a "big brother or sister" who takes them on an occasional outing or spends time with them at home. (Boys with boys and girls with girls, of course.) Meetings can be focused on a specific topic or simply be an occasion to have fun and walk alongside an older person of integrity. These mentors should be carefully chosen as they may well become heroes in your child's life. They should be mature enough to recognize teachable moments and handle them wisely.

During the teen years, mentors provide a safe way for a youth to vent privately when "Mom and Dad just don't get it." A trusted mentor should know how to keep a child's confidence and when to alert a parent of serious danger. Our daughters have adult mentors outside the family they can talk to when they feel they can't talk to us. This has been one of the most helpful strategies we have practiced to keep communication healthy during the teen years.

When a parent and child just seem to be locking horns, a mentor can provide other options and give both a parent and a young person a safe way to talk things through while supporting family standards.

Are you a single mom who has the tall order of providing mentoring for a son? The Mentoring Project (www.thementoringproject.org) may help when there is no man in the home or in the picture. Our sons especially need this input to become the people they've been created to be.

Sexual Purity Maintenance Questions

When a child is in the teen years, sexual purity should be added to the mindset of purity that was established from a young age. We've found that the best way to keep teens accountable for sexual purity is for them to talk about it openly and directly with a trusted mentor.

The main purpose of mentoring is not just to reveal, but to rescue.

A mentor should keep their conversations with the child private unless the child is in danger.

The following are suggested maintenance questions for sexual purity we used in training with a group of teenagers from tough family backgrounds. The questions were on a laminated card that the teen could give to a mentor. The mentor was to ask the teen the questions at decided-upon intervals.

But remember, purity is about so much more than sex. A more comprehensive approach would include questions that could expose lying, overeating, financial irresponsibility, laziness —the list can be as individual and broad as necessary, depending on the mentoring relationship and purpose. Please don't forget that the main purpose of mentoring is not just to reveal issues but to encourage change—to *rescue*.

But let's just start with sexual purity for now. The mentor can ask:

- Have you interacted with someone of the opposite or same sex this past week in a way that was questionable or that tempted either of you to be irresponsible in your sexuality or intimacy? (This includes flirting and "captivating with the eyes," "hanging" on each other, making out, or any sexual interaction.)

- Have you read, watched, repeatedly looked at, or listened to any sexually explicit material?

- (Girls) Have you dressed in clothes that reveal cleavage, tummy or upper thighs, or are skin tight, or draw attention to your body instead of your face and personality?

- (Guys) Have you misled a girl in any way by teasing her with words or touch, or by using her as a way of getting attention or pleasure?

- Are you monitoring your thought life and replacing inappropriate thoughts with productive thoughts as often as needed?

- Have you spent regular time reading the Bible, having heart-to-hearts with God and listening for his voice? (Your partner needs to know what is "regular" for you.)

- Have you made your family a priority?

- Are you doing your best to be honest, trustworthy, respectful, and honoring to yourself and others?

- Have you just lied to me when you answered any of these questions?

- Can I pray with you for forgiveness, strength, or a new start?

Did you break into a cold sweat reading that list? Breathe!

Yes, it's a challenge, but this authentic kind of knowing, acceptance, and mentoring is the roof that keeps the Planned Purity "house" dry and safely covered.

Mentors for Parents

And remember, parents, the hard questions aren't just for the teens. We also need accountability about sexual purity in our lives. What friend(s) do we have who can ask us the hard questions? With Planned Purity, mentoring is for both parents and children.

As you set up mentors for your children, find the same kind of relationships for yourself. Adults are human and need to admit that they need help themselves.

Throughout my life and our many moves, I've been fortunate to pair up with certain individuals for my accountability and general growth. Sometimes these people have been introduced to me in spite of my independence, and I'm grateful. I actually have two dear friends, both named Jan, who help balance me right now. They're a part of a group of six women who get prayer requests from me regularly. I visit with them and stay in touch online, and they are allowed to ask hard questions of me. One Jan is in my face with her direct comments, and the other is extremely gentle. Both are wise. I need both Jans to get good perspective on my life!

Wisdom says: Don't think you are better than you really are. Be honest in your evaluation of yourselves.[1] When we are honest about where we are, we will find mentors who will help us. As we grow personally, we are then capable of providing accountability for our children and finding mentors for them, too.

Starting a Purity Mentoring Group

Finally, consider being a mentor yourself! You may be more ready than you think to reach out to others and simply share what you have learned, and what you're learning. Your experience and willingness to host a group are invaluable! Purity affects everyone, and most people are very curious about it.

Mentoring outside your family can be a great way to train both your family and others. Anyone can start a purity study at church or with a small group in their home, using *Planned Purity* small group studies,

Princess groups for girls, *Squire* groups for boys, or any number of other resources.

Mentoring Opportunities

- You can help your younger child understand a mentoring relationship simply by having an evening routine of praying together and evaluating the day. Confess faults to each other (yours, too, parent) and receive grace as a habit.

- Consider who might function as a mentor for your child. Give your child the person's phone number with the permission to call anytime. Discuss possible accountability questions the mentor can ask your child.

- Find a mentor who will ask the hard "maintenance" questions about your life. Observe those around you and ask for recommendations. Make a plan to pursue accountability with this person, and consider the questions you would want them to pose.

- _____

  _____

  _____

Chapter 9

Authentic Parenting

Remember, as parents, we are the foremost mentors for our children. This fact actually stresses many of us because we think we need to be perfect to be good mentors. Here's some good news: We don't need to be perfect; we just need to be real. We need to be authentic.

When we own up to our weaknesses and look for help, this is authenticity.

When I think of an authentic person, I think of Pastor Bob, who made a powerful impact on my husband and me when we were newly married. From time to time before the sermon on Sunday, he would ask the whole congregation to pray for him. On one particular Sunday, he said, "I had a disagreement with my wife on the way to church, and I do not have the right attitude to preach. I need to ask your forgiveness and my wife's. And I need you to pray for me." Now that's real. Bob's simple, direct example of confession still affects us today.

When we own up to our weaknesses and look for help, this is authenticity.

Another person I think of is my friend Becki, one of the most authentic people I know. She is the first person I remember giving me permission to struggle with my weaknesses. She did so by saying a few simple words about a difficult matter in her life. She ended by admitting frankly, "I know what I need to do. I know the right thing to do, but I don't want to do it! I don't like it!" (Becki ultimately did what needed to be done.)

Ah, to be as honest and transparent as Bob and Becki.

Snapshots of Authentic Parents

As authentic parents we must refuse to be phonies to our kids. Seeing and hearing about our failures is extremely productive for them. The child cannot relate to a parent who pretends to be perfect when the child knows the parent is imperfect. Just as our pastor asked the congregation for forgiveness, children need to see us ask for forgiveness as often as necessary, especially when it comes to offenses against them. Children's potential for compassion is huge, but how will they implement it if they don't see our pain? How will children know we can relate to their pain if they never see us deal with pain ourselves? How will children learn to ask forgiveness if they don't see humility and grace modeled by their own moms and dads? (For an example, see appendix D, script 19, Parent Asking Forgiveness.)

How will children learn to ask forgiveness if they don't see humility and grace modeled by their own moms and dads?

In my own case, I am a recovering perfectionist. I do things in an orderly way, and for most of my life I have believed that my way is the only right way to do things. I sometimes try too hard to control my family with urgency that is unnecessary.

My husband is much less a perfectionist than I am—in some ways. Randy makes piles, and that's his idea of organization, except when it comes to DVDs, which are in alphabetical order. He works hard and plays hard and does everything with passion.

If you come to see my husband and me at a conference or event, we will look as professional as possible, but we may have just had a disagreement before we came, and we'll probably tell you so if we did! (At the time of this writing, we had just returned from a marriage retreat—and we had a fight on the way there!)

When parents disagree, children often see it or at least feel the repercussions of that disagreement. It's up to the parents to explain that disagreement (when appropriate), assure children that the parents are committed to the relationship, and ask forgiveness for upsetting the children because of a lack of respect or self-control on their parts. When parents are honest about their "holes," children gain the confidence and authenticity to recognize their own shortcomings as well.

Authentic Relationships with Children

I once heard a parenting teacher say, "If your kids aren't angry with you or rolling their eyes at you at some point, you're doing it wrong." You may think, on particular days (or years) that you are the last person your child wants to hear from. But a number of studies show that nothing could be further from the truth.

In statistics relating to children's growth and development, the parent/child relationship is shown to be of paramount importance. Children want a good relationship with their parents, even if the children don't act like it. A report from the National Longitudinal Survey of Youth states: "Adolescents, in general, respect, admire, and like their parents and enjoy spending time with them." The report also noted: "There is evidence from numerous research studies…that positive parent-child relationships and interactions enhance the development of children and adolescents."[1] A positive parental relationship improves academics, behavior, and mental, social, and emotional well being. The benefits extend into adulthood. The bottom line is: Children do better when they have strong relationships with their parents.

Authentic relationship is the only bridge across which truth and instruction can travel.

Authentic relationship is the greatest tool given to us for protecting, pursuing, and practicing honorable living. It is the only bridge across which truth and instruction can travel.

Don't miss this truth: You can learn all the principles in this book, but if you don't have a strong relationship with your child, you will not be able to communicate them. Relationship is the bridge that brings truth into a child's life.

What does it mean to have an authentic relationship with a child? An honest-to-goodness relationship with a child *of any age* means:

- Respecting a child as a person, being willing to enter into the child's world and spend time with the child there

- Playing with the child

- Talking to the child on a conversational level, not just presenting rules

- Taking an interest in the child and listening to his or her opinions

- Approaching thorny questions with a willingness to say, "I don't know," and seeking out answers

- Asking forgiveness when we are harsh or grouchy

- Looking for opportunities for the child to follow a dream

- Nurturing the child in a faith that will carry him or her through the many times in life where nothing else makes sense

- Preparing the child to handle life without us

The responsibility of a relationship with a child is great, but isn't closeness and intimacy what we are all hoping for? The joy that results will bless both our children and us in the future.

We Are the Right Parents

When we are authentic about our parenting challenges, we will have moments when we think: *Help! We aren't cut out to be parents!*

Remember this truth: No matter our foibles, we are the right parents for our children. Our children are ours for a reason. I firmly believe that each parent, upon the birth or adoption of a child, is specifically equipped for raising that particular child.

Many parents wonder if, how, and when to share their past mistakes with their children. Timing and emotional connection are key. Does the situation call for a loving explanation of our past? Will we be willing to *We are the right parents for our children.* cry or share emotionally our regrets? Our honest remorse can be an unforgettable lesson.

When our daughter turned fourteen, my husband seemed to be on edge when he talked with her, especially about relationships with boys.

This obvious change became a wedge between them. Finally, my husband sat down with our daughter to confess that he lost his virginity at fourteen. Because of his own regret, it was hard for him not to be overprotective. This emotional conversation opened my daughter's heart to him and has strengthened her resolve not to fall into the same trap.

Many feel so invincible and grown up already that they find it hard to obey parents. Do you remember that feeling? When our children learn about the pitfalls that we *didn't* avoid, they have the opportunity to do better than we did.

Average people learn from their mistakes; wise people learn from the mistakes of others. We share our experiences in an effort to make our children wise.

Parents Grow Together

It's extremely helpful to meet with other parents so that we don't feel alone in our struggles. We are always fumbling, but still improving if we are willing to be honestly accountable. Parental accountability often looks like a small group of parents who meet together to share war stories and learn new skills. These groups often benefit from books and programs like *Growing Kids God's Way, Shepherding a Child's Heart,* and *Age of Opportunity.* (For more details, see appendix A, "Books and Web Sites," especially the section titled "Resources for Parenting.")

Never Too Late

Maybe you're a parent who is wrestling with feeling as if you've "blown it" irreparably with your child. You've made so many mistakes in relating to your child that you feel as if it's too late to start a meaningful relationship.

This quote from the National Campaign to Prevent Teen Pregnancy is a special encouragement to all of us: "Know that it's never too late to work on a good relationship with your child. Even though your teen may be acting like she doesn't want to have anything to do with you, those are probably not her real feelings. Children of all ages want a close relationship with their parents, and they yearn for their parents' help, approval, and support."[2]

If you feel badly about your present relationship with your child, the first step is to ask forgiveness in a very authentic conversation.

(For an example, see appendix D, script 19, "Parent Asking Forgiveness.") Take your son or daughter somewhere out of the ordinary. Make a commitment to be different, and then *be* different. Live and interact authentically, keep giving and receiving forgiveness. Be gracious, patient, and firm in your beliefs.

So much can change by this simple step. Start setting an example your child can trust and choose to follow through. Do what you can, and watch what happens with the rest.

A need to ask forgiveness is especially appropriate and amazingly effective if there is a wall between you and an adult child. Go to them now, and do what you can to let healing begin. Then let them see the transformation of honorable living in your life.

Authentic Relationships with Spouses

We've looked at authentic parenting and authentic relationship with our children. Now let's look at being authentic with our spouses.

Our lives are a training video that our children see over and over.

Think about the answer to this question: Where will your child learn how to treat his or her spouse? The answer is inescapable: From the parent. Whether you are married or single, your example is going to have more impact than any other source.

Our lives are a training video that our children see over and over. When our children mature and go to out to live on their own, the memory of our choices will be with them. They will consider that catalog of information when they do the choosing.

If you are a single parent, don't skip this section about marriage principles. These ideas apply to all relationships; plus, God may have marriage in your future, too.

My husband and I don't consider ourselves marriage experts by any means, but here's what has been most helpful to us as we have grown together in an authentic relationship.

1. Be spouses first; parents second.

First and foremost, do not focus so much on parenting that you neglect your relationship with your spouse! It's so easy to get so busy with all the details of parenting that we forget to take care of the parents' relationship with each other. When the marriage is strong, the parenting will be stronger, too.

If you are a single parent, it's tempting to pour everything into parenting, but remember to give yourself permission to take care of your needs, too. Your children will learn about relationships through the friends that you have and the choices you make about dating. Time spent with supportive friends benefits your children because it models healthy relationships for them.

2. Play together.

My husband Randy loves music and instrument stores. He's a musician—it makes sense. But I used to balk at accompanying him on these trips because in a music store I wander around as aimlessly as a man in a dress shop.

Later on I recognized the importance of entering into Randy's world. Instead of telling myself I was bored, I made an effort to engage. I still don't know a lot about music stores, but I can ask Randy what he likes about a certain guitar, even though I don't understand the difference between a humbucker and a single coil pickup (not a truck).

Our connections on a daily basis help guard the marriage against selfishness and indiscretion.

3. Learn together.

Regular devotions, studies, or readings also help draw you and your spouse together, protecting you from unfaithfulness physically or emotionally.

Do you like to read together? Couple devotionals or studies may help. Does one or both of you prefer learning by listening? Conferences or videos may work better. (We recommend Gary Smalley's *Keys to Loving Relationships* series.) See a complete list of suggested books and resources for adults in appendix A.

Do you enjoy other couples? Seek out a small-group study.

How long has it been since you and your spouse have enjoyed a marriage retreat? The Kathy family, founders of Chik-Fil-A, believe so strongly in strengthening marriages they sponsor the wonderful Win-Shape program in northern Georgia (www.winshape.org/marriage/). They recommend a marriage retreat once a year as a gift to your spouse and yourself. Another good option is a *Weekend to Remember* through FamilyLife (www.familylife.com). Invest in a healthy marriage because it will have a tremendous impact on your children's pursuit of purity, as well as your own.

4. Serve together.

Does one of you have a heart for the homeless, or enjoy the elderly? Do you want to volunteer as a sports coach or work in the background at a thrift store, sorting? Find what works for one or both of you and go together.

5. Go out together.

Dating your spouse is an important aspect of nurturing closeness. Our teenage children are old enough to know that a grumpy mom and dad mean the parents aren't getting enough alone time together. During these times, one of them may say, "Mom and Dad, you need to go on a date!" When my husband and I go out, we're practically shoved out the door, hearing our daughters behind us saying, "Don't worry about us. We'll be fine. Go and have fun!"

You can date, no matter your age or the number of years you have been married. Go for walks together, out to eat, to a concert, or favorite event. Be at your best for your spouse that night and "court" each other. Childcare may be an issue, but make the sacrifice to find trustworthy sitters.

6. If married, enjoy sexuality with your spouse.

Do your best to show a vibrant, living example to your children of how to show love to a spouse, so when they mentally rewind the "training video" you've made, they see how to show love to their spouses, too.

A joyful sex life is necessary for you to portray true affection for each other in day-to-day interactions that your children see. Although your children don't need to know what goes on in the bedroom, they will not experience the same warmth in your household if you and your spouse are not sexually active, healthy, and happy. A lack of sexual bonding between parents cheats the whole family.

That being said, healthy sexuality in a marriage does not always come easily or naturally. If you struggle with porn, marital infidelity, issues of intimacy or even if you just don't feel close to your spouse, *do not hesitate to get help*, either as a couple or as an individual if your spouse is not ready. It is a shame if you live your life crippled because of being too proud to ask for help.

I want to speak directly for a moment to those who have an addiction to pornography. You may think that looking at porn in secret isn't hurting anyone, but it hurts you and your whole family. If you are a consumer, stop now, before you become an addict. If you can't stop, get help before it gets worse. (Visit purehope.net to learn how to protect children from pornography and to deal with family issues caused by porn.) Lock down your computer or get rid of it. Talk to a counselor. You aren't the only one struggling, and you can't do this on your own.

A lack of sexual bonding between parents cheats the whole family.

An authentic parent who wants to pursue and teach sexual purity absolutely must be personally honest about their own sexual condition.

7. If you're a single parent, model a pure life as a single person.

If you're an unmarried parent, model purity in your singleness. Desperate dating at any age is not an effective model. Protect your heart and body in relationships with the opposite sex.

Yes, you are an adult, but the same boundaries of sexuality apply to you as to younger people. To put it succinctly: Single parents need to be celibate. Whenever I say this in an adult sexuality seminar, the room gets very quiet. It will be a struggle, but this is the only option for singles.

Modeling contentedness and acting with sexual integrity are necessities of setting an example as a single parent, just as they are in a two-parent household. The special challenges of facing these standards alone call for strong accountability and specific help from outside the household. Focus on the Family offers a number of online and book resources for single parenting. (Go to focusonthefamily.com and search for "Single Parenting.")

Network with those who will keep you accountable in your own life as you pray for guidance. Studies like *Every Man's/Woman's Battle* will be helpful in setting standards for yourself personally.

Summary

Remember that we're in the midst of constructing a roof in our Planned Purity diagram. This roof is created through accountability with three groups: mentors, parents, and community. We've looked at mentors and parents, so we'll finish with community in the next section.

Parenting Opportunities

- How have you been an "authentic" parent? How have you pressured yourself unnecessarily to be "perfect"?

- Think about the "training video" your parents presented to you. How does yours compare? How can you improve it to benefit your children?

- Are you a parent who is thinking it may be too late to establish an authentic relationship with your child? It's not. Ask forgiveness in transparent conversation and then show by your actions that you are committed to building a relationship with your child.

- Choose one of these activities to pursue right away to build relationship with one or all of your children:

  * Write a love note or letter of encouragement. (Facebook or email is a second choice—handwritten is better.)

  * Take a child on a fun day (or part of a day) for quality time with you.

* Learn what your child's love language is, and express love to them that way. (See http://www.5lovelanguages.com/learn-the-languages/the-five-love-languages/)

* Think of a creative, unexpected way simply to surprise or delight your child.

* _____

_____

_____

Building Materials

Books and Web Sites
See Appendix A for more details.
Raising Maidens of Virtue, Stacy McDonald (39)
★*Raising a Modern Day Knight*, Robert Lewis (40)
★*Age of Opportunity*, Paul David Tripp (41)
★*Every Parent Needs to Know About...*, iCare (42)
★*Battlefield of the Mind*, Joyce Meyer (43)
★www.cpyu.org, Center for Parent/Youth Understanding (44)

Chapter 10

Community Support

Take a look at your family's weekly schedule. Pretty full? That means your family interacts with a number of communities on a weekly basis. Stretch to the monthly schedule and take another look. Your communities might include friends, neighbors, coworkers, churches, schools, clubs, sports teams, and others. I like to use the term *distributed community* to describe this network and its influences. I see a distributed community as:

the groups with which we interact regularly

and which affect us and our children

in their character formation, attitudes, understanding,

and pursuit of a good heart and life.

Our family has an unusually diverse distributed community because we've traveled so much and presented Planned Purity in so many communities. Here's a snapshot of our distributed community at this writing:

- A home megachurch with a small group hosted in our home
- Youth group through that church
- A class I provide in youth group or to adults, from our church and others

- A second church family in which my husband serves as worship leader
- A Bible study where my daughter helps mentor Ukrainian girls
- Our daughters' Christian school, where I contribute Planned Purity training
- A community of Planned Purity friends who have attended a seminar or become friends
- Neighborhood and town friends from all ethnic backgrounds
- Overseas friends from mission trips that we contact online
- Our closest relatives back home in Ohio

This is just a part of our community. See how much we can learn from each other, share values, and model virtues?

I admit that our life is probably a little out-of-the-ordinary, but all of us have more opportunities to interact with different individuals and groups than we may think, and the more we reach out, the more people we get to know. As we actively evaluate our involvement with individuals and groups, we can build a community locally and even abroad that supports us and our children in pursuit of pure lives. This community will also provide opportunities for sharing what we learn with others.

Who do you and your family interact with regularly? Friends from Scouts, soccer, or ballet? Friends from church? Next-door neighbors? Relatives? People you interact with regularly online count, too.

Take some time to make a list below of the groups in your family's distributed community. You may be surprised at how many circles of influence you have!

_____

_____

_____

_____

Evaluating Community

Now that you've listed your family's distributed community, think about how these groups support or undermine a pursuit of good hearts and life choices. Is your involvement in each group a helpful experience overall, or are examples of respect, honor, and sexual purity hard to find?

We want to guide our children into healthy community relationships, helping them evaluate what is in agreement with the philosophies at home and what isn't, and showing them how to deal with situations where home values conflict with community values. *You may be surprised at how many circles of influence you have!* We will always encounter people with different values than we have. But as we model integrity and sexual purity, we may well be able to influence others to embrace healthy values, too.

In this chapter we'll look at two important communities that affect our children greatly—the church and the school—and apply what we learn there to other groups like sports teams, scouting groups, leadership programs, school clubs, dance or instrument lessons. Before we talk about specific groups, however, let's look at how the idea of authenticity is very important for community.

Groups Valuing Authenticity

Any community group—whether a church, school, or club—will be better for your family if it is authentic. Authentic groups are simply *real.* Any group that values authenticity will be diverse, or open to diversity in backgrounds, ethnicities, and tax brackets. They will see mistakes as valuable chances to learn, and not expect perfection over enthusiastic participation and commitment to ongoing change. A group that is known for presenting itself as perfect cannot be authentic.

Authentic groups understand that both individual identity and community identities are important. They welcome newcomers and don't try to force them into molds. They build relationships to strengthen the individuals involved. They value honesty and transparency while maintaining an environment committed to truth, goodness, and beauty.

The Authentic Christian Church

A church that is following the biblical model must be truly authentic. Be patient as you search for an authentic church. Just as many parents try to appear perfect, rather than authentic, so do many churches. Outer appearances and legalistic rules lead the congregation to hide struggles instead of working through them together. Without authenticity, people can't trust one another. They may try to appear as though they have it all together spiritually, only to be exposed again and again as simply human.

Authentic groups are simply real.

An authentic church is not perfect, but honest, presenting the truth, and full of grace. Imperfections are viewed as opportunities for growth, not as measurements of spirituality.

During our early married years, my husband and I visited JPUSA (Jesus People USA) in Chicago. This church and community were very different from the traditional congregations in which we spent our early years. Made up mostly of the homeless and the poor, the group lived in the same area, shared all things in common (including a clothes closet from which anyone could choose), and no one dressed up for church. If a member were an alcoholic, he might show up after a drinking binge. If a prostitute came in, no one pointed her out as such. The facilitator of the service dressed simply in jeans and a T-shirt, and gave a practical, biblical message. Outside church services, the community ate together, worked together, planned events together, and held one another accountable for their choices as they matured in faith.

This example helped us reevaluate the American middle-class church. The church must be willing to walk alongside people in the struggle to live in purity. Many of us fight an addiction to pornography. Our children are dealing with a constant onslaught of media lies. A church must be authentic enough to be relevant to today's world and encourage members to admit that they are struggling just as those outside the church do, but with hope and help. Then we must reach out to each other in love and accountability, drawing each other to greater grace and integrity.

American churches (and churches in other countries as well) with that kind of family relationship are precious. Be wary of churches where tradition alone rules, or where the pastor seems to be building his own empire. This can happen both in small churches as well as large.

That said, the shortcomings of believers themselves should not cause us to write church involvement off as a negative and unnecessary influence. Individual churches are made up of imperfect people who know or are realizing they need a greater Power than themselves to live a life of goodness, purity, and meaning. Thus, we must choose a church not only because we want to be asked questions of accountability, but also because we know the people there will discuss our hard questions as well. This sharpening process makes the whole church what it should be.

An authentic church is not perfect, but honest, presenting the truth, and full of grace.

If you are evaluating or looking for a local church, here are some characteristics I believe will be demonstrated (imperfectly) in an authentic church:

- An authentic church loves the Bible and is not afraid to discuss its contents with anyone of any opinion. They are not afraid of those who disagree with them but willingly give a reason for their hope—not always perfectly, but humbly. Thus they welcome those who are not Christians into their lives.

- An authentic church recognizes they are part of a greater whole. They welcome partnerships with other churches and organizations, and work hard individually and as a whole to maintain relationships outside their particular place of worship.

- An authentic church has a pastor who is unwilling to be the star of the show but is a humble servant who submits himself to others and confesses his faults. When a pastor sets this example, the church will often follow suit.

- An authentic church has sound doctrine but does not focus on loving the doctrine. The church focuses on loving people and seeing them become all they're meant to be.

- An authentic church will not make you stay if you don't want to. They are more concerned with sending people out to help others than building a congregation.

- An authentic church is not in a hurry to "get you involved." They respect your right to make choices, and the church wants to contribute to your growth. If you feel passionately led to complete a specific task, they eagerly encourage you to prepare and do it.

- An authentic church sees beyond innocent mistakes. The pastor may preach too long sometimes or forget your name. The office may need some help getting organized, and the worship pastor may occasionally forget his words or play a wrong chord and laugh right onstage. That's OK in an authentic church.

- There are always tears in an authentic church, and there is always someone with a free shoulder to cry on.

If you can't find a church that's just right, don't give up. Jump in and become one of the agents of change to create a truly authentic church. In time, you will find ways to exchange accountability.

Evidence of Purity Accountability in a Local Church

A local church can provide a powerful level of accountability for sexual purity. Here are some points to questions to ask about this type of accountability:

- Does your church speak openly about the importance of biblical purity of both heart and body?

- Are there efforts to understand the effects of modern culture, both in guarding the heart and relating to those outside church involvement in a relevant and loving way?

- Do members seem to be guarding themselves against what is destructive?

- Does the staff set an example of modesty and uphold standards for modest dress and behavior in youth and adults alike?

- Do the members seem to take into consideration that some people are learning new habits, showing grace to those who are still discovering the importance of purity?

Christian life is messy. We are all trying to get cleaned up. So grace and acceptance should be present, as well as clear standards and openness in speaking about issues of heart and sexual purity, both from the platform and in the congregation.

Discretion and Good Judgment

Compromising situations can crop up in a church community when you least expect it.

The shortcomings of believers themselves should not cause us to write church involvement off.

The key is to deal with what happened openly and directly. Here's a great example of a dangerous situation that thankfully ended with a positive outcome because a person in leadership behaved authentically.

During a mission trip overseas, one of our leaders took a walk with a leader of the opposite sex. The two ended up lost in the remote fields of a foreign country. They eventually found their way back to the church, after being soaked in a rain and wandering for miles.

That night our exhausted leader repented with tears. This person took responsibility for the situation and the example that was set for our team. Nothing out of line had really happened, but the appearance of indiscretion was briefly voiced by team members.

As our leader asked forgiveness, trust—and even admiration— was restored. The leader confessed openly, was shown grace, and the mission trip continued. Complete restoration took place because the leader confessed a lack of judgment—and because the team was ready to forgive and move on.

This story also underscores the necessity of setting specific boundaries between men and women during church activities. Whether on the platform, in the office, or during events, discretion should always be modeled between men and women. For example, in prayer, counseling and mentoring, men should be paired with men, and women with women. (This guideline especially applies to the pastor himself, even though the pastor may feel pressure to pray for everyone.)

The youth group is a place where discretion must be taught in an ongoing, practical way. Youth events should not turn into pairing functions. Limits on dress (not too tight, too revealing, or too short) should be discussed. Young men can be reminded to cover boxers or remove hats as a show of respect to God and the group. Boundaries may then be gently enforced, one-on-one, by people full of grace. In this way we guard the eyes, hold each other accountable, show respect for others, and reduce temptation.

Discretion, modesty and purity must be taught in a youth group in an ongoing, practical way.

If your church does not make a strong stand on sexual purity, perhaps you can initiate studies on the subject, using this book or another. You may want to recommend *The Princess and the Kiss* or *The Squire and the Scroll Life Lessons* for younger children, preparing them to be examples as they grow. Perhaps your purpose in being at the church is to spearhead something that can benefit the entire congregation's understanding. But do be polite, speak in love, and be patient.

School as an Opportunity

Your child will spend thirty to forty hours per week at school—similar to the time spent at a full-time job. No matter what kind of school your child attends, it is a community of influence. Here's how to use any school situation as an opportunity for accountability, based on my experience.

When we moved to a metropolitan area, both of our daughters attended large public junior and high schools for a time. This was quite a change from the little school in a literal cornfield we left in the Midwest.

Academically, the schools had a reputation for high standards; socially they were minefields of loose standards. Our sixth-grader was appalled to see students kissing and groping each other in the hallways when adults weren't present. Our older daughter in high school said students used the restrooms for trysts so often that she wouldn't use the bathroom at school, stating emphatically, "The restrooms at school aren't safe!"

These comments from our daughters led to many productive discussions about interaction between men and women. Our children learned that our standards are not the norm, and that their desire to live by a higher bar set them apart. They also grew in compassion for those who used sex as a substitute for love because they were not experiencing love at home.

I don't use these examples because public schools are all bad. I would say public schools have worsened because of a lack of discipline for students at school and at home. The sexualization of culture has amplified the effect. However, if parents use public school experiences as teaching tools, then public school can be a useful introduction to the "real" world. In fact, students who are mentored with an understanding of justice and service can make wonderful leaders in a public school.

As a matter of fact, children who attend a private or Christian school will need the same discussion about appropriate behavior between boys and girls as public school students. Even if you home-school your child, at some point he or she will also be exposed to intimate matters. *No matter how your child is educated, he or she will be exposed to negative influences and choices.* I would like to have as many of these important conversations as possible at home before my children jump into the social soup of college or career.

In the best case scenario, a school can be an accountability partner as your child practices sexual purity. If you have a choice as to what school your child attends, *The responsibility for* remember to look beyond academics. Consider *education is the* whether the faculty work on the development of *parents' in the end.* character and truth, goodness and beauty. Observe the children and families, and attend a day of classes. Is each child simply ingesting and regurgitating information, or is character being formed?

If public school is the best option for your child, educate yourself about the school system. What hostilities toward good character and sexual purity will they face? Consider how you may strengthen your child to handle possible situations. Be as involved as you possibly can, and make time to train your child on your own. (This should happen no matter where your child is schooled.) Even if a school does a good job, the responsibility for education is the parents' in the end. At all times, the school's training, influence, and accountability is secondary to yours.

Purity and Character Training in Schools

A school environment can be an excellent accountability partner when it rewards character formation and gives sexual purity training. On the positive side, some public schools include character training, and at our children's Christian schools, character formation was stressed at every turn. Unfortunately, however, most schools, including Christian schools, have no training for sexual purity.

If your child attends a Christian school, try talking to the administration about including sexual purity training. You will probably get a positive response. For example, when I approached the administration at my children's Christian school, they were very open to this kind of help and immediately scheduled a Planned Purity seminar. They had been looking for something appropriate and simply needed a parent to spearhead an event. At the seminar, we saw that many parents longed for the school to provide training for sexual purity to reinforce the parents' training at home. Now a group of other parents is planning for continuing education in sexual purity.

If your child's school overlooks character formation and sexual purity training completely, be willing to talk with an administrator about the value of this type of material. You may also work with the PTA to bring in a speaker or event. Administrators are often over-loaded and may be delighted with a parent's clearly focused, graciously presented ideas.

Sex-Ed: You Can Handle This!

When it comes to our children's sexual education, again, parents should be the main source of their children's information. If your school provides sexual education, review it thoroughly and explain to your child what agrees with your family's standards or doesn't. If the school isn't particularly teaching virtuous living, find ways for your child to build community with other like-minded children in youth groups or family small groups.

In some religious schools, discussion of sexual issues is considered taboo. If the school is unwilling to present new information, have discussions one-on-one with your child and in other settings as well. Perhaps you can begin a parents' group for discussion in your home, using Planned Purity materials or other books in the resource section of this book.

Rather than discussing sexuality on a regular school day, school leaders may be willing to host a sexual purity training seminar outside of school. You can be the one to start a tradition that benefits many children.

Accountability and Growth in Other Communities

Besides the church and school, your child may be involved in community groups in the form of sports teams, scouting groups, leadership programs, school clubs, music lessons, or dance classes. In each case, evaluate the integrity/purity temperature of the environment and how it affects your child. Assist your children in guarding their hearts and in finding ways to affect others in the groups for good. Discuss dress and song choices in dance classes. Look for integrity in leadership. Volunteer if you can.

Our daughter took ballet classes for almost ten years. In the course of her study, she constantly built relationships with girls whom she invited to church. She took a lot of teasing for not being interested in boys when other girls were sexually active, but she bravely explained the advantages of her decision to wait. Although she no longer studies ballet, her ballet friends still stay in touch and often ask her for advice.

We were proud of her example and stepped in many times to ensure balance between the work ethic of her Ukrainian instructor and our daughter's desire to study ballet seriously without becoming a star soloist. I served on the board of the company for a while to build relationships with the artistic director and the head instructor, and we still consider them family friends. The board was able to begin a relationship with the family that led to performances at our large Orlando church, which improved business for the company and gave the church the opportunity to build relationships with this family. The artistic director said at the end of a performance that we had "changed all his ideas about religion." Community-building can lead to many wonderful opportunities to make friends, learn, and grow.

If you enjoy special relationships with other families, consider how you may partner with them to start a small study/discussion group relating to issues of honorable living. My Hindu neighbor and I don't share religious beliefs, but we do share the values of honorable living and respect for life. We also both like Indian food and Bollywood movies. We have attended each others' religious services. Being her friend is a joy and adventure, and when I explain what I do for a living, she is always interested and thoughtful.

My daughter babysits and cleans for another neighbor with two young boys. We don't know everything about the family's specific values, but when my daughter is there she is modeling the lifestyle of a pure-hearted young woman to the boys and their parents. Through modesty, patience, working hard, and requiring obedience from the children in her care, she strengthens that family with her participation in the household.

A Living, Expanding Network

No matter where you and your child are involved, a general awareness of community influences will open your eyes to new opportunities to guard, grow, and share. These new opportunities are often more fun than we expect. Sometimes they're as simple as discovering a new perspective. At other times, we may discover that other like-minded parents want to work together and form a new effort.

We can all use as many Planned Purity communities as possible, and many more parents are looking for them than we think. As more groups grow and connect, we will change not only our own lives but the world around us as well!

Church, School, and Community Opportunities

- If you attend church, evaluate your congregation and how they function when it comes to purity and accountability. Are there ways you can speak into your church's present system with grace to make it stronger?

- If your children are in a school system, find out what opportunities are presented for character training and sexual purity training. How may you help strengthen your school's ability to be a purity accountability partner?

- Talk to other parents about the possibility of a training seminar for parents. Could you present the idea to your school administration or organize an independent event?

- Make sure your volunteering efforts stay in balance. If you are volunteering yourself to death, pull back and evaluate. Where can you make the most direct impact and still have some time for yourself and your children?

- _____

_____

_____

Building Materials

Books and Web Sites
See Appendix A for more details.
Raising Maidens of Virtue, Stacy McDonald (39)
★*Raising a Modern Day Knight*, Robert Lewis (40)
★*Age of Opportunity*, Paul David Tripp (41)
★*Every Parent Needs to Know About...*, iCare (42)
★*Battlefield of the Mind*, Joyce Meyer (43)
★www.cpyu.org, Center for Parent/Youth Understanding (44)

Part 6

The Fence—Security in Grace

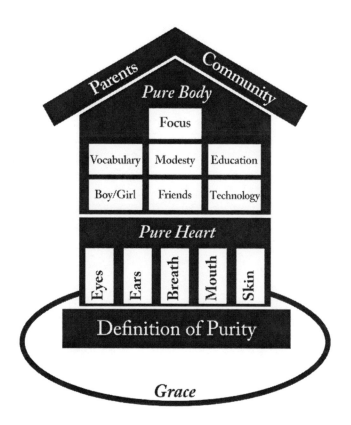

Chapter 11

Surrounding Grace

Τhe classic symbol of a happy home has come to be the white picket fence. In the Planned Purity diagram, you can see that the circle surrounding the house represents grace, as secure as the "white picket fence." What imperfect human can survive a journey toward purity—or life in general—without the freedom to fail and be restored?

Whether you are building purity in your home from the ground up, or doing some remodeling to what is already in place, you will need grace to keep the process joyful. Just like a physical construction project, you may experience setbacks that surprise and frustrate.

For example, a small church where my husband served decided to restore an older house on their property. First they just wanted to make the master closet bigger. Then they discovered that the floor wasn't solid, and the sub floor was rotted out. Once they got underneath the house, they found that the plumbing pipes had been connected poorly; they had burst apart and soaked the crawl space with raw sewage. The construction team truly needed a sense of humor to keep going!

Grace is the divine generosity that no family can survive without.

At times, you may feel your pursuit of purity in your home is stalled, or even moving backwards. Does that mean you shouldn't try, or that your house won't be beautiful in the end? Absolutely not. As we freely give and receive grace, we become part of a plan that only God may see clearly right now.

A lot of people think they understand grace—until they are the ones who need it. Don't skip this chapter because you think you already understand grace or you think that grace doesn't apply to your situation. Grace is the divine generosity that no family can survive without.

Free Will

The most heartrending stories I hear are from parents who "did it all"—they were available, engaged, guarded the hearts of their children, and set up boundaries. The children seemed committed to everything they were taught. They had supportive communities around them. Yet the kids *still* made choices that astounded the parents. They lied intentionally. They had secret pornography addictions. They got pregnant.

Free will.

One of these stories is about a teenage girl from a Christian school. She was a leader in the youth group and knew all the answers. Purity was a common topic in the household, and she encouraged her friends to stay pure, but she was also hearing a lot about sexual experimentation from her friends—both at church and elsewhere.

The same girl planned a secret meeting with a young man. She told her parents she was going for a walk alone, but in reality, she had arranged for a young man to drive to another part of the neighborhood and meet her there. Then she allowed the young man to perform oral sex on her.

The parents were devastated. What happened?

A curious girl.

A willing young man without boundaries.

Free will.

Thankfully, the parents were able to confront their daughter and speak frankly with the young man's parents. They sought counseling. They walked with their daughter through the implications—heart and body—of her actions. The daughter is on a much better path today. Heart issues were exposed that needed attention and healing, in both the girl and her parents.

Your child may make a decision just as dramatic and surprising as this daughter's was to her parents. An unexpected pregnancy or a disease may be involved. Partners in the activity may need to be confronted in an uncomfortable way. Heart-wrenching secrets may be exposed.

The fact is, no matter what comes, we have an opportunity to practice grace, which our children will desperately need. On the negative side, during a crisis, an unguarded response can scar our children permanently. While we should not free children from responsibility for their actions or try to protect them from painful consequences, we should also walk with them through the dilemmas while reminding them that there is a bigger plan for it all. In fact, a nosedive may provide a perfect opportunity for growth that they've never experienced before. They may be forced into a new work ethic, lifestyle, or debt repayment that they need to learn, leading them to realize that they are not the center of the universe and that life is not like a video game or movie.

Please, for your children's sakes, remember that setbacks of any kind are a normal part of life, different for everyone. And life will continue afterward. *Part of real life is real trouble. Overcoming conflicts and unexpected circumstances makes us stronger and wiser.*

Parents Fail, Too

What if we do react unlovingly when a crisis comes? I know I have already! Is it the end of your credibility as a parent?

I'm so glad to say, "No, it's not." In fact, besides giving me the opportunity to model humility and ask forgiveness of my children, my outbursts also functioned, at times, as a way of showing my family how deeply their actions hurt me. Not that I still didn't ask forgiveness. Not that I should ever allow myself to overreact just because "they need to see how I feel." But even our most desperate failures can be redeemed. Let me share a very personal example about my own struggles.

A nosedive may provide a perfect opportunity for growth.

As an adult, I finally was able to recognize that I have a significant struggle with anxiety and depression. A simple situation, such as a drive in the rain, or being alone in a swimming pool, could cause a panic attack. At these times I became so afraid that my family didn't know how to help. As my anxiety spiraled out of control, sometimes I wound up in bed or in a closet, wound up in a ball and not wanting to talk with anyone.

At the peak of my struggle, I packed a bag and walked out of our home. I went to stay with a lady pastor friend who did not judge me and provided a safe place for me to work through some tough decisions and emotions. This happened after more than twenty years of marriage, during which I promised our children many times that their father and I would never separate.

My family suffered. I suffered. One of my daughters wanted to come stay with me, and the other was furious, saying, "If you loved us, you wouldn't be gone!" My husband took down a meaningful piece of art from over our bed and put it in the closet as he worked though his own anger. Our whole family was thrown into chaos.

I was emotionally not well. I needed to ask forgiveness for specific incidents and attitudes. I cried until I became physically ill. I called other relatives to ask their forgiveness for past wrongs that came to mind. I cried out for help. I also needed some professional assistance. I saw the appropriate doctors and started medication to help control and heal my anxiety and depression. (Medication may not be the answer for everyone who has anxiety or depression, but it helped me.)

After a few weeks, when we had talked through the issues and I came home, what a mess awaited me. My family was a shambles. They didn't think they could trust me. I asked their forgiveness many times. My angry daughter kept her distance. It took months for our family to move toward healing.

I would never want that situation to repeat itself. But I will say that we all learned from it. I felt great remorse for how I had handled things, and I became more honest about my condition and needs. I'm more content now with being human rather than pretending to be superwoman. After my daughter got over her anger, she realized she wasn't superwoman, either, and could accept her own shortcomings more easily. My husband and I came back together and recognized we had no desire to live without each other. We struggled through my healing season, which required a good deal more sleep and quiet time for me in a family environment that was constantly active.

Miraculously, today the thing I most often hear from my family members is, "We have the best family in the world!"

Our hearts broke for many days as we slogged through the mud of our messes, but grace pulled us through. My family and other friends rescued me with their grace. As a result, I did my best to show grace and patience toward the daughter who held on to anger for such a long time. (When I looked at her situation, she certainly deserved grace as much as me.)

Maybe as a parent you think you have gone too far to be forgiven, or you have been unwilling to admit that you are making choices that hurt your children. Don't be stuck in that place. Choose differently. Humble yourself. Get help from those you can trust. Start over again right now. *No matter what* happens, there is grace available. We can show it. We can receive it. And life can move forward to a better place—sometimes unexpectedly, even supernaturally.

Second Chances

Maybe the concept of grace is hard for you to grasp. *Grace simply means that we are given another chance.* It means that we accept our human nature as well as others', that we are ready to forgive, that we can learn from both our failures and successes. Grace is *not* a doormat where we thoughtlessly wipe our feet and go out to trudge through the mud again, but a gift that must be offered freely and accepted with humility.

> *Grace simply means that we are given another chance.*

Say your child makes a bad decision (or a series of them) and ends up with a huge text messaging bill, as happened during one season of cell phone use at our house. Yes, the bill was painfully paid by the offender, who had just received a good amount of money for another task and had to give it up. But forgiveness also took place. A chance to start over (grace) was given with the understanding that, as trust is built, more freedom would be offered. So far, so good.

Now, say that you make a blunder. Recently I watched a portion of a movie with my daughter. After viewing what I thought was a funny scene, my fourteen-year-old stood up and said, "Why am I watching this?" and left the room. To her, I had not edited the material strictly enough to guard her eyes. Big oops. I immediately asked forgiveness for offending her, which was easily granted—she was painfully gracious. Whew. I received the message, loud and clear, that I needed to do a better job of editing such images in the future.

What about raising our voices when we are communicating to family members in times of stress? Are we willing to humble ourselves, admit our own poor choices, and ask forgiveness? How many times? Seventy times seven?[1] Grace has to be given and received by both parent and child often and regularly for healthy communication to grow.

Dealing with Mistakes

When our daughters were younger, one of the hardest concepts for them to understand was that mistakes or wrong answers are as valuable as right answers. They would agonize over test scores or missing three math problems out of twenty. But right answers only show what we know. Mistakes are helpful because they reveal what we don't know and give us the opportunity to learn. Celebrate the seventeen right answers, yes, but also ask, "What can I learn from the three I missed?"

It's the same way with purity training. Mistakes are not the end of the world, although there can be definite consequences. Working through those consequences can happen in a productive way, depending on our choices as parents.

Recently a mom came to me, heartbroken because her older daughter had become pregnant. She was raising two younger daughters and was trying hard to train them to save sex for marriage.

"What will I do now?" she asked. "What will I say to my younger girls about their older sister?"

This is a situation that would be painful for anyone. But this mom took the high road. First of all, she decided that the baby would be a blessing no matter how the little one had come into the world. She decided to walk with her daughter through the difficulty of single parenting rather than demand her right to have an empty nest after raising her own children.

Her younger daughters are seeing firsthand the difficult results of becoming a mother without a father involved, which is an encouragement to them to make different choices. Yet the family is forgiving and loving in spite of these unexpected developments, and the child is a delight. Grace has come to their household, and life is going on in sometimes complicated, but beautiful ways.

Life won't be perfect. Life is messy and sometimes chaotic. We will never be able to avoid that. But crisis situations show us how to walk with peaceful hearts through the storms of life, if we're willing. And crises can develop into unexpected blessings, which also build character in us. Without learning to handle crisis and conflict, we are weak, anxious, and ill-equipped. Difficulties make us stronger. We certainly don't want to intentionally cause problems for ourselves or our families, but we must remember that when adversity mixes with strong relationships, the result is strong families and strong children. This applies in issues of purity and any other issues of life as well.

A Trade Secret

One of the most powerful "secrets" I know for opening a child's heart is asking *their* forgiveness. Even in the case of a walled-up teenager, sincere remorse can construct a ladder taller than the obstacle. Like a tightly closed bud, an angry child's heart can open and blossom in the light of such humility.

As parents, we can practice grace as we seek to understand our child's heart and needs. We can't assume that our young man or woman is being deliberately disobedient to irritate us. We can't simply chalk their behavior up to our mistakes as a parent. If we take the time to listen, we will find out what's really going on.

Ask your children's forgiveness when you fail them. The parent who humbly seeks forgiveness not only opens a child's heart but also provides an example of remorse for wrongdoing that a child can follow. Learning to ask forgiveness with humility is an invaluable lesson.

The Greatest Example

The best way to finish this chapter about grace is to look at grace's most perfect picture—Jesus on the cross. Remember when Jesus prayed, "Father, forgive them for they do not know what they are doing"?[2] When Jesus looked down from the cross at the jeering mass of humanity below him, he saw them as children. They didn't know what they were doing. They were still learning. They hadn't figured out what was going on yet. They didn't realize he was willingly dying on their behalf.

That's the ultimate example. And we, as parents, have the same responsibility to "lay down our lives" for our children, recognizing that they haven't quite gotten it yet. In fact, many people haven't quite gotten it yet—we haven't either. So that puts us all in the same boat, doesn't it?

Opportunities for Grace and Forgiveness

- Do you admit your mistakes? When was the last time you failed your child and asked forgiveness? How about other family members or friends? Ask forgiveness now for wrongs you've committed or grudges you've carried. You deserve to heal, and you will have trouble helping your children until you do. (See #40, Appendix E, for a practical object lesson, and the sample script for asking forgiveness below.)

Sample Script: Asking Forgiveness (Parent)

Single incident: I need to ask your forgiveness. I'm sorry I yelled at you—especially in front of your friends. That was inappropriate. I lost my temper and it was wrong to take it out on you. Will you forgive me?

Longer term: Can I talk to you? I need to ask you a really important question. (Get child's OK or at least a nod.)

I need to ask your forgiveness. I haven't been a perfect parent, and I need to take responsibility for that. I haven't taken the time to be with you the way I should, and I'm sorry. [Describe your situation in detail.] I'm ready to do things differently. I may not do it perfectly every time, but I really want to try. Will you forgive me?

(If child says no or responds with anger, calmly reassure the child that his or her feelings are understandable.) I'm sorry you're not ready to forgive me, and I don't blame you for being angry. I just want you to know that I'm truly sorry, and I love you. I hope you can forgive me soon. In the meantime, I'm going to do my best to make different choices. Thanks for listening.

(If the child says yes, then express your gratitude for the grace they have given you.) Thank you. I am truly sorry, and I love you. I'm going to do my best to make different choices. Thank you for giving me grace today. (This would be a great time for hugs!)

- Are you nursing a grudge against your child because you feel you have done so much for them and "this is how they've thanked you"? Maybe you feel their actions have reflected poorly on your parenting and your reputation in the community. Realize that you are the parent and he or she is a child who is still learning. Stop taking it personally. Your attitude *must* be one of love and grace, and you must ask forgiveness for bitterness or your own desire for comfort or respect.

- If you or your child is nursing a grudge, begin praying for the person(s). Let your heart soften toward them. What can you do to show kindness to them?

- If there has been an unplanned pregnancy in your family, show kindness and not judgment to those involved. Do not enable irresponsible behavior, but rejoice over the new life and take responsibility for your own actions. Pray about what you need to do.

- _____

_____

_____

Part 7

Starting Construction—Practical Steps

Chapter 12

Ages and Stages

How do we approach a surly teenage boy, and at the same time manage the needs of an innocent six-year-old girl? Just as we would decorate their rooms differently, we can plan our strategies of heart and life development individually.

Every family has individual needs when it comes to the number of children, age spans, personality traits, and seasons of life. You'll take into account your schedules, the ages of children, and each person's needs. Assess your family's situation by answering these questions:

- What ages are you dealing with?

- Who needs the most attention right now?

- Is there anyone who just wouldn't want to be a part of such discussions at present?

- Is your spouse willing to participate?

If one family member needs extra attention, it's OK to focus on that need first. Make a special effort to be warm toward and pray for family members who don't want to participate. Explain to your older children the great example they can set for the younger ones (or vice versa).

Realistic Scheduling

Whose calendar is overbooked? I see that hand!

Families today operate with very small margins of free time. I personally am an over-responsible, anxious, too-ambitious kind of person. I tend to do too much and lose steam (or overheat!). This is not helpful to my family. In some of my past efforts, my husband and children have felt that I was a nag and more than a little self-righteous. I had to ask forgiveness, regroup, and take some time off to consider a new approach.

For one thing, I needed to submit to my husband. For another, I needed to calm down. And last, but not least, I needed to control my schedule and start saying *no*. I am still in that process.

It isn't easy to make family time a priority, no matter the purpose. My family and I live in Orlando, where we have entertainment options everywhere, all the time—but that may not be good for us. When we first moved to Orlando we went to Disney World once a month because we could get free passes. We almost killed ourselves doing that! It took awhile to relax and recognize that although all things were lawful, not all things were beneficial.[1]

To find time to ensure growth in character and sexual purity, you'll need to make sacrifices. But your sacrifices will seem small compared to the payoffs.

Consider these questions as you begin:

- How will we make time to do a study or discuss questions?

- Can we choose one time slot that can be set aside weekly or bi-weekly?

- Would it be best to begin with short sessions at bedtime with a single child a couple of nights a week?

- Could a short discussion or object lesson be shared at selected family meals?

- Might it be best to start with some simple memorization, accompanied by discussions about what the verses mean and how to practice them?

- How much of our children's time is already spent on homework and extracurricular activities? We need to avoid planning a study that requires so much that it leads to resentment.

- What extracurricular activities might need to be dropped for the greater good of an individual child or the whole family?

Too often we commit to sports or music lessons in a greater way than we do lessons in personal formation that will affect our children much more foundationally. We want to give our best in this effort and be as thorough as possible.

On the other hand, don't start out so ambitiously that you lose steam and stop entirely.

If you are making an effort, give yourself credit. If one approach fizzles out, just start another. If for some reason you have to skip a week or a month, use that time to plan and pray more specifically for the needs of your family. Start again when you can.

Find a schedule that works for you. It might be best to start a study with one child, and do the study with another child when the first one is completed, holding a couple of family discussions a month in the meantime.

Chapter 13

A Family Kick-Off Meeting

Y ou're just about to head to the store to obtain the necessary materials to begin a purity plan in your home. But you may want to visualize yourself in the foreman's position, so to speak, before you make that trip. When you step to the front of the room to give the whole building crew (the family) a vision for what's about to take place, what will that event look like? It's an occasion, to be sure.

A meeting for the whole family is a landmark event that gathers your family to begin new efforts toward a good heart and honorable living. Following are family kick-off formats that might be helpful to you. As always, your imagination is the limit!

In the next section, you'll find helpful suggestions for materials as you gather what you need not only for this event but the ongoing work days to come.

Family Event Planning 101

As you plan your family kick-off, discuss with your spouse the possibilities you're considering. You and your spouse might have very different ideas, and it's important that you present a united front.

If you and your spouse are in a rough place, make your plans with sensitivity to your spouse's heart condition. If you're single, you may plan accordingly. (Any of the following activities may be changed slightly to be practical for a parent working alone.)

Write down a plan showing what you'd like to accomplish first, second, third and so on as you build a household of purity. (Start a family study? Spend some one-on-one time with your teen? Write new rules for technology?) Be ready to present this plan in a fun, enthusiastic way. An object lesson is a great way to make your presentation enjoyable and help the point to stick (see the list of object lessons in appendix E).

After you have a plan, think about a setting. You could take the family out to a meal at a restaurant to help mark an historic family event. A special meal could also be prepared at home. Don't stress out over what to eat, but make the details memorable so your family knows something unique is starting.

Gifts could also be given. Options include family friendship bracelets, a framed verse or quote for each person's room (see appendix B "Truths to Memorize" for helpful verses), or any other gift that would make family members feel valued.

To start the meeting, it's good to share how much each family member means to you. Write down your ideas and read them if you like. Next, if you feel it's appropriate, you can really get your family's attention by confessing your shortcomings (see more about this later in this chapter). Then explain the Planned Purity diagram briefly and what you feel is important for your family to know as you begin to pursue purity together.

If you have older children, use the house diagram as a visual aid. If your children are younger, use just the Five Doors of the heart. (See object lessons in appendix E or the *Preschool Purity of Heart* booklet, appendix A, #3. Instructions show how to create a simple visual aid.) Talk about the analogy of good food for your body, especially if a meal is involved, and tie it in with the concept of good food for the heart. If you want to start a family study on purity, the dedication meeting is the time to introduce it. Tell the family about the study and then work together (especially with teens) to choose where and when you will do it. You could end with a prayer or by sharing a special thought.

A family kick-off is a great way to begin a new chapter in the life of your household, and the meeting can be as individual as your family is. Scribble some ideas here if you like.

Family Kick-Off Notes

Our family goals _____

_____

Our first step_____

_____

Our next step _____

_____

Date and location of the Family Kick-Off

_____

_____

Main points of the Family Kick-Off

_____

_____

In appendix D, I've scripted two possible scenarios for your family kick-off. A third possible script also appears for inviting an older child to a special event that might follow a family meeting. (See scripts 20, 21, and 22.) I hope these examples will serve as a launching pad for your own unique family experience. *Please* don't use the scripts word for word—the message has to come from you personally.

As long as you are doing something, you are making progress.

In addition to the scripts, you can also include an object lesson to make the occasion even more memorable. See appendix E for the object lesson descriptions. Good choices include the lessons in the General Purity section:

1. Clean Cups, Dirty Dishes
2. Pick Your Poison
3. Be Good to Your Boat

And the Sexual Purity section:

5. Apple Analogy
6. Rose Analogy
7. Gift Analogy
8. Treasure Box

Make your plans as involved or simple as you like. Remember, *as long as you are doing something, you are making progress.*

A Tough Consideration

As I mentioned earlier, you may want to ask forgiveness from your children during your family dedication meeting. Although this thought may make parents squirm, beginning with a fresh slate can make a deep impression on your children and create a fine foundation for trust and new teaching to begin. Here's an example of the type of apology you might make:

> We (I) need to ask your forgiveness. There are a lot of things that we didn't understand about our own choices until now. We've made some mistakes and haven't given you all the information you'll need.

> Will you forgive us?

> We want to start a new journey in our family to learn about pure hearts and good lives. Here's our plan: [explain]. We're going to do this as a family so everyone can learn, including us. Do you have any questions we can answer right now?

Most likely your child(ren) will be ready to give you a second chance. However, there may have been other hurts between you and your child in the past that are still healing. If so, be sensitive if they seem threatened or hesitant. Allow your child to forgive when he/she is ready. Continue to show through your actions that you care for them and are ready to offer the same forgiveness to them if appropriate.

Whew! Asking forgiveness is a lot like throwing up (please excuse the earthy example!). No one wants to do it, but we feel so much better afterward! In addition, we've also given our children a living training video for how they can also ask forgiveness.

A Family Mission Statement

One goal you might consider during kick-off and other family meetings is the formation of a family mission statement that reflects your new awareness of a pursuit of pure hearts and honorable lives. One family we know painted their mission statement on the back of their kitchen cupboards (which faces the family table). Every day their family can read or be reminded of their purpose together. Deciding on just the right words and purpose as a family can take some time, but the eventual result will bring your family together and create a strong "team" atmosphere in the home. Here is our friends' kitchen cupboard statement:

The Mitchell Family Mission
To bear witness to the love of Christ
and encourage others to live godly, healthy and financially secure lives
through compassion, hospitality, acts of service,
teaching and creative expression.

Sharon, the mother, says, "We read the family mission together before family meetings. It helps us decide what we say 'yes' to and what doesn't fit with who we are."

Each family will have a unique mission statement. This statement doesn't use the word "purity," but it obviously describes aspects of a good heart such as the focus on helping others to live godly, healthy lives. No matter how you choose to word your statement, think about how a pure heart and life are reflected in it.

Families in Process

All families are in process, and many of us just don't look as neatly put together as the families in these examples might seem to you. Maybe mom or dad is absent, or doesn't really want to be there. Maybe a teenager is in a place where they seem to resent any efforts to help them grow. Every family is dealing with their own unique and sometimes very difficult circumstances.

If your spouse is not ready to be involved in new efforts at all, at least try to gain his or her consent to move ahead with a plan. Gently continue to invite your spouse to participate (but don't nag!). Cheerfully present material to your family, and treat your spouse lovingly as well. Never belittle a spouse for not participating—this will only drive them away from you and cause problems for the rest of the family as well.

This isn't a race; it's a relationship.

If a kick-off is too much fuss for the state of your family at this time, then skip the meeting and teach children either at appointed times or by taking advantage of teachable moments and implementing small changes over time. Even simple interactions can be powerful if they present truth lovingly.

An Ongoing Process

As you carry out these lessons and plans, be willing to flex if emergencies arise (rather than unhappily "pushing through"). This isn't a race; it's a relationship. Make the relationship a priority at all times. Share personal stories when they're appropriate, and take time to listen to your children's stories, too. Enjoy each other's company.

Building a solid house happens brick by brick, not all at once. It's an ongoing process that happens through everyday experiences as well as special events.

The following chapter will introduce you to the rest of this book, which contains all kinds of tools for finishing up the house for building your family's personal household of purity. You've come a long way, but don't stop reading now. Just ahead are the vital tools to make your family training fun and stress-free!

Chapter 14

Toolbox Overview

In order to build a household of purity, you need tools, and this book ends with a well-stocked toolbox (the appendices). You'll be able to use this resource section for years to come. Read these brief descriptions so you will know how to get the most out of your tools.

Appendix A: Books and Web Sites

While remembering that truth is our foundation, we can also benefit greatly from using books and other resources for our family training. In appendix A, I give you an overview of selected materials, based on age. I've reviewed these sources myself and included a brief description of each one. In addition, outstanding resources are marked with a star (★).

Once you see this list, you'll recognize how much good stuff is out there, and you'll be able to find more sources on your own.

Appendix B: Truths to Memorize

When it comes to a good heart, honor and purity, the Bible contains the greatest wisdom in the world. Included here are many specific verses, grouped according to the Five Doors and Seven Windows of the Planned Purity diagram.

Choose the verses that are meaningful to your family and get started with some creative memorizing. I like to have my children write the passages on index cards or sticky notes so that we can post them on the refrigerator or in the car. (We do a lot in the car!) Sometimes we write verses on the bathroom mirrors in lipstick or washable paint.

My family will take a week or longer to memorize a portion. Remember to keep it low-pressure, so that memorization doesn't cause resentment.

Hint: Don't look for perfection, but focus on understanding. Do you and your kids know what the verses mean and how to practice them?

Some people argue that memorization is ineffective because memorization does not equal understanding. But memorization can play an important role in character formation: Words become instantly accessible so that their meaning can grow and deepen with time. For example, some of us memorized Bible verses as children when we had only a simple understanding of the words. But as we matured, those words connected much more deeply with our experiences.

Appendix C: Events and Rites of Passage

Like a climber, your child needs footholds as he or she becomes mature. These footholds are special events or rights of passage. Keep your parental antennae up, and you'll pick up on how far it should be from one of these mile markers to the next.

Purity events of all sorts are becoming popular. Father/daughter dances, purity balls, and other events are all great opportunities. Take advantage of the events that are available for you to join, and plan additional events you feel are important. I mentioned the ceremonies that are in the *Life Lessons* books.

Getaways are also popular, where a parent and a preteen take a weekend to talk about purity. You can plan your own weekend or use a resource that's already available. Getaway weekends are like the "big talk" done one better, but recognize that preparatory and ongoing conversation on the subject will still be necessary.

Appendix D: Scripts

We've all had situations where we need some help with wording what we want to say to our children. It may be when our children ask a question about sexuality out of the blue. Or we're shocked to find our child viewing pornography. Or we get into a turf war about what our daughter can wear out of the house. These scenarios have already taken place in many of our households. If not, they're very likely to happen at some point.

Things like this have happened in our home. That's why I've written a few scripts as examples of how to navigate such minefield conversations. (Keep in mind that these are some of the conversations I wish I'd had—I've had quite a few counter-productive talks myself!) Because it's impossible to touch on every situation in a family, I hope these scripts not only give you ideas about specific scenarios but also give you a feel for the spirit in which a child should be engaged and spoken to—with respect and honor, truthfulness and firmness, love and authority. I tried to choose subjects that might arouse the greatest apprehension for parents.

These scripts are not for being read out loud, but they will give you your own ideas and thoughts about how to have a conversation with your child.

Appendix E: Object Lessons

Few things are more memorable to children and adults alike than an object lesson. That's why I've listed forty object lessons that are coordinated with the subjects in the book. We've had lots of fun with them. I hope they will be fun for you, too, and inspire new ideas of your own.

Appendix F: The Bishop Family Contracts

As a family, we have found that the form of a contract helps to show how serious we are about making intentional choices. I am providing you with three of the contracts my family used in order to give you a starting point to make your own family contracts. Do *not* feel you must use our guidelines. They are for our family. Consider each point in light of your individual family situation and child.

When you have prepared your contract, have a family meeting where you can intentionally review each boundary, in a friendly but businesslike manner. Enforce your "guard rails" with confidence.

A Vision of the Future

What an amazing building project we have begun! We can see both the beauty of the house we are creating, as well as the work yet to be done. Just as a builder envisions the finished project as he is working, we can move forward now with a beautiful picture in our minds of the home we're constructing.

Maintaining a home is a process. We will be pursuing a good heart and sexual purity for a lifetime, and now we have tools to do it well and wisely. Let's overview all the stages of construction that result in a pursuit of purity in a family and in a life.

The Ground

We know that the ground has to be prepared to build a house. In the same way, our pursuit of a deep, engaged relationship with our children will set the stage for all our training, purity and otherwise.

The Foundation

We've defined purity. It's about more than sex, and not just about teenagers. Purity is pursued over a lifetime and has to begin with the pursuit of a right heart.

The First Floor

The first step to develop a good heart is simply guarding our senses (the Five Doors). Even our youngest children can be taught to develop into people of honor and integrity, ready to embrace sexual purity as they grow and learn more about it.

The Second Floor

We have many windows of opportunity to set up boundaries for our children as they learn to pursue purity in action. We can refer back to the boundaries in this book, and trust that we'll come up with our own ideas as well.

The Roof
Accountability for ourselves and our children protects our entire house from hostile elements. We provide good examples for our children, evaluate our family's distributed community, and set examples for others as well.

The Fence
We and our children are human and fallible. When we fail, we can ask forgiveness and be forgiven. We can teach from failures as well as successes, so no experience is ever wasted.

We are building an amazing community of households committed to purity. Our community is capable of not just changing our own lives, but the world. *Love fearlessly to pursue these goals with wisdom and graciousness.* Pour out your life and love on your children's behalves, and enjoy your spouse and your relationship with God to the fullest. Make intentional choices and confidently assert the boundaries you set.

You are the right parent! Your child is in your home for a specific purpose, and you have the opportunity to teach the child from both your failures and successes. Humbly use both. There is no magic formula, but there is a blueprint to follow that allows for the greatest measure of successful, honorable living.

Love fearlessly to pursue these goals with wisdom and graciousness.

And there is grace. If it were not so, I could not be writing this book.

In a recent interview, I was asked how to encourage parents who felt they had failed in their child rearing. As one of those parents who has experienced failure, I responded, "Sometimes I burn my toast. But that doesn't mean I can't teach my children to cook."

Using our building analogy, maybe you have left some holes in your foundation, or tried to build a second floor without a first, or any number of oversights. That's how my house looks, too. I have my own feelings of inadequacy as I present Planned Purity to you. However, as a result of redemption, as a result of grace, because of the gift of starting where we are and beginning again, I am able to present these thoughts to you. May you take courage from our family's fumbling example and find strength to make something beautiful of your own as well. You may be astounded at the beautiful structure that appears.

Appendix A

Books and Web Sites

Generations of Virtue offers an excellent selection of resources on their web site at www.generationsofvirtue.org. You may also get good ideas by talking to staffers at your local Christian bookstore. As you find good sources, add them to the lists in this book and refer others to these sources as well.

★ Denotes books especially recommended by the author

Preschool

The preschool age is where a pure heart must be developed, which will result in the character necessary to make good choices as a child becomes older. Look for stories and books about integrity, honor, and goodness (like William Bennett's *The Book of Virtues*). Steer clear of buying books simply because the characters are popular in the media. Instead, look for content about good character and right choices.

Simple Bible stories can also capture a child's heart.

To provide an additional preschool resource, I wrote a booklet titled *Preschool Purity of Heart.* It uses song, role play, discussion and visual aids to explain the concept of purity and the Five Doors of the heart.

Remember that the time you spend on virtue-based stories with your young one will open doors of communication you will definitely need later.

Resources for Preschool

1. *Toddler's Bible*, V. Gilbert Beers, Cook Communications—a simple, sweet version of Bible stories and truths to draw the littlest child into truth and purity of heart
★2. *Read-Aloud Bible Stories* (four-book series), Ella Lindvall, Moody Publishers—the single most engaging toddler-level Bible stories we know of, plus simple questions
3. *Preschool Purity of Heart*, Jennie Bishop—six repeatable lessons on purity and the Five Doors of the heart for the very young; includes role play, songs, discussion and scripting

Elementary School

Planned Purity was birthed out of the creation of two children's books that teach purity. I wrote these books because I needed them for my own family! My first book, *The Princess and the Kiss,* tells the story of a princess who saves her kiss for a prince (and ends up choosing one who saves his kiss for her.) This story especially appeals to girls, but it also gives examples of suitors that are helpful for boys. The companion book, *The Squire and the Scroll,* teaches about the Five Doors of the heart from a boy's perspective. To retrieve the Lantern of Purest Light for his kingdom, the young squire must take on five quests, each one involving one of the five senses.

You can go a step further by using the companion devotionals for these books, which include twenty-one lessons especially for ages eight to twelve. Lessons include crafts, verses to memorize, and lots of creative ideas—even tips for a meaningful purity ceremony.

Resources for Elementary School

4. *The Princess and the Kiss*, Jennie Bishop, Warner Press—best-selling picture book for girls featuring a princess who saves her kiss (portrayed as a ball of light) for a prince
5. *The Squire and the Scroll,* Jennie Bishop, Warner Press—picture book for boys featuring a squire who must retrieve the Lantern of Purest Light for his kingdom by completing five quests (the Five Doors of the heart) and conquering a dragon

6. *The Garden Wall*, Jennie Bishop, Warner Press—children's picture book about a girl building a garden and a boy building a wall to protect it; shows a model of lasting friendship leading to lasting love

7. *A Child's Book of Virtues*, William Bennett, Simon and Schuster—best-seller presenting various classic stories of virtue

8. *A Child's Book of Heroes*, William Bennett, Simon and Schuster—classic stories of heroes

9. *A Little Book of Manners*, Elizabeth George, Harvest House—sweet, beautiful book with tons of fun tips and stories about manners for girls

10. *A Little Hero in the Making*, Elizabeth George, Harvest House—training and stories about manners, especially for boys

11. *Battlefield of the Mind for Kids*, Joyce Meyer, FaithWords—primer for kids on managing the thought life

Especially For/About Elementary-Age Boys

★12. *Boys Adrift*, Dr. Leonard Sax, M.D., Ph. D., Basic Books—incredible book on boys; highly researched and very readable—don't miss it

13. *Life Lessons from The Squire and the Scroll*, Jennie Bishop, Revive Our Hearts—Twenty-one lessons for boys based on the storybook *The Squire and the Scroll*, for use with parent and child or in a small group, ceremony included

14. *The Naked Truth*, Bill Perkins, Zondervan—facts that explain how boys function in relationships

15. *What He Must Be...If He Wants to Marry My Daughter*, Voddie Baucham, Jr., Crossway Books—a comprehensive treatment of a young man's preparation to be considered ready for marriage.

NOTE: If you are a parent of a girl, it would be wise to read some resources on boys.

Especially for Elementary-Age Girls

★16. *The Body Book*, Nancy Rue—cutest-ever, practical guide for young girls, introducing them to hygiene, body facts, and answering common questions

17. Life Lessons from The Princess and the Kiss, Jennie Bishop, Revive Our Hearts—Twenty-one lessons for girls based on the storybook *The Princess and the Kiss* for use with parent and child or in a small group, ceremony included

18. Before You Meet Prince Charming, Sarah Mally, Tomorrow's Forefathers—story and teaching format attractive to many preteens

19. Secret Keepers, Dannah Gresh, Moody—probably the best-known book on modesty on the market

NOTE: *If you are a parent of a boy, it would be wise to read some resources on girls.*

Teenagers and Beyond

Many books on sexual purity for teens, college students and singles are readily available, as are a number of books on marriage issues. Ask for your teen's opinion before you purchase a book for him or her. Read a chapter at a time and talk about it.

As an introduction to the topic of purity, you may want to start off by talking through the Planned Purity diagram in this book.

Resources for Preteens, Teens, College Students, and Single Adults

Sexuality

★*20. If You Really Loved Me*, Jason Evert, St. Anthony Messenger Press—one of the best question-and-answer books available on sexuality

★*21. Unprotected*, Miriam Grossman, Sentinel Trade—excellent, readable report on the devastating effects of promiscuity (the "hooking up" culture) on college campuses

22. Battlefield of the Mind for Teens, Joyce Meyer, Faithwords—primer on disciplining the mind for teens

23. Theology of the Body for Teens, Brian Butler, Jason and Crystalina Evert, Ascension Press—comprehensive teen study based on the above

24. Theology of the Body for Beginners, Christopher West, Ascension Press—Pope John Paul II's Humana Vitae scaled down and in modern language

Emotional Purity

★*25. Eyes Wide Open: Avoiding the Heartbreak of Emotional Promiscuity,* Brienne Murk, Regal—excellent treatment of guarding the heart and emotions, especially in relationships via technology; a must-read
26. Emotional Purity: An Affair of the Heart, Heather Arnel Paulsen, Crossway—goes beyond physical purity to questions of keeping emotions in check and guarding the heart

Courtship Compared to Dating

27. I Kissed Dating Goodbye, Joshua Harris, Multnomah— best-seller asking readers to consider courtship over dating; very readable
28. www.beforethekiss.com: courtship information
29. www.doorposts.com: comprehensive studies on preparing to be a wife or husband
30. www.stayinthecastle.com: courtship suggestions and creative story resources

Especially for Young Women

31. And the Bride Wore White, Dannah Gresh, Moody—best-seller including Dannah's story and "secrets" to sexual purity
32. Sexy Girls: How Hot Is Too Hot?, Hayley DiMarco, Baker—thought-provoking and a great read; modesty from a marketing view; what should we be selling?
33. For Young Women Only, Shaunti Feldhahn, Multnomah—highly researched information important to young women's sexuality. See also www.shaunti.com.

Especially for Young Men

34. For Young Men Only, Shaunti Feldhahn, Multnomah—as above, for young men. See also www.shaunti.com.

Resources for Parenting

Below are parenting materials that I have personally reviewed and found to be very helpful.

35. *I Want to Teach My Child About Manners,* Jennie Bishop, Standard Publishing—a carry-along book of many short, practical tips and information on teaching manners

36. ★*Talking to Your Kids About Sex,* Mark Laaser, Random House—wonderful scripted answers for parents to consider for intimate talks with their own children

37. ★*Shepherding a Child's Heart,* Ted Tripp, Shepherd Press—goes beyond reacting to a child's actions to examining the intentions of the heart

38. *Growing Kids God's Way—The Child Wise Series,* Gary and Anne Marie Ezzo, Multnomah—well-known practical biblical parenting series

39. *Raising Maidens of Virtue,* Stacy McDonald, Books on the Path—more conservative approach to guarding femininity and purity with practical ideas

40. ★*Raising a Modern Day Knight,* Robert Lewis, Tyndale House—great for dads who want to know more about raising sons of integrity

41. ★*Age of Opportunity,* Paul David Tripp, P & R Publishing—challenging call to parents to see the preteen/teen years as opportunity instead of dreading them

42. ★*Every Parent Needs to Know About* ... four-book series from iCare on technology/pornography issues—exceptional value and wonderful research for parents seeking to understand technology and set healthy boundaries (see web site below)

43. ★*Battlefield of the Mind,* Joyce Meyer, Faithwords (also available in teen and kids' versions)—the primer in understanding how to discipline the thought life

44. ★www.cpyu.org (Center for Parent/Youth Understanding): excellent youth culture information

45. www.focusonthefamily.com: parenting resources galore online and in print

46. www.thementoringproject.org: a program especially for sons without dads, for those who are looking to mentor or single parents looking for mentors for boys

For Singles or Married Couples (Biblical Sexuality)

47. *Kissed the Girls and Made Them Cry*, Lisa Bevere, Nelson—healthy sexuality and relationships

48. ★*Every Man's Battle*, Stephen Arterburn and Fred Stoeker, Water-Brook—healthy sexuality and guarding against pornography for men

For Married Couples (Sexual relationship issues)

49. *Good News About Sex and Marriage*, Christopher West, St. Anthony Messenger Press—excellent Catholic (Protestants should read as well!) explaining biblical marriage; very readable

50. *Every Woman's Marriage*, Shannon and Steve Ethridge, Water-Brook—healthy sexuality for married women

51. *Every Man's Marriage*, Steve Arterburn and Fred Stoeker, Water-Brook—healthy sexuality for married men

52. *Keys to Loving Relationships* video series, Gary Smalley—comprehensive lessons on the basics of relationships; very practical (http://smalleyonlinestore.com/keystolovingrelationshipsondvd.aspx)

53. *Every Woman's Battle*, Shannon Ethridge, WaterBrook—as above, for women

54. *For Women Only*, Shaunti Feldhahn, Multnomah—highly researched information on sexuality women need to know

55. *For Men Only*, Shaunti Feldhahn, Multnomah—as above, for men

56. www.christopherwest.com: incredible writer/speaker on human sexuality, *Theology of the Body* books—Catholic theology and super purity material for all denominations

57. www.theologyofthebody.net: more of the wonderful series and reflecting on Pope John Paul II's Theology of the Body.

58. www.sexuallyconfidentwife.com: Shannon Etheridge on healthy sexuality and spirituality

Movie/Music Review Sites

Become an expert in building up your child according to his or her personal media bent. What style of music do they like? Do they appreciate comedy or drama?

Every family will make different choices about media. Try to come to an agreement with your spouse on how much and what is appropriate. Remember to leave room for discussion.

In general, use movies and music as special treats (not constant habits). When you choose to enjoy media, load up with "good stuff." The following review sites may help you determine what's right for your family.

59. ★www.pluggedinonline.org
60. www.dove.org

Marriage Retreat Organization Sites

61. ★Chik-Fil-A's WinShape: www.winshape.org/marriage/
62. FamilyLife Weekend to Remember: www.familylife.com/site/c.dnJHKLNnFoG/b.5846045/k.F479/Attend_a_conference.htm
63. ★www.icarecoalition.org/icare.asp
64. www.defenderministries.com
65. www.imom.com
66. www.allprodad.com

Appendix B

Truths to Memorize

B elow are forty-two verses and passages that are great choices for memorization. They are presented in the New International Version, but please use the version you feel most comfortable with. The materials are organized into two parts. The first part gives the definition of purity and the key verses from the Planned Purity diagram. The second part gives the best verses about purity found throughout Scripture, grouped into the following topics:

Benefits of Purity
Purpose of Purity
Practice of Purity
Purity of Body
Purity for Youth

Highlight the verses that most relevant to your family and then write down the dates when you have learned them together.

Definition of Purity:

Purity is a lifestyle of inner housekeeping

that is taught over a lifetime,

beginning with a good heart

and working its way from the mind and thoughts

into the life and actions.

Planned Purity Verses

The Foundation
1. Wellspring of Life. Above all else, guard your heart, for it is the wellspring of life (Proverbs 4:23).

The First Floor: The Five Doors

Overview
2. The Five Senses of Purity. My son, pay attention to what I say; listen closely to my words **(Ears).**
Do not let them out of your sight, keep them within your heart; for they are life to those who find them and health to a man's whole body **(Breath)....**
Put away perversity from your mouth; keep corrupt talk far from your lips **(Mouth).**
Let your eyes look straight ahead, fix your gaze directly before you **(Eyes).**
Make level paths for your feet and take only ways that are firm. Do not swerve to the right or the left; keep your foot from evil **(Skin)** (Proverbs 4:20-22, 24-27).

Specific Verses for Each Door
3. Eyes: The eye is the lamp of the body. If your eyes are good, your whole body will be full of light. But if your eyes are bad, your whole body will be full of darkness. If then the light within you is darkness, how great is that darkness! (Matthew 6:22-23)
4. Ears: Listen to advice and accept instruction, and in the end you will be wise (Proverbs 19:20).
5. Breath: The Lord God formed the man from the dust of the ground and breathed into his nostrils the breath of life, and the man became a living being (Genesis 2:7).
6. Mouth: What goes into a man's mouth does not make him "unclean," but what comes out of his mouth, that is what makes him "unclean" (Matthew 15:11).
7. Skin: There is a time for everything ... a time to embrace, and a time to refrain (Ecclesiastes 3:1, 5b).

The Second Floor: The Seven Windows

Overview
8. First clean the inside of the cup and dish, and then the outside also will be clean (Matthew 23:26).

Specific Verses for Each Window
9. Focus: Do nothing out of selfish ambition or vain conceit, but in humility consider others better than yourselves (Philippians 2:3).

10. Vocabulary: Do not let any unwholesome talk come out of your mouths, but only what is helpful for building others up according to their needs, that it may benefit those who listen (Ephesians 4:29, NIV).

11. Dress: Your beauty should not come from outward adornment, such as braided hair and the wearing of gold jewelry and fine clothes. Instead, it should be that of your inner self (1 Peter 3:3-4a).

12. Education: Then you will know the truth, and the truth will set you free (John 8:32).

13. Boy/Girl Interaction: Treat younger men as brothers, older women as mothers, and younger women as sisters, with absolute purity (1 Timothy 5:1b-2).

14. Friends: Do not be misled: "Bad company corrupts good character" (1 Corinthians 15:33).

15. Technology: Dear children, keep yourselves from idols (1 John 5:21).

The Roof: Mentoring
16. Strong Together: Though one may be overpowered, two can defend themselves. A cord of three strands is not quickly broken (Ecclesiastes 4:12).

The Fence: The Security of Grace
17. If we confess our sins, he is faithful and just to forgive us our sins and purify us from all unrighteousness (1 John 1:9).

General Purity Verses

Benefits of Purity

18. Who may ascend the hill of the Lord? Who may stand in his holy place? He who has clean hands and a pure heart (Psalm 24:3-4a).
19. Create in me a pure heart, O God, and renew a steadfast spirit within me (Psalm 51:10).
20. Surely God is good to Israel, to those who are pure in heart (Psalm 73:1).
21. The Lord detests the thoughts of the wicked, but those of the pure are pleasing to him (Proverbs 15:26).
22. He who loves a pure heart and whose speech is gracious will have the king for his friend (Proverbs 22:11).
23. Blessed are the pure in heart, for they will see God (Matthew 5:8).
24. "Therefore come out from them and be separate, says the Lord. Touch no unclean thing, and I will receive you. I will be a Father to you, and you will be my sons and daughters, says the Lord Almighty" (2 Corinthians 6:17-18).

Purpose of Purity

25. I promised you to one husband, to Christ, so that I might present you as a pure virgin to him (2 Corinthians 11:2b).
26. And this is my prayer: that your love may abound more and more in knowledge and depth of insight, so that you may be able to discern what is best and may be pure and blameless until the day of Christ, filled with the fruit of righteousness that comes through Jesus Christ— to the glory and praise of God (Philippians 1:9-11).
27. Religion that God our Father accepts as pure and faultless is this: to look after orphans and widows in their distress and to keep oneself from being polluted by the world (James 1:27).

Practice of Purity

28. **Best Thoughts.** Finally, brothers, whatever is true, whatever is noble, whatever is right, whatever is pure, whatever is lovely, whatever is admirable—if anything is excellent or praiseworthy—think about such things (Philippians 4:8).
29. **Sincere Faith.** Love ... comes from a pure heart and a good conscience and a sincere faith (1 Timothy 1:5).

30. Others' Sins: Do not share in the sins of others. Keep yourself pure (1 Timothy 5:22).

31. You have purified yourselves by obeying the truth (1 Peter 1:22).

32. Pure from Contamination. Since we have these promises, dear friends, let us purify ourselves from everything that contaminates body and spirit, perfecting holiness out of reverence for God (2 Corinthians 7:1).

33. If we confess our sins, he is faithful and just and will forgive us our sins and purify us from all unrighteousness (1 John 1:9).

Purity of the Body

34. No Hint of Immorality. But among you there must not be even a hint of sexual immorality, or of any kind of impurity, or of greed, because these are improper for God's holy people (Ephesians 5:3).

35. The Marriage Bed. Marriage should be honored by all, and the marriage bed kept pure, for God will judge the adulterer and all the sexually immoral (Hebrews 13:4).

36. The Sister Attitude. Treat younger men as brothers, older women as mothers, and younger women as sisters with absolute purity (1 Timothy 5:1b-2).

37. Purpose of the Body. The body is not meant for sexual immorality, but for the Lord (1 Corinthians 6:13b).

38. Flee Immorality. Flee from sexual immorality. All other sins a man commits are outside his body, but he who sins sexually sins against his own body (1 Corinthians 6:18).

Purity for Youth

39. How can a young man keep his way pure? By living according to your word (Psalm 119:9).

40. Known by Actions. Even a child is known by his actions, by whether his conduct is pure and right (Proverbs 20:11).

41. Flee Evil Desires. Flee the evil desires of youth, and pursue righteousness, faith, love and peace, along with those who call on the Lord out of a pure heart (2 Timothy 2:22).

42. A Good Example When Young. Don't let anyone look down on you because you are young, but set an example for the believers in speech, in life, in love, in faith and in purity (1 Timothy 4:12).

Appendix C

Events and Rites of Passage

For Parents to Study/Plan Event with Children

★*1. Passport 2 Purity weekend packet,* Family Life (boys and girls)—weekend away to introduce sexuality basics, includes "passport" with gold stamps to show progress

2. Preschool Purity of Heart, Jennie Bishop—six repeatable lessons on purity and the Five Doors of the heart for the very young; includes role play, songs, discussion and scripting

3. How You Are Changing (series), Jane Graver, Concordia (boys and girls)—excellent series to introduce the facts of life, including scripting suggestions

★*4. Battlefield of the Mind for Kids,* Joyce Meyer, Faithwords—super basics on the discipline of the thought life for kids

Especially for Girls

★*5. Secret Keepers* date packet, Dannah Gresh, Moody (girls)—Eight dates on modesty and femininity for girls and moms, including CD with stories to listen to in the driveway before you leave, options for low-cost alternatives, stickers and journal; exceptional

6. Life Lessons from The Princess and the Kiss, Jennie Bishop, Revive Our Hearts—Twenty-one lessons for girls based on the storybook, ceremony included

7. www.purefreedom.org: Dannah Gresh Secret Keepers web site for help with femininity, modesty and purity

8. Preparing Your Daughter for Every Young Woman's Battle, Shannon Ethridge, WaterBrook—patterned after Every Woman's Battle but specifically for girls; very explicit, preview and/or edit for your child

Especially for Boys

9. Life Lessons from The Squire and the Scroll, Jennie Bishop, Revive Our Hearts—Twenty-one lessons for boys based on the storybook, ceremony included

10. Every Young Man's Battle, Stephen Arterburn and Fred Stoeker, Random House—patterned after *Every Man's Battle*, for boys specifically; very explicit, preview and/or edit for your child

Appendix D

Scripts

Remember, these scripts are *only* examples. You may not agree with some of the approaches. If not, use them as discussion starters to decide how you would handle the situation differently. If we can think about the way we will communicate before a difficult incident comes to pass, we'll be much better prepared to handle it well when that incident or a similar one arises.

Also be aware that age categories given are very general. Only you know what your child is ready for, so if the material is appropriate for you, ignore the age recommendation.

IMPORTANT NOTE: It's always best to answer a child's initial question by asking: "What do you think?" This immediately clarifies what information they need. It's so easy to respond inappropriately because you assume the child's question means one thing when it means something else. Also, when in doubt, err on the side of "talk less, listen more."

When your child asks a question, stop what you're doing and sit with the child somewhere quiet and private to give an answer.

Contents of this Appendix:

Sexuality

Mass Media

7. Making Movie Choices
8. Editing Inappropriate Movie Scenes
9. Speaking to a Host Parent About Media
10. Social Networking Modesty
11. Social Networking Chats

Personal Media

12. Maintaining Cell Phone Boundaries
13. Responding to Unwanted Phone Calls
14. Making Music Choices

Modesty

15. Diffusing Dress Code Wars

Relationships

16. Bullying
17. Online Bullying
18. Sexual Bullying
19. Parent Asking Forgiveness

Family Kick-Off Meetings

20. A Family Kick-Off Meeting at Home with Multiple Ages
21. A Family Kick-Off Meeting at a Restaurant
22. A Follow-Up Meeting with an Older Child

Sexuality

1. *How Children Come Into Being*
Age: seven and under

Child: Where do babies come from?

Parent: Where do you think they come from?

Child: Billy said you find them in the cabbage patch.

Parent (smiling): Well, that would make a nice story, wouldn't it? But that's not exactly right. Babies come from a man and a woman. It takes a man and a woman to have a baby.

Child: Oh. (No further questions? Stop here. That may be all the child needs at the moment.)

2. *How Children Come Into Being*
Age: Elementary school or older

Child: But how do a man and a woman make a baby?

Parent: That's a good question. I'm glad you asked *me*. Well, first they should be married, right? A baby needs a mom and dad that won't leave him or each other. (Hesitate and answer any questions about marriage here.)
How do you think a man and woman make a baby?

Child: I think maybe they take their clothes off and snuggle in bed.

Parent: Well, that's part of the process most of the time. What part are you curious about?

(Child may answer in regard to the parts of the bodies, what else happens, how the baby gets in the mother's body, and so on.)

Parent: Can you tell me how men's and women's bodies are different? (Hopefully this has already been discussed, but if the child answers, "no," proceed ...) OK. Let's look at a picture of a man and a woman (any modest magazine picture will do). What do you notice?

(Draw the child into conversation about the differences—breasts, broad shoulders, dress, hair may be part of what the child notices.)

Parent: You're right! And men and women cover up certain parts of their bodies with their clothes, too, don't they? Breasts are like that—at least they should be. (smile) And a man and a woman have special parts of their bodies that fit together perfectly when they lie close together. The woman has an opening called a vagina, and the man has a penis that fits inside a woman's vagina. When a man and woman put their bodies together like that, it's called sex. And that's what makes a baby.

(Let child comment and answer questions simply and succinctly.)

Parent: Now, I need to tell you one more thing. Because sex is a very special and private thing between a husband and wife, it's not something we talk about with just anybody. A lot of people your age are learning about sex, and it's their parents' job to talk to them about that. So if anyone asks you questions about it, the right thing to say is, "You should ask your mom or dad about that. It's their special job to tell you." And if you have any questions about it, I want you to come to me. I will always tell you the truth. And if I don't know the answer, I'll find it for you. Okay?

3. *Explaining Sex ... and More*
Age: Elementary school

IMPORTANT NOTE: Please recognize that many of our children are talking about "sex" as intercourse only. They don't necessarily know that abstaining from oral sex and foreplay activities are part of sexual purity. This talk involves helping a child understand aspects of sexual purity including "how babies are made."

Child: Mom, what does sex mean?

Mom: Let's go sit down in your room to talk about that question.

(Take child to a place where privacy is ensured.)

Mom: Okay, let's start this way—tell me what you think sex means.

Child: Well, I think a man and a woman get in bed together with their clothes off.

Mom: That's part of it. What part are you curious about?

(Answers will vary, of course. Listen carefully and answer just what the child wants to know in simple terms.)

Child: What happens when they're in bed together?

Mom: There are a lot of ways to answer that question. When a man and woman are married, they can enjoy each other's bodies in lots of ways. Some of the things they do just make the man and woman feel close and very happy, and other things can make a wonderful child, like you (smile). But God says all of this can only happen when a man and woman are married.

Child: Oh.

Mom: Did you hear something specific that made you curious?

Child: Some kids at school were talking about it.

Mom: What did they say?

Child: Um ...

(So many answers may come here, from the simplest "someone mentioned the word" to "my friend says her brother is having sex with her." Don't be alarmed. Every exposure to the world's depraved state is an opportunity to arm our children for purity. See the scripts for "How Children Come into Being" and "Explaining Oral Sex" for some help if your child is ready for those discussions. I recommend not giving specific information until the child is at least age nine. If you feel your child is not ready for the information they're asking, see page 145-153 to review Corrie ten Boom's father's response about the "heavy suitcase" that a child may not be ready to carry or open yet. But be aware that if they don't get the answers they seek from you, they may seek them from friends who give wrong information. Be looking into friendships where the conversation is taking place, and make it clear that this kind of discussion is extra-private, between a parent and child. Encourage the child to tell others the same if they try to bring up intimate subjects.)

4. *Explaining Oral Sex*
Age: eight and up

Older child: I don't understand the sex thing. How does it work again?

Parent: I'll try to help. What do you know so far?

Child: I know about the body parts that fit together. But I heard that boys have sperm and girls have eggs. What does that mean?

Parent: Well, you're right about that! When a man and a woman have sex, sperm come through the penis into the vagina and into the uterus, which is where a baby can grow. At a certain time each month, a woman's body produces ova. When one sperm connects to one of these eggs, a new life is begun.

Child: I heard someone talk about oral sex. What's that?

Parent: Hmmm. What do you think it is?

(answers, corrections)

Parent: Oral sex happens when a man or woman puts their mouth on their partner's private parts. That's another thing that is only OK if a man and woman are married. It's very dangerous if someone does it outside of marriage, because you can catch serious diseases from people who have had oral sex with others. Not having oral sex before marriage is part of keeping ourselves pure.

(Might add) Touching anyone in private areas or in ways that bring on really intense feelings makes emotions start that are very hard to control. So we always want to respect others by not touching them or even speaking to them in a way that may start feelings we can't finish. Does that make sense?

5. *Explaining Pornography: Son*
Age: Elementary school and older

NOTE: The following example begins as though the parent has discovered the child in the process of viewing pornography. You may be approaching a child at a different time, or having a simple talk regarding a commercial, movie, or ad.

If you are caught off guard, you may need to give yourself time to calm down and talk later. Practice wisdom and self-control in your response. Your child is most likely simply curious.

Parent: (calmly) Son?

(Give child time to calm down, or whatever is needed. It's vital that you are calm. This is an opportunity to teach, or to scar your child with shame. Be careful! Breathe!)

Parent: I'm not going to say what you think I'm going to say. But tell me, is this the first time you've seen this sort of thing?

Son: Ah—well—I've seen a few other things—

Parent: Okay. So you must be curious about what you saw, and I want you to know that your curiosity is perfectly normal. Those pictures aren't the way to get the answer, but it's important to understand why you feel drawn to them. Nobody's here right now, so I can answer your questions.
How do you feel when you look at these pictures?

Son: It's embarrassing. But I keep looking.

(Continue conversation if the time is good; otherwise, agree on a time to talk privately.)

Parent: God made something amazing when he made the female body. It's beautiful, and it gets an amazing response out of men, too. The appreciation you have for a woman's beauty is normal and good. But it's been given for a special purpose—so you can appreciate and cherish one woman and care for her and any children you have with her. When a man doesn't guard his eyes from looking at women's bodies, he starts to think of women as objects, and he ruins his ability to really appreciate his future wife.

(Questions?)

When a man does guard his eyes, he gives himself the gift of one day enjoying his wife's body to the fullest, because hers will be the only body he sees. And she will know that he has saved himself for her, so she trusts him with her body. That man can enjoy his wife's body without guilt, for the rest of his life.

(Questions?)

Don't underestimate the power of these pictures. Pornography is addicting. It releases a chemical in your brain that will make you want to see more and more, and maybe even act it out. It's like poison. Steer clear of it completely, and don't hesitate to turn off a TV or computer, or step out of a store or movie theater because of it. It's that important to being a good man and a good husband someday.

Son: But it's everywhere. How do I do that?

Parent: One way is to shut off the technology if that's where you see it. But if you see an immodest woman on a billboard, try to "bounce" your eyes away. Look at something else immediately and remind yourself that you're an honorable man who is saving your eyes for your wife. And let me know if you're struggling. We can talk about this anytime.

6. *Explaining Pornography: Daughter*
Age: Elementary school and older

NOTE: The following example begins as though the parent has discovered the child in the process of viewing pornography. You may be approaching a child at a different time, or having a simple talk regarding a commercial, movie, or ad.

If you are caught off guard, you may need to give yourself time to calm down and talk later. Practice wisdom and self-control in your response. Your child is most likely simply curious.

Parent: (calmly) Sweetheart?

(Give child time to calm down, or whatever is needed. It's vital that you are calm. This is an opportunity to teach, or to scar your child with shame. Be careful! Breathe!)

Parent: I'm not going to say what you think I'm going to say. But tell me, is this the first time you've seen this sort of thing?

Daughter: Yes! It was an accident! It popped up on my screen at the beginning of a video I wanted to watch! I'm sorry!

Parent: It's okay. I understand. This stuff is everywhere, and you can easily stumble across it.

Daughter: I feel awful!

Parent: I'm so sorry you had to see this, honey. Don't worry, I'm right here, and I don't think any less of you. These things happen.

(Take time for comfort.)

Parent: I want you to know that your curiosity is perfectly normal. Those pictures aren't the way to get the answer, but it's important to understand why you feel drawn to them.

(Continue conversation if the time is good; otherwise, agree on a time to talk privately.)

Parent: God made something amazing when he made the human body. It's beautiful. The appreciation we have for the beauty of the body is normal and good. But it's been given for a special purpose—to be guarded and saved for the appreciation and caring of one special person who will care for a spouse and a family. When we don't guard our eyes from looking at others' bodies, we start to think of ourselves as objects, and we ruin our ability to really appreciate our future spouse.

(Questions?)

When a woman guards her eyes, she protects herself from believing that she has to behave or dress or pose the same way to be attractive. She can be satisfied with who she is and be a woman of modesty and beautiful mystery, someone with a heart and soul and not just a body to look at. This confidence will make her a delight her husband someday. She hopes for a man who has saved himself in the same way, so all the love they enjoy will be their personal joy and celebration—no one else's. A couple like that can easily trust each other with their bodies. That woman can enjoy her husband's body without guilt, for the rest of her life.

(Questions?)

Don't underestimate the power of these pictures. Pornography is addicting. It makes you want to see more and more, and maybe even act it out. It's like poison. Steer clear of it completely, and don't hesitate to turn off a TV or computer, or step out of a store or movie theater because of it. It's that important to being a good wife and a good mother someday.

Mass Media

7. *Making Movie Choices*
Age: All

NOTE: Boundaries with movies will not be the same for every family. Have a reason for the limits you set, and be consistent and willing to talk. Be aware of movie review sites where you can check the content of a film.

Child: Mom, I want to go with my friends to see that new movie that's out.

Parent: Did you check the review online to see what it's about?

Child: No, my friends said it was good, though.

Parent: Hmmm. Well, I haven't seen it myself. Let's look online and see what it says. (Parent and child look together.) Whoa. What do you think about the sexual content it talks about here?

Child: Oh. Well, maybe it's not so bad.

Parent: Sorry, hon. I can't give you permission for that one.

Child: But, Mom!

Parent: How about asking if your friends would like to see a different, more appropriate movie? That might be better than staying home. Or we could ask your friends over to watch one of our movies here. I'll make popcorn if you want.

Child: Mom, why do you have to be so picky about everything?

Parent: I'm sorry I seem picky to you. But I love you, and I'm more concerned about your character than I am about you being able to go to every event you're asked to. That seems like it would be more comfortable, but the movies you watch affect the person you are. Sorry to disappoint you this time. Would you like to consider one of the options I just mentioned? Or you can just have a quiet evening on your own if you want to.

NOTE: *Again, be prepared for a negative response and give space or respond lovingly as best you can. You are the parent, not a teenage friend.*

8. *Editing Inappropriate Movie Scenes*
Age: Seven and older

Parent: We're going to just skip right over this scene.

Child (old enough to know what sex is): Why?

Parent: That's a good question. Let me pause this for a moment while I answer. (Hit pause.) The scene I'm skipping has two actors in it who are acting just like they are having sex. Sex is always meant to be private. It isn't meant for anyone else to watch. Some people who make movies don't agree with that, so they pay actors to act those scenes out. It isn't okay to pay people to act like they're having sex, and it isn't okay for us to watch. It's a good story otherwise, so I think we can watch most of it. But this scene isn't necessary.

Age: Younger than seven

Parent: Sometimes the people who make movies aren't really thinking about how some scenes aren't good for families. I want to guard your eyes so your heart stays clean and healthy. I'll teach you how to do that for yourself someday, but right now I need to choose for you. The rest of the story is pretty good. Maybe we can talk about what we learned from it when it's over.

9. *Speaking to a Host Parent About Media*

NOTE: This should be a phone conversation between parents prior to accepting an invitation to sleep over or visit, edited as necessary.

You: Good morning, Mrs. Smith. James tells me that you and Patrick have asked him over to play on Saturday. Is that right?

Mrs. Smith: Why, yes. Will James be able to come?

You: I think he'd like that. Can we talk about some details first?

Mrs. Smith: Sure. I was thinking of coming to get James about noon and bringing him home after supper.

You: Our schedule is free then. Can you tell me what you have planned for the boys to do?

Mrs. Smith: Oh, we don't have any particular plans. We have a pool, so they can swim, and our street is safe for biking.

You: Will you be supervising them in the pool, or riding with them?

Mrs. Smith: We usually let Patrick play on his own. He's a good swimmer and knows the bike rules. We have a helmet for James.

(NOTE: At this point, depending on James' age, you would respond that it sounds great or ask that you'd be more comfortable if he were supervised. If the parent can't supervise, graciously try to reschedule at a time when they can be available.)

You: Will the boys be watching movies or using the Internet?

Mrs. Smith: They may be.

You: Okay. Would you mind having James call me to okay whatever movie they might watch? We're trying to be careful to steer him clear of movies where women are wearing too little, or intimate scenes are acted out, blood and gore, that kind of stuff.

Mrs. Smith: Sure. We have some rules about those things, too. I'll be glad to have him call you. (Don't be surprised if the parent is a little more surprised than this one.)

You: Great! Do you have the same standards for the Internet?

Mrs. Smith: Well, Patrick pretty much knows his way around. His computer is in his room. (Red flag!)

You: All right. Well, if it would be okay with you, maybe the boys could steer clear of the computer while James is there. We're trying to encourage him to spend time paying attention to his friends instead of their computers at this stage.

Mrs. Smith: You make a good point. That's not a problem. We have lots of things they can do besides use the computer. Are Wii games okay with you?

(NOTE: Again, you would give your personal response or ask about specific games. If you still feel uneasy, you may suggest sending one of your family's games along, or simply reiterate your desire to steer clear of "screentime" during a visit.)

You: Thanks for filling me in, Mrs. Smith. And I'll actually be in your area, so I can drop James off—then you won't have to drive both ways. (This is a great strategy for meeting a parent and getting a feel for the home environment if you need to. Meeting parents beforehand is always better if you can manage it, maybe at a school function or elsewhere. This is where involvement at school really helps. Don't be afraid to ask others who know the family for references, i.e. "Do you know the Smiths? They've asked James over to play, and we haven't had the chance to meet them yet." Again, it's all about gracious wording and tone.)

10. *Social Networking Modesty*
A talk with Mom

NOTE: Again, before the right to use a social networking system is given, a number of safeguards and standards must be discussed. Parents must always have passwords and adhere to a "no privacy" policy. Anything that must be hidden is inappropriate. The right to view a child's online material at any time is a given. Again, it's a privilege, not a right.

Interact with your child online and learn to use the systems they do. The experience will educate you better as you set standards, keep lines open between you and your child, and remind them that you're keeping track of their activity.

Mom (addressing daughter who is online): Amy?

Amy (not looking up): Yeah, Mom?

Mom: I need your eyes, honey.

Amy (sighing): OK. What's up?

Mom: Honey, I've noticed some things on your Facebook that concern me. We need to talk about them.

Amy: Not again! Gosh, I hate that you can look at whatever I do. Don't I ever get any privacy?

Mom (smiling wanly): Not online, honey. We discussed that when we started this, right? It's ...

Amy: I know—"it's not a right, it's a privilege."

Mom (smiling again): Well, I'm glad you've got that in mind. So let's talk about these photos from your sleepover at Kim's.

Amy: What's the matter with them?

Mom: Well, you both look cute, but the camera angle looks right down into your bra. That's a modesty boundary we set, remember?

Amy: Mom, that is SO not a big deal. Other girls take a lot more immodest pictures. Do you want me to look like a grandma?

Mom: Honey, you are beautiful, and you could never look like a grandma at this age. Besides, what's wrong with a grandma?

Amy: You know what I mean!

Mom (chuckling): I know. Just trying to lighten the air. But you can't post these pictures, hon. They need to come off your Facebook.

Amy: Nobody else's parents have such strict rules!

Mom: Mmmm—I think you'd be surprised how many parents do. I know it doesn't feel that way because of the culture around you, and I know that's a hard thing. But we have higher standards because we believe you're more than your body. No one should be looking at your breasts. They should be looking at your heart. It's pretty hard for guys to do that if you put your chest right there in front of them. Guys aren't bad, but they're built to be visually stimulated, remember? We talked about this before.

Amy: Well, none of my guy friends are like that.

Mom: Honey, they're ALL boys. And yes, they are biologically built like that. It doesn't mean they want to take advantage of you. It just means that you're making it hard for them to become honorable young men when you're giving them the chance to view your body. They have enough immodesty to deal with every day without their friends adding to it. Your dad and grandpa would tell you the same thing.

Amy: Hmmmm.

Mom: So pull the pictures, OK? I'll check your site later to keep you accountable.

Amy: OK, Mom. I'll do it, you won't have to check. I want as few of these conversations as possible.

Mom: Me, too! We have so many things that are so much more fun to talk about! Thanks, honey. (Hug if you can.)

11. *Social Networking Chats*
A talk with Dad

Dad: Emily, we need to talk about your Facebook.

Emily: OK.

Dad: You know I love you, and I know you've set high standards for yourself. I'm proud of you for that. That's why I'm disappointed by the conversation on your site lately.

Emily: Um, ok.

Dad: Do you have an idea of what I might be talking about?

Emily: Maybe.

Dad: Tell me.

Emily: Well … I'm thinking maybe it has to do with Zach.

Dad: Yep. Why do you think that?

Emily: You don't like him.

Dad: I didn't say that. Why don't you tell me what kinds of things you've been talking about lately? After all, you know I can see those conversations.

Emily: Um—well—he said I'm hot, and I said—this is embarrassing, Dad.

Dad: Well, I think that may be the point. When you feel as though you have to hide something, you might want to double check what you're talking about with mom or me. It sounds like you know you've stepped over the line and gotten a little too personal.

Emily: Well, lots of other girls talk to guys that way.

Dad: Not everyone's families set the same boundaries, it's true. But for our family, you'll need to back off on the personal conversations. I'm going to ask you and Zach to only talk at school for a couple of weeks so you can cool it. No phone or internet for awhile, okay?

Emily: But, Dad!

Dad: I know that doesn't make you happy, Em. But it's part of learning to be responsible with your heart and staying in friendship-based conversations online. Those are the standards we set when you got the phone and the computer, and those are the standards we're sticking to. I'll call Zach tonight and let him know what we decided— we've talked before, and he knows the standards, too.

Emily: (silent)

Dad: I know you don't understand it entirely, Em. But I love you, and it's my job to protect you and guide you in your relationships. Not every parent does that, but at our house, we do. I'll give you some time to adjust to these new arrangements, and we can talk about it a little later when you're up to it.

(Dad leaves quietly.)

Personal Media

12. *Maintaining Cell Phone Boundaries*
Age: Elementary and older

NOTE: First of all, have clear, written rules about what you expect from cell phone use before your child receives one. Does your child absolutely need a phone? Is it clear that YOU own the phone and set the rules regarding its use? Do you understand all the phone's operations? When may it be used? (At the table, at a gathering at a friend's house, at an overnighter?) For what purposes may it be used? (Homework, checking in with parents, conversations of a certain length, romantic conversation, gossip?) If the phone takes pictures, what are the boundaries of pictures that may be taken or shared? When may the phone be taken away? Note our family's sample agreement. (Please take time to talk as a couple or consider as a parent what your family needs – don't just use ours!)

Dad to daughter on phone: Sarah?

Sarah: Yeah? (to caller) Just a minute, my dad is here.

Dad: You've been on the phone for forty-five minutes, hon. Time to say goodbye.

Sarah: (to caller) Sorry, I have to go. I'll call you back. Yeah, Dad?

Dad: Sarah, I've had to remind you again and again to limit calls to thirty minutes if they're just "chat sessions." We want you to be home and present with us after school.

Sarah: I know, but thirty minutes is so short. I hate that rule!

Dad: I know it's not easy for you to follow, but it's important to our family.

Sarah: Nobody else I know has rules like this.

Dad: Well, we're not anybody else's family. And since it won't be long before you're out on your own, we want to spend as much time together as possible. Is your homework done?

Sarah: (roll of eyes) No.

Dad: Okay, hon. I know this is hard, but I'm going to take the phone for the evening so you can focus. Once you get your work done we'll do something together, okay?

Sarah: Dad!

Sarah: Like I said, I know this is hard. But I own the phone, and we set the rules. If you can deal with it cheerfully tonight, I'll give it back tomorrow. If we keep seeing you stepping over the boundaries, I'll have to take it away for longer. We discussed this when we got you the phone, right?

Sarah: Yes. (hands over phone)

Dad: I know you're strong enough to make good choices, honey. Until you can do it on your own, I'll help you out. That's why I'm here. I'm hoping to see a good attitude the rest of the night. Now, do you need any help with your homework?

(Stay or go as needed, showing a spirit of helpfulness and support.)

13. *Responding to Unwanted Phone Calls*
Age: Elementary school and older

NOTE: An increasing number of mothers are concerned about young ladies approaching their young sons, even in elementary schools. Cultural influences and lack of good fathers contribute to girls being hungry for affection. These boys or girls need both our clear "no" and our guidance.

Don't hesitate to call a parent and ask them to intervene if calls are repeated frequently in spite of your requests. Obviously, this conversation is not on a cell phone. It's helpful to "check in" cell phones at home to help a child focus on the family and homework. This also makes calls easier to screen. Thus, the parent would answer and pass the phone to the child. Phone use is a privilege, not a right! Each family will need to set their own boundaries in this area.

Caller: Can I talk to Jason?

Parent: Who's calling, please?

Caller: This is Melissa, from school.

Parent: (friendly) Hi, Melissa. Can I ask why you're calling? (Every parent is allowed to ask this question!)

Caller: Oh, uh, I just wanted to talk.

Parent: Melissa, I'm sorry. Jason doesn't take calls from girls unless it's about homework. Is there something I can help you with?

Caller: Um, no, not really.

Parent: Okay, Jason will see you at school tomorrow, then. Have a good night!

(May be followed up with a talk with your child to clarify boundaries and explore what may be going on at school, and so on.)

14. *Making Music Choices*
Age: Elementary and older

NOTE: Before your child is given the rights to ANY technology, there should be clear communication about how the technology is used and what is acceptable. Do not give your child any technology that you do not know how to operate yourself. Also keep a strong understanding that all communication must be safe for the whole family and may be checked by a parent at any time—if you have to hide it, it shouldn't be spoken or typed. Technology is a privilege, not a right, that may be removed at any time.

Parent: (gently tapping child on shoulder) Hello?

Child: (parent should have child remove headphones) Yeah?

Parent: I'm going to ask you to turn the music down, OK? If I can hear it, it's really hard on your ears, and you'll need to be able to hear when you're forty.

Child: (rolls eyes) Okay.

Parent: (authentically interested) What are you listening to?

Child: It's a new band. I downloaded this song I really like today.

Parent: What's it called?

Child: (answers)

Parent: What's it about?

(If child knows, take the opportunity to discuss – take time to look up lyrics online later.)

Parent: (Later, when headphones are off) Hey, I looked up that band today.

Child: OK, Dad, what's wrong with them?

Parent: Sorry to clue you in, but the lyrics are about (degrading women, sexual content, violent, suicidal, and so forth). I'm going to have to ask you to delete that one.

Child: (heavy, hopeless sigh)

Parent: We agreed that you could get the iPod under the condition that I would be able to help you monitor the music you listened to, remember?

Child: Yeah.

Parent: So getting rid of a song is better than giving up the iPod, right?

Child: Yeah.

Parent: OK, so give me the iPod for a bit so I can take care of that. I know it's a pain, but I love you and I care about who you become. Try to remember our agreement from here so you can keep your iPod, all right?

Child: (Shrugs, "whatever")

NOTE: Don't be afraid to enforce and take the iPod back! Your child WILL survive and be better for it!
Technology demands so many types of discussions and boundaries—just a few are covered here. For more terrific ideas on modern technology and your kids, see icarecoalition.org/ icare.asp.

Modesty

15. *Diffusing Dress Code Wars*
Age: Elementary and above—or younger

First rule: Shop with your child. Children should learn how to shop and what to shop for from parents, not only in terms of modesty, but economy and practicality.

Child: But, Mom, all the other kids are wearing these skirts.

Parent: I know it's important to you to fit in, honey. But some standards are important enough that we have to be willing to stand apart from what the rest of the crowd is doing. I'll be glad to buy you one of those hoodies the kids are wearing.

Child: But these skirts are so cute!

Parent: Well, cute is fine, but revealing so much of your body isn't. Guys who look at you when you wear those clothes will be thinking only of your body and not of you as a person.

Child: Oh, Mom, guys aren't like that.

Parent: Honey, guys don't always mean to focus on your body. It's just how they're wired. They were made to appreciate women's bodies. But if you respect them, you won't flaunt your body in front of them. It's disrespectful to tease a boy with your body. And just remember, it isn't just those boys who are looking—it's older men, too.

Child: Gross.

Parent: Your beauty is powerful, honey, and it's up to you to use it wisely. Save your body for a husband to enjoy. It's not something for sale in a store window. And some clothes really draw attention to it like that. How is a guy ever going to appreciate your ideas and dreams when all he can think of is your thighs?

Child: Oh, Mom!

Parent: (smile) Hey, it's the truth. Now, do you want to look at one of these hoodies, or are we through shopping for tonight?

NOTE: Be prepared. It's OK for your child to be angry or sullen for awhile.

Relationships

16. *Bullying*
Age: Elementary and above—or younger

Child comes home crying or looking glum.

Parent: Hi, honey! Oh, you don't look very happy today. (hug) Did something happen at school?

Child: (shakes head)

Parent: Hmmm. Did you get a bad grade?

Child: (shakes head again)

Parent: Maybe someone was mean to you. Is that it?

Child: (bursts out) Timmy said I was ugly!

Parent: (hug) Oh, honey, I'm sorry. Do you feel ugly now?

Child: (sobbing) Yes!

Parent: Daddy and I tell you all the time how pretty we think you are, don't we?

Child: (nods)

Parent: Sometimes people have mean days, and they say mean things. Maybe Timmy had a bad day, or maybe someone was unkind to him before he came to school. Usually when someone is hurting they hurt others, too.
I need to ask you something. What did you say to Timmy after he was mean?

Child: I told him he was a big pig!

Parent: Oh, my. So you said some pretty unkind words, too. Hmm. (Facing child) When I look at you, I see someone beautiful. I don't know who Timmy saw. Let's forgive him for this bad day he's having and see if he doesn't act better tomorrow. But if he doesn't, I'll be sure to talk to someone about it, okay?

Child: (starting to feel a little hope) Do I have to forgive Timmy? He's so mean.

Parent: Yes, I think we do. Because if we don't, our hearts will be dirty with anger, and that won't make us pretty inside or out, will it? And I know it might not be easy, but you will have to tell Timmy tomorrow that you're sorry, too. I can come with you if you want me to.

Child: I don't want to say I'm sorry.

Parent: I know it's not easy, honey. But it isn't right for you to call Timmy names just because he started it. To keep your heart pure and clean, you'll have to ask forgiveness. But don't worry. I'll be right there to help.

Pray together and move on. Walk them gently through the process of humbling themselves as you insist on right behavior. Be aware and go to bat for your child if the situation doesn't improve.

NOTE: If you have a son, be especially careful to teach him to stand up with courage and ask forgiveness. His ability to communicate honorably is an important part of his development as a man. Don't be too quick to step in, but ask what he thinks should be done and guide him away from revenge. Getting him to communicate in this situation and come to a conclusion about how it should be handled is invaluable. (See below.)

Parent: So Clay hit you in the arm today. Gosh, I'm sorry. Why do you think he hit you?

Child: He called me a shrimp.

Parent: Ouch. That didn't make you feel good, huh? What do you think we should do about this?

Child: I want to hit him back!

Parent: Do you think that's the right thing to do?

Child: Well, no. Maybe I could write him a letter.

Parent: Do you think that would help?

Child: Um … no. But I could stay out of his way for awhile.

Parent: That might be okay. But what if he hits you again?

Child: I might hit him back… but that might start a fight. (sighs) I'm not sure what to do.

Parent: Well, maybe take a couple of days and see how it goes. We can ask God to show you what's best to do. And you can let me know if he does it again. How's that?

Continue discussion as necessary.

17. *Online Bullying*
Age: Preteen or older

NOTE: It's always best to set standards of use and talk about the dangers of technology when the child first is allowed to visit online sites or begin a social networking page (like Facebook). Please see the Bishop Family Technology Agreement (contract C) for ideas.

Mara: (enters with laptop) Uh, mom ...?

Mom: Yes?

Mara: I ... um ... I think you need to see something online.

Mom: Did you run into some pornography ads?

Mara: No, mom, it's not that. It's my friends at school.

Mom: Oh. Okay. Let me see. What do you think is going on?

Mara: Well, there's some mean talk going on about a girl at school.

Mom: Tell me about it.

Mara: (sitting down) Look. One of the girls called Maria a fat, ugly cow. And some of the girls are using even worse words.

Mom: Wow. That's some ugly language.

Mara: I know. I didn't even know those girls could talk like that. I want to say something to them about it, but I'm afraid they'll post things like that about me.

Mom: Well, I think this is something for the grown-ups to figure out. I'm glad you want to protect your friend. First I'll talk to the school about it and see what they can do. In the meantime, let's unfriend the girls who are talking this way so you don't risk any nasty posts. And I'll call Maria's mom. I don't know her, but if it was me I'd want to know about this right away.

Mara: Mom, don't tell them I told, okay?

Mom: I'll be very careful. I don't want you to get mixed up in this, either. But I think we should start praying for those girls right now. Remember what I always tell you?

Mara: Hurt people hurt people?

Mom: Yes. And these girls are definitely hurting. I'm sure you can be a big encouragement to Maria at school, too. If you see something getting out of control with her and these girls, don't be afraid to call a teacher. I know you're afraid, but be brave and stand up for this girl when you need to. I'm glad you feel compassion for her. That means your heart is healthy. (hug)

Mara: Okay, mom. I'm going to unfriend those girls now.

Walk closely alongside your child if she is dealing with bullies online and/or at school. Name-calling and other mean posts can be devastating to your daughter. Discuss how to choose wisely whom you "friend" and whom you don't. Never let your child "friend" someone they don't know personally. An unknown "friend" could be a predator.

18. *Sexual Bullying*
Age: Preteen or older

NOTE: It is never right to bully anyone *for their sexual preferences. Every person demands respect, no matter their stance on homosexuality. Teach your child to love and share their views with respect, seeking to understand instead of starting a fight.*

(locker room)

Mike: Hey, punk. Some of my friends are telling me you don't have a girlfriend. What's the matter with you?

Sam: Nothing. I just have a lot of girls who are friends, that's all.

Mike: (taunting) Uh-huh. Well, you know what I think? I think you don't really like *girls*. Maybe you like guys better, huh?

Sam: (chuckles) No, Mike. I *really* like girls. I think they're beautiful. But I respect them and want to wait for one specific girl. I don't want to spread myself around, you know?

Mike: That's crazy. Why not have some fun? There are plenty of girls here at school who like to party.

Sam: I like getting together with friends. We just had a blast last week at the beach.

Mike: Oh, but man, your parents were there. That's a lame party.

Sam: (laughing) It wasn't lame. It was fun. Everybody had a great time. You should have seen Ted try to surf for the first time. Oh, man!

Mike: Hmmph.

Sam: Mike, people don't have to have sex to have fun. Girls like guys who respect them. And no one gets to be a man by sleeping with as many girls as they can.

Mike: Hey, what are you saying?

Sam: I'm just saying—I know you like girls and all—but do you ever think about how they feel when you use them and move on? And what if one of them got pregnant, or got a disease because you've got one?

Mike: I haven't got a disease.

Sam: How do you know? Some diseases don't show symptoms, especially in guys. But girls can get infected and get sick a lot more easily. Some of them might not even be able to have babies.

Mike: How do you know all this stuff?

Sam: My dad and I talked to the doctor about it.

Mike: You talk to your dad about this stuff? Man, I can't talk to my dad about anything.

Sam: Gosh, I'm sorry about that. I'm sure my dad would talk to you sometime if you needed to know anything.

Mike: Nah, man. (waves him off) I gotta go.

Sam: Hey, Mike?

Mike: (turns) Yeah?

Sam: Think about what I said next time you're with a girl, okay?

(Mike shrugs and walks off)

Sam: (calling after him) And remember, I LIKE GIRLS!

Obviously, there are so many ways this scenario could go. First and foremost, teach your young men to celebrate their friendships with both girls and guys, and to 1) not to be ashamed to say they like girls as well as 2) saying wholeheartedly that they respect and honor girls.

19. *Parent Asking Forgiveness*

Single incident: I need to ask your forgiveness. I'm sorry I yelled at you—especially in front of your friends. That was inappropriate. I lost my temper, and it was wrong to take it out on you. Will you forgive me?

Longer term: Can I talk to you? I need to ask you a really important question.

(get child's OK or at least a nod)

I need to ask your forgiveness. I haven't been a perfect parent, and I need to take responsibility for that. I haven't taken the time to be with you the way I should, and I'm sorry (or insert situation – be detailed). I'm ready to do things differently. I may not do it perfectly every time, but I really want to try. Will you forgive me?

(NO, or angry response – engage as necessary, calmly)

I'm sorry you're not ready for that, and I don't blame you for being angry. I just want you to know that I'm truly sorry, and I love you. I hope you can find it in your heart to forgive me soon. In the meantime, I'm going to do my best to make different choices. Thanks for listening.

(YES)

Thanks. I want you to know that I'm truly sorry, and I love you. I'm going to do my best to make different choices. Thanks for giving me grace today. (Hugs as needed!)

Family Kick Off Meetings

20. *A Family Kick-Off Meeting at Home with Multiple Ages*

Setting: At home. A favorite meal is served. Mom has secretly made a white cake with white frosting and the word *purity* written on top. (You could add sparkler candles—fun!) After dinner, Dad reveals the special dessert and says a few words, incorporating an object lesson (see object lessons in appendix E for prep). For example:

Dad: We have a special dessert tonight because we have something special to talk about. Your mom and I have always tried to do our best to teach you how to be good kids, right?

We just read a book that taught us some great things that we want to learn together as a family. So we are going to have some family meetings on Tuesday nights to study how to have a good heart and an honorable life.

Let me show you a quick example that explains what the word *purity* means. This coffee cup is clean inside (show) and outside, right? Purity means that our hearts are clean (show inside) and our actions are pure and good as well (show outside).

Sometimes we can look good on the outside and do all the right things to look pure, but we don't keep our thoughts and attitudes pure in our hearts. Then we look like this. (Show a cup that is clean on the outside, but smeared with chocolate syrup on the inside.)

If we don't keep our hearts clean, then we end up with a cup like this. (Show third cup that's smeared inside and out.) That's because wrong thoughts and attitudes turn into wrong actions. If we keep thinking bad thoughts, we'll start doing bad things.

If we think about how much we want a candy bar (show cup 2), we could end up putting one in our pocket at the store when no one is looking (show cup 3). If we think about how much we don't like someone (show cup 2), it's likely that we'll say bad things about them or do something nasty to hurt their feelings (show cup 3). If we constantly think about how much we want a girl or boy to like us (show cup 2), we will probably end up doing something foolish to get their attention (show cup 3).

What we really want is to have right thoughts and attitudes on the inside and right actions on the outside (show cup 1). That's what it means to have a good heart and a good life.

We want our family to be like a construction team, building our lives like good, strong houses. Here's a picture that explains what I mean. [Explain the Planned Purity diagram briefly at this time. Respond to all comments.]

We'll also do some special events with each of you one-on-one.

Karen [age 3] is going to go through some fun lessons with Mom during the day.

Jordan [age 9], you and I will work on Life Lessons from the *Squire and the Scroll.* Here's your copy of the book. You'll like it.

Jaime [age 16], we can go out for coffee and look at some online sites about guarding your heart and life. I'd like you to give me your input on that after our meeting tonight.

When you understand what a pure heart is and you want to make a more serious commitment to purity, we'll celebrate by holding a party for each of you. We can invite a lot of friends to those parties, or just celebrate together as a family.

Mom and I are going to be learning, too. Mr. and Mrs. Johnson, our good friends, will get together with us once a month or so.

Mom: We wish we would have grown up knowing more about what it means to really be good and pure from the inside out, so we want to make sure you get all your questions answered! You're so precious to us, and we want to begin this journey with a gift that ties us together as a family. [Give bracelets as gifts, or choose a different option.] These bracelets are for us to wear all the time to remind us of things we've talked about.

Dad: So now we're a team! Does anyone have questions? [Allow time for answers.] We'll meet this coming Tuesday after supper. Now I'll pray and we will eat this cake!

[Sample prayer] Lord, thanks for your purity that makes us as white as this cake. Help us learn to be good like you, in our hearts and actions. Thanks for this great meal and this great family we love. Amen.

Your discussion may continue after dessert.

21. *A Family Kick-Off Meeting at a Restaurant*

Setting: A favorite restaurant. Dad clinks his glass with a spoon at the end of the meal.

Dad: Mom and I have a special announcement to make tonight, and that's why we're all having a night out on the town!

Your mom and I have always tried to do our best to teach you how to be good kids, and there's more to learn for all of us. We all (Mom and me included) need to learn more about having a pure heart and honorable lives. Mom's going to tell you more about that.

Mom: We just read a book that taught us some great things about strong, good hearts and lives, and we are going to have some meetings on Tuesday nights to learn together as a family. We'll be like a construction team, building a Planned Purity house. [Show the diagram at this time. Respond to all comments.]

We'll talk about what this picture means in our time together, piece by piece.

We'll also do some special events with each of you one-on-one. A couple of nights a month, Dad or I will take you out individually. We have some books to read together, but we can just talk, too.

At some point we'll hold a special ceremony for each of you, when you feel ready to make some more serious commitments to a pure, good life. These will be special private times for our family.

Dad: We wish we would have grown up knowing more about having right hearts and making good choices, so we want to make sure you get all your questions answered. We're happy to be your parents and have the privilege of helping you do well.

Mom: So now we're a team! Does anyone have questions? [Allow time for comments.] OK. We'll meet this coming Tuesday after supper. And now, dessert!

[Sample prayer] Lord, thanks for our family. Help us learn to be pure and clean as you are, in our hearts and our choices. Thanks for this great meal and this great family we love. Amen.

Continue discussion during dessert if the family wants to talk. When you arrive home that night, it would be fun to have a surprise waiting for each of the kids on their pillows. The surprise could be some white chocolate with a note about how you'll be praying for the child, or a small gift. You may want to present a study or storybook for each child this way.

22. *A Follow-Up Meeting with an Older Child*

If you have younger children and older children, you will probably want to have a separate meeting with your older children after the family meeting. This meeting might be needed to invite an older child to a special event such as *Passport 2 Purity* from FamilyLife (see appendix A). The following example features a boy and a dad but can easily be tweaked for daughters as well.

Setting: A favorite restaurant with a table that keeps the conversation private.

Dad: It's really good to have this time together. We're proud of you and how you're growing up. And now that you're [insert age], you're ready for some serious information.

When I was a teenager, my parents had some talks with me about the things in life that really mattered. Even so, I still had a lot to learn when I went out on my own—especially about sex and what it means to be a good man. That's why it's so important to me to tell you information that I wish I knew.

Here's how I see it. When you're born, you get a kind of boat that you travel in for the rest of your life. It's up to you to keep it maintained so you can have a safe trip on the river of your life.

That's why you and I are going to take a weekend trip alone and talk about what it means to be a man of integrity and honor. You may have noticed how some guys respect girls, and other guys don't. In our house, we respect women, and that makes you and I men of honor. And now you're ready to understand more about that.

We're going to _____ [name the hotel, resort, beach house, camp, and so forth]. We're not just going to talk; we're also going to have a lot of fun [swim, see a movie, hike, fish, hunt, canoe, etc.]. But this is a trip just for us guys. What do you think?

Not every child will be excited about the prospect, but explain that this is the beginning of a new season of "grown-up" information. Promise to answer questions anytime, not just during the weekend. Have a plan ready for follow-up meetings, and talk about them with your child at the beginning and end of the weekend. Keep the event private between you and the child unless the child wants to talk about it with someone else. This weekend trip isn't an end to itself, but it is an important mile marker.

Appendix E

Object Lessons

Following are some simple examples of lessons in purity that could coincide with your discussion of the Planned Purity diagram, or to prepare a family member for its introduction later. Remember, teachings don't have to be long or involved, and they don't have to come from this book. They just have to be *personal*. If you put your own touch into your discussions in some way every session, your kids will respond to the material. Be sensitive, listen, notice, and get the family involved.

General Purity
1. Clean Cups, Dirty Dishes
2. Pick Your Poison
3. Be Good to Your Boat
4. Pure Premium

Sexual Purity
5. Apple Analogy
6. Rose Analogy
7. Gift Analogy
8. Treasure Box

Door 1— The Eyes
9. Dark Inside
10. Real or Not? (Movies)
11. Real or Not? (Games)
12. Text the Love
13. Online Study
14. Screen Time Log
15. Pioneer Night

Window 6 — Friends

Window 7 — Technology

Grace

General Purity

1. Clean Cups, Dirty Dishes

Use three white cappuccino cups or large coffee cups for this lesson. Smear the inside of one with mud or melted chocolate to make it look dirty. Smear one with mud or chocolate on the inside and outside. Put the two dirty cups where they can't be seen. Then read Matthew 23:26 to your child(ren): "First clean the inside of the cup and dish, and then the outside also will be clean."

Now, talk about how we have to start from the inside out to be pure in heart and body. We want to be like the clean cup, with clean thoughts and plans (inside), and clean actions as well (outside). Discuss how sometimes we can look clean on the outside, but inside we are full of wrong thoughts and selfishness. If we don't have a pure heart inside, what will eventually happen? (Pull out the dirty cup here.) Our thoughts and plans start to affect what we do. For example, we think about how much we want to hit someone, and then we do. Or we think about how much we want a candy bar, and then we swipe it from the grocery. Now our cup is dirty inside and out. We really need to clean up our act!

Discuss the image of a person who *looks* good, but doesn't *do* good. Then stress how our hearts must be pure to truly *be* good.

2. Pick Your Poison

Put a number of food choices on the kitchen table. Include healthy choices, not-so-healthy choices, and junk food. Discuss which foods will make a person physically the healthiest. Now talk about what "foods" make the heart the healthiest, as it relates to the Five Doors (i.e., gossip is a junk food, encouragement is healthy for the heart). Good food makes your body healthy, just as good spiritual food makes your heart healthy. Bad food in either case can cause sickness or death.

Next, pour a glass of water and put a drop of food coloring into it, pretending it's poison. Put the glass in amongst the other foods. Now talk to the child about how a good parent would never let their child

310

choose something that would harm them. This is true of the body as well as the heart.

3. Be Good to Your Boat

Use a boat or a model to explain that each one of us is given a "purity boat" for use as we travel down the river of life. If we make good choices, we keep the boat free of leaks. Bad choices make our boat spring leaks. How long do you want your boat to last?

4. Pure Premium

Ever notice how items that are "pure" command more attention and more money on grocery shelves? Buy some pure maple syrup and some generic syrup and taste the difference. Why is "extra virgin" olive oil more expensive? (The obvious analogy can be drawn that virginity is very valuable if the child is old enough.) Set a time limit and have a contest to see who can find the most "pure" items at the grocery store in a certain aisle. Why are fresh fruits more than canned fruits with additives? Why is organic meat more costly than "regular"? Think of other examples you may want to use in your family, and discuss the value of purity of all types, whether it applies to groceries, soap, precious metals, or the heart.

Sexual Purity

5. Apple Analogy

Start with a shiny red apple. Explain that the apple is given to you by God as a gift to represent your heart. You are to keep it only for your spouse. What happens every time you give your heart or body to someone else? (Name different relationships, i.e., "This is your first girlfriend – this is your second girlfriend" or "This is a kiss given to someone else – this is holding hands with another boy" and take a bite or two from the apple each time you do.) Would you be proud to give the apple as a gift to your husband or wife now?

You may also let the apple set and get brown, bringing up the lesson on another day to show how giving yourself away leads to the decay of your gift or the decay of your heart.

6. Rose Analogy

As above, you can use a rose or other flower to show how, each time you give yourself away, the flower loses petals. What condition will it be in when you present it to your spouse?

7. Gift Analogy

As above, you may also use a beautifully wrapped gift box or a box containing "treasures." Rip the paper and ribbon of the box to show its condition after various people open it or tear pieces off.

8. Treasure Box

Begin with some kind of valuable-looking box with treasures. (Chocolate is good!) Explain that each piece of chocolate is a "first" (first time holding hands, first time walking on a beach, first long look right into the eyes, first kiss, and so on.) Remove one treasure at a time for every "first" that is spent on someone other than the coming spouse. Explain that we are in control of how many "firsts" we save for our marriage partner at the altar.

Door 1—Eyes

9. Dark Inside

If everyone has their own sunglasses, put them on. Talk about how dark it is when you wear sunglasses inside. Then talk about what it means to have eyes full of darkness, or to be full of darkness, spiritually.

10. Real or Not? (Movies)

For older children—using a cover from a favorite live-action family movie (choose one not based on a true story), ask what things in the movie are real, and what things aren't. (Ideas: story, actors and actresses not portraying real people, actors' portrayed feelings, set, costumes) Discuss why it's important to know what's real and what's not. How do movies shape our thoughts about things? Do we sometimes believe that something "fake" is real? Computer graphic imaging, for example, distorts real images into fake images, or vice versa.

Plugged In (Focus on the Family online publication) offers discussions for specific movies. Ken Gire's book, *Reflections on the Movies*, goes a little deeper for parents.

11. Real or Not? (Games)

Again, with older children, discuss a favorite video game. Obviously, the game is animated, but what about the game is very real? (Ideas: our heart races when we're excited, our reactions when we "shoot" a character, our desire to play on and on) God meant for us to live real lives, not just lives on computer. Are there ways we can enjoy our favorite games and still stay tuned in to reality? How?

12. Text the Love

Have a family challenge to send ten texts of encouragement on a particular day. Messages must say something specifically uplifting about the recipient. At the end of the day, discuss what happened. If you like, up the ante to challenge each family member to send one encouraging text per day for a week, or month. Make lists of people who might really need a kind word.

13. Online Study

If you have two computers or more, have part of your family go to one part of the house and the other go to another. Have a family discussion of some aspect of a pure heart or body online. Afterwards, have a snack at the table together and talk about what was harder or easier about talking that way. What other understandings could happen in online conversation that could be avoided by talking on the phone? In person?

14. Screen Time Log

Do a family challenge. For a week or a month, write down the amount of minutes spent watching TV or movies. (The same could be done with a computer, games, phone, or all of the above.) At the end of the time period, look at the hours spent. Talk about whether it's too much or okay. Why? How do we decide?

15. Pioneer Night

Do a little online research to find games pioneers played when there was no TV or family entertainment. Then take a tech-free night to play such games, sing songs, or read by candlelight. Discuss how interaction with your family is different from screen time and why it's important to have time where technology is turned off. You may want to make this exercise a regular habit!

Door 2—The Ears

16. Loving Listening

Spend some time listening with your child to their favorite song. Ask them what they like about their song. Now share your favorite song, and tell them why. Absolutely no judgment allowed! (Ideally, limits on music allowed in the family should already be set.) Just listen. What can you learn about your child through the experience? Do this often as tastes change.

If you haven't set limits on music, listening together may bring up discussion points that help prepare a child for coming changes. Make sure you share your own healthy listening habits. Perhaps a general family meeting at some point would help with further discussion on guarding the ears and setting new boundaries, if needed.

17. Cell Phone 101

Spend time letting your child explain how his or her phone works, even if you already know. Ask questions like, "So what do you use that for?" and "Have you ever gotten a text that made you smile/feel bad?" Show an interest in your child's phone conversations and friendships. Discuss how to use the phone for encouragement, for helping others, and dangers of irresponsible use (destroyed friendships, indecent photos being passed along and posted on the Internet, paying for charges for overuse, and so on). Again, listen!

18. Plug Your Ears

Show your children a pair of earplugs. Ask what they'd like to keep out of their ears. Direct the discussion toward things they might hear that could dirty their hearts. What specifically might those things be?

19. CD Frenzy

Gather up a number of CD cases around the house. Take some time to study the covers. What are the photos like? Are they real? (Talk about PhotoShop and airbrushing.) What do they make you think about that person? Who does the person thank? Read some of your favorite lyrics and talk about what they mean.

Door 3—The Breath

20. Tissue Talk

Blow on tissues to remind a child of how the breath is invisible, but we can't live without it. If we get sick, our breath spreads germs, so we use a tissue to cover our mouth and nose when we sneeze.

In the same way, when we care for our lives and others', our breath brings life. But when we only care about ourselves, we pass on germs of selfishness.

21. God's Breath

Blow on tissues to show a small child his invisible breath. Ask if they can see God's breath when the tissues moves—it's their own! Then discuss how God breathed his breath into Adam and that gift has been passed on to us today—we are only alive because we breathe God's breath.

22. Breath Collage

Use magazines, online sources and photos of real people (not exclusively models, movie, music or sports stars) and create a collage of as many types of people as you can find. Include different races, ethnic groups, children, third-world children, babies, pregnant moms, elderly, those with disabilities, family members, and so on. Talk about how we're all made in God's image and loved, and then how we must respect, honor and love others as well, no matter our differences.

Door 4—The Mouth

23. Tie It Up!

Use a bandanna to gently tie over a child's mouth. (This is a good exercise for those "constant chatter" days!) Hint that "maybe there are some times we all need to keep our mouths closed." Then talk about when we should be quiet or what language or unkind words or jokes we should keep to ourselves. Be prepared to be direct and specific when questions arise!

24. Sweet or Sour

Use items like lemon juice, grapefruit juice, vinegar, sugar, honey, chocolate, ultra-sour candy, a strawberry, and so forth to talk about the different tastes and the faces we make when we taste them. How can our words be "sweet" or "sour"? Why does the face we make when we say the words matter? What kinds of words do we think others would like to hear us say? Can we think of any recent examples of "sweet" or "sour" words that came out of our mouths? How are those connected with sweet or sour attitudes? Do we need to ask forgiveness for any of our words?

Door 5—The Skin

25. Hot Potato

Ask how an oven mitt protects a cook or baker. Then discuss how we can use our hands to protect others.

26. Shopping for Love

For older children—have a large *paper* grocery bag handy, along with a few grocery items, including a couple of things that look *very* good, a couple of items that are okay, but not favorites, and a couple that seem a little strange or unfamiliar. Lay the items out and put them in the bag as you ask the following questions:

- Which of these would you want to eat even if you weren't very hungry?

- Which of these would you buy if you were just shopping and not so hungry?

- Which of these would you buy if you hadn't eaten in a week and that's all there was to choose from?

Next, talk about our need to be loved. Just like we'll eat almost anything when we're starved, we sometimes will take attention from anyone if we're feeling needy or lonely. How do we get the right kind of love and attention when we feel that way? (Hopefully, the answer will include family and safe friends.) Talk about who can be trusted to be safe in their loving attention, and why.

Window 1—Focus

27. Service!
Serve a yummy dessert. While you're enjoying it, make a list of all the ways others had to serve in order for you to enjoy the treat. For example, Dad may have made the income to buy the ingredients. Mom may have baked it. What about the farmer who grew the beans for the chocolate or vanilla, or grain for flour? How about the person who experimented to come up with the recipe? See how many more you can think of, and then ask what service can be performed next? (putting dishes in sink, and so on) First person who volunteers gets a second helping of dessert! Talk about how many people serving equals a "sweetness" in so many ways.

Window 2—Vocabulary

28. What Does It Mean?
This simple exercise can be done with note cards. Simply use a marker to write words like *pure, integrity, honor, noble,* and any others you'd like your children to be able to define. Let each family member make some of their own if you like. Or, if your children are ready, write down some terms more closely related to relationships or sexuality, i.e., "going out," "breaking up," "dating," "hot," "cool," and other modern slang. (Be prepared with your sense of humor and dictionary,

and remind your children that there are no "dumb" answers.) So many of us know so little of what the words we use really mean.

This exercise could also take the form of cards at the kitchen table, picking one up per night for discussion.

Window 3—Modesty

29. Advertising Analysis

Start by cutting some pictures out of a fashion magazine that, in your household's opinion, do not reflect modesty. Now compare those clothes to the clothes in your wardrobe. How does your wardrobe differ? What are some changes that may need to be made? How do we know what is modest or appropriate, biblically and in our personal household?

30. Bikini Bare

(NOTE: This is for families who have decided that bikinis are too bare for women.)

Borrow a bikini. Now, compare it to a bra and underwear of the same size. How different are they? What's the difference? Why can one be worn in public and the other can't? Should bikinis be okay if underwear isn't? Why or why not?

One mom I know took the opportunity to use this lesson in the middle of an argument with her preteen daughter. The daughter was whining the question, "Why can't I wear a bikini?" Her mother said, "Okay. Go into your room and take off everything except your panties and underwear. Then we'll go to the beach." The daughter stopped dead in her tracks with a thoughtful, "Oh." It may work for you, too!

31. Fashion Power

Look online or check out books that show how fashions have changed in the last hundred years or so. Have fun looking at "crazy" styles, and talk about what is modest. (Bathing suits from the 1920s provide a great conversation starter!) Look at both women's and men's clothing. Note how clothing has become more androgynous, and how appealing femininity and modesty can be. How have these changes affected what we believe about men and women? About beauty? About sex and temptation? Look at the body types of models as well. Explain that almost all photos now are retouched to create smaller thighs, perfect faces, and other features. How does this make real people feel? Remind your child that he or she is accepted and loved as they are because of who they are, and that God finds them beautiful or handsome.

Window 4—Education

32. Private Question Journal

At times a preteen or teen might be close-mouthed about sexuality, either feeling it's a private matter or not feeling quite comfortable about talking with you face-to-face. In that case, it might be a good idea to start a Private Question Journal for that particular child. Let him or her know where the book will be (in a private spot in their room where only you or they can find it). Tell your child that they may ask ANY question by writing it at the top of a page in the book and replacing it in their hiding spot. When they're out of the house, you will check the book and write answers whenever they need them. This private means of communication may start to open doors for personal talks later on.

Window 5—Boy/Girl Interaction

33. Staying Afloat

Visit the ocean, a lake or wide river. Talk about how much fun it is to swim, boat, surf, fish, and so forth on the water. Then discuss the rules for safely enjoying the water (life jacket, good weather, knowing how to swim). Discuss what happens if rules for water recreation aren't followed. Talk about our emotions and desires and compare them to the bodies of water. We love how they feel, but what rules should we follow so we don't get carried away? (Ideas: parent's help or soothing music when you're afraid at night, talking to the opposite sex like brothers or sisters instead of romantic partners, hitting a pillow instead of someone else if you're angry, and so on.)

34. Sticking Together

Begin this example for older children by talking about why too many romantic escapades ("going out" and breaking up) might be better practice for divorce than a happy marriage someday. Tear off a piece of duct tape (about a foot) and stick it to someone's clothing, saying, "This is what happened the first time you give your heart away or fall in love. It sticks well, doesn't it?" Then stick the tape to another person. "But if you get bored with that person, you tear off the tape and stick it to them." Keep removing and reapplying the tape until it doesn't stick anymore.

Now talk about how commitment works, and about the fact that, the more we give ourselves away, the greater possibility that we won't be able to "stick" with a marriage partner.

35. Wild Fire

This lesson is similar to "Staying Afloat," above. Spend time next to a fireplace or campfire. Notice how the fire looks beautiful, provides warmth and light. But what happens if the fire gets outside of its boundaries and falls on grass, leaves, paper or carpet? Look online at pictures of a forest fire aftermath or a burn victim. Burns are some of the hardest, most painful wounds to treat because they have to be constantly scrubbed. Fire spreads fast if it gets out of control, especially in dry conditions.

Human sexual desire is like that. We love feeling wanted and precious by a boy or girl, but especially in certain conditions (being alone, listening to romantic music or watching a sensual movie or video) our desires can break through their boundaries and get out of control, spreading fast. If we get burned, we'll be hurt deeply. Discuss this analogy as it applies to your child at his or her age.

Window 6—Friends

36. Good Friend, Bad Friend

Do some role playing with your children to help them explore how a good friend or bad friend acts. Be a friend who says, "Hey, let's try to steal something from the dollar store. It'll be fun!" or "I'd like to have you come to my house to play, but I have to ask my mom first." Let the child answer with what he would say in that situation. Then move from such obvious examples to friends who say things like, "Jason is such a loser," or, "I hate math. Mr. Seaton is the worst teacher," or "Wasn't Mike awesome today in gym? Did you see him make that basket?" Talk about which friends are best, and how to turn a conversation to something positive when negative or gossipy things are said.

37. Family Friendship

Friendship bracelets are easy to make, simply by braiding yarn or embroidery thread. (If you're good at the fancier patterns, you can plan your own family craft fest!) The purpose of the bracelets in this lesson is to make bracelets that only the members of your family have, creating a kind of team spirit and security. As you're braiding away, talk about how your family is a team and some of the things you like best about your family, the things that make it unique.

Window 7—Technology

38. Because the TV Said So

With younger children who watch TV, talk about some of their favorite commercial products they have seen. Why do they like them? Do the TV commercials always tell the truth? Why are commercials made? Why or why can't we trust them?

39. Hero or Idol?

For older children, find a (modest) poster of a movie star, singer or pro sports figure that your whole family is familiar with, but does not know personally. Now, begin to list everything you know about that person. The list will probably be short or have nothing to do with the person's character. Next, work on a list of what you don't know about them (i.e., Have they ever taken drugs? Are they a good father or mother? Do they love their family? Are they unselfish? How do they spend their money?) From there, talk about how we choose heroes sometimes just because of they way they look, without knowing much about them.

Who is someone your family could put on a poster whom you all really know something about? Is there a teacher, family member, or friend about whom you could answer those questions? Who is really worthy of being a hero and why?

Examples: Have pictures available of parents as kids and show how they became examples at church or school or in their communities or groups, even as children. It's good for the family to remember that they even *were* children once!

The Fence—Grace

40. Wiped Clean

Use a white erase board or a regular chalkboard or even a piece of paper. Write a personal statement about something bad that could be done (i.e., "Today I cheated on a test," "I pulled my sister's hair," "I made fun of Jamie," "I yelled at my husband," and so on). Make sure they could apply to anyone in the family. Then talk about how when we feel sorry and say so, grace and forgiveness wipes our failures away. Erase the statements one by one as you explain, or crumple the papers and throw them in the trash. If anyone would like to ask forgiveness for anything, allow them to do so and have the family show grace and forgiveness with hugs.

Appendix F

Bishop Family Contracts

These contracts are family agreements that we've used successfully in our home. We tried to craft them so they were clear and reflected our values, our desire to protect and our love for our kids.

Your contracts don't have to look anything like ours, but reading these examples will help you begin to consider how yours may develop. Presenting your document to the family may evoke excitement, eye-rolling, interest or groans. No matter what, explain that having something written down will prevent misunderstandings and help the family run better. As everyone begins to understand the family goals, a spirit of teamwork can ensue that is positive and helpful.

You may want to keep your documents in a family notebook. Or you could frame and hang them. Or you may want everyone to have a copy to refer to. Gently refer back to your contracts as needed, and remind everyone of the benefits of pursuing a pure heart and life.

Contract A

PREPARATION FOR COURTSHIP AGREEMENT

*N*ote: *These guidelines are for the high school years as a healthy, balanced friendship develops. We call them "preparation for courtship," since at this point education takes a priority over relationships that can distract from life goals.*

Adherence to and submission to these guidelines may result in more freedom as time passes. Failure to comply may result in further boundaries.

The main qualities we are looking to develop and prove will be strong, loving, and respectful family ties, obedience, honesty and respect of time, since (girl) and (boy) have already set very strict boundaries for physical interaction. All these disciplines contribute not only in the present situation but in other relationships that develop.

Preparation for Courtship Guard Rails

Open door communication: All phone and other communication is appropriate for any ears in the family, and emails and instant messages are open to family review. Phone and computer interaction are privileges, not rights, and will sometimes be shut down for a time for scheduled quiet/down time or for family interaction.

Communication Guidelines

- Communication (phone and computer) days off per week: Tuesday, Thursday

- Number of calls per weekday (excluding off days): 2

- Phone time during weekday: 30 minutes for all friends/(boys) limited to 15 (50%)

- Instant messaging: 30 minutes for all friends/limit 15 for (boy/ girl)

- Weekends: 1 hour phone/1 hour computer interaction (limit ½ hour each for boy/girl)

- Boy does the calling during week when he is free

- No calls during homework

- One form of communication at a time

- Absolutely no calls or interaction after 9 p.m.

Other Guidelines

- No prayer/romantic feelings, pet names, or saying, "I love you." The goal is to guard the friendship.

- No exclusive or "coupling" dates; i.e., any gathering where you are paired off because others are paired off.

- No frontal hugs with males.

- Dance discipline: (girl) will complete her ballet training four nights a week as a non-negotiable. Youth group and dance are approved activities this year. Extra time is family time.

- If you are getting a ride after youth group with the boy's parents, no sitting next to the boy.

- Two social events outside youth group a month at most; this includes outings after youth group. Girlfriends can visit or sleep over often.

- Continuing communication between parents of families as needed.

Thanks for respecting the rules we feel as necessary for our family's health and well-being. We appreciate your patience and friendship!

Contract B

HOUSE RULES

*N*OTE: *In our personal experience we found that starting with very specific rules on paper helped, but in day-to-day acting out we offered a lot of leniency as long as attitudes were good. We wanted to share duties, yes, but even more important was everyone's attitude. The heart is what we're all really trying to shape, so we recommend not being a "family rule Nazi."*

These boundaries are being set to encourage our family to find more opportunities to talk together, work together, and play together. They are also to encourage us to respect and honor each other and to work together cheerfully to be good stewards of the many good things God has given us. "Everything is permissible"--but not everything is beneficial. "Everything is permissible"--but not everything is constructive. (See 1 Corinthians 10:23.)

There will be grace and flexibility in these rules, but we ask that everyone adhere to them as much as possible and respectfully ask for exceptions when needed, with a cheerful heart no matter the situation. This should help make our home more peaceful and help us to interact better day to day.

TECHNOLOGY

- No computer/screen 5-9 on school nights

- No movies during week (unless family night)

- Two DVD movies per weekend (one viewing)

- Xbox: Dance pad program for workouts anytime (with parents' approval)

NOTE: Exceptions on computer time must be approved by Mom and Dad; parents may also need exceptions for business and otherwise

HOMEWORK

- ALL homework must be finished before other activities (volunteering, staying overnight, youth group, pool, and so on).

BEDTIME

- Lights out by 9:30 for (12-year-old), 10:30 for (15-year-old)

- No phone after 9:30

TRASH

- Monday evening: (12-year-old) take out all trash and put by the curb, empty recycle basin

- Thursday evening: (15-year-old) take out all trash and recycling to curb

MEALTIME HELP

Weekday dinners: Since mealtimes vary, we will expect turns to be taken in cleaning up after meals. Mom will assist as needed. Meals will be at 5:30 on Wednesday and Thursday because of evening activities.

- Dessert master: (12-year-old) will provide at least one dessert per week

- Bread master: (15-year-old) will provide one homemade bread per week

DISHWASHER

We will expect CHEERFUL unloading and reloading of the dishwasher whenever asked. We will all get a chance to help with this, but we will not be taking actual turns. Just be prepared to help when asked without complaining.

LAUNDRY

- Mon:

- Tues: Dad shirts

- Wed:

- Thurs: (12-year-old)

- Fri: (14-year-old)

- Sat: Mom and Dad (may flex as needed)

GUESTS or OVERNIGHT STAYS

- Parents must be contacted at least 24 hours in advance.

EXTRA EVENTS

- Activities outside regular youth group or volunteering must be approved by a parent. Drivers must also be parent-approved. No more than two extra special events per month.

NOTE: Any of these guidelines may be changed or added to as we find need to.

"Do everything without complaining or arguing." See Philippians 2:14.

"A cheerful heart has a continual feast." See Proverbs 15:15.

"God loves a cheerful giver." See 2 Corinthians 9:7.

"Whatever you do, work at it with all your heart, as working for the Lord, not for men." See Colossians 3:23.

Contract C

TECHNOLOGY AGREEMENT

*I*MPORTANT NOTE: *Again, DO NOT feel you must use our guidelines. This example is given only as a jumping off point. Consider each point in light of your individual family situation and child. Be very intentional in reviewing each boundary, then introduce with a friendly but businesslike meeting. Enforce your "guard rails" with confidence.*

OUR PRIORITIES:
God
Family
Work/School
Friends

FACEBOOK

- No social networking without mom and dad's access. If we don't have the password, it shouldn't exist.

- NO obscenity. If someone sends obscenity, immediately delete it and block the person if it continues.

- Photos must be appropriate. No cleavage, sexy poses, unnecessary posing with girlfriends, bra straps, and so on. If you are in doubt, leave it out.

- Limit the number of photos on your Facebook. Limit 15 events with 20 pictures each. Choose the best, leave the rest.

- Limit number of friends to 110 + family and mentors.

- Applications must be appropriate. Check with Mom and Dad as needed.

- Remember, Mom and Dad will be checking pages regularly. If we ask you to remove something, the instruction should be received with a good attitude.

- Time limits: half hour segments. Use your time wisely.

PHONE

- No sending pictures unless to parents or sis.

- Purposeful texting. Limit "What's up?" "I don't know. What's up with you?" type interaction.

- Purposeful calling. Time limits for boy/girl conversation. No calls after 9:30 unless approved by Mom or Dad.

- No phone calls at table or during family time (including car time or family trips in car, and so on).

DISCIPLINE

- Three warnings will be issued for negative attitude in following these guidelines. Upon the third warning, the device involved will be off limits for 24 hours. Days will be added for further infractions.

NOTES

Chapter 1
Planned Purity

1. Jan Faull, "Is My Child Having Sex?" (Parents.com, November 2004), http://www.parents.com/parenting/better-parenting/teen-agers/is-my-child-having-sex/ (accessed May 6, 2010).

2. Bill Albert, Sarah Brown, and Christine Flanigan, eds. (2003), 14 and Younger: The Sexual Behavior of Young Adolescents (Summary) (Washington, DC: National Campaign to Prevent Teen Pregnancy), pp. 8-9, http://www.thenationalcampaign.org/resources/pdf/pubs/14summary.pdf (accessed June 28, 2010).

3. Gene Veith, "Sex and the Evangelical Teen" (Worldmag.com, August 11, 2007), http://www.worldmag.com/articles/13208 (accessed May 6, 2010).

Chapter 2
Loving Relationships

1. Bill Albert. (2009). With One Voice (lite): A 2009 Survey of Adults and Teens on Parental Influence, Abstinence, Contraception, and the Increase in the Teen Birth Rate (Washington, DC: National Campaign to Prevent Teen Pregnancy) p. 2, http://www.thenationalcampaign.org/resources/pdf/pubs/WOV_Lite_2009.pdf (accessed June 28, 2010).

2. Lynn Okagaki, *Journal of Applied Developmental Psychology* (2000) quoted in Janice Shaw Crouse, "What Works: Why Teens Choose Purity" (Christianity.com, n.d.), http://www.christianity.com/christian%20living/features/1394540/ (accessed May 6, 2010).

Chapter 3
Purity Defined

1. Proverbs 4:23

2. Matthew 23:26

3. Exodus 25, Leviticus 24:7, Malachi 1:11

4. Amy Norton, "Sex of Any Kind Harms Teens Emotionally" (Cape Times, February 9, 2007), http://www.capetimes.co.za/index.php?fArticleId=3671938 (accessed May 6, 2010).

Chapter 4
The Purity Continuum

1. Shana Schutte, "TV and Your Child's Ability to Think and Learn" (focusonthefamily.com, 2007). http://www.focusonthefamily.com/entertainment/mediawise/tv-and-todays-family/tv-and-your-childs-ability-to-think-and-learn.aspx (accessed March 3, 2011).

2. Jerry Ropelato, "Internet Pornography Statistics" (Internet-Filter-Reviews.toptenreviews.com, 2011) http://internet-filter-review.toptenreviews.com/internet-pornography-statistics-pg5.html (accessed February 26, 2011).

3. Seth Lubove, "Sex, Lies and Statistics" (Forbes.com, November 23, 2005) http://www.forbes.com/2005/11/22/internet-pornography-children-cz_sl_1123internet.html (accessed February 23, 2011).

4. Song of Solomon 2:7, 3:5, 8:4

5. Bill Albert, With One Voice (lite) A 2009 Survey of Adults and Teens on Parental Influence, Abstinence, Contraception, and the Increase in the Teen Birth Rate (Washington, DC: National Campaign to Prevent Teen Pregnancy) p. 2, http://www.thenationalcampaign. org/resources/pdf/pubs/WOV_Lite_2009.pdf (accessed June 28, 2010).

Chapter 5
Emotions and Thought Life

1. Beth Moore, *Breaking Free: Making Liberty in Christ a Reality in Life* (Nashville, Tenn.: LifeWay Church Resources, June 1999), p. 193.

2. Karen Newby and Anastasia Snyder, "Teen Risk Behavior" (Ohioline, 2009), p. 6, http://ohioline.osu.edu/hyg-fact/5000/pdf/5240EP.pdf (accessed May 6, 2010).

Chapter 6
The Inner Person—A Pure Heart

1. Philippians 4:8

2. John Piper, *Don't Waste Your Life* (Wheaton, Ill.: Crossway, 2003), p. 120.

3. "Pornography" (The Free Dictionary by Farlex, Inc.), http:// legal-dictionary.thefreedictionary.com/pornography (accessed June 22, 2010).

4. Sonya Thompson, "One in Three Boys Heavy Porn Users, Study Shows" (Sciencedaily.com, February 25, 2007), http://www.sciencedaily.com/releases/2007/02/070223142813.htm (accessed May 6, 2010).

5. Albert Mohler, Jr., "First Person: The Culture of Pornography" (sbcbaptistpress.com, December 28, 2005), http://www.sbcbaptist-press.org/bpnews.asp?ID=22367 (accessed May 6, 2010).

6. Jerry Ropelato, "Internet Pornography Statistics" (internet-filter-review.toptenreviews.com, 2011), http://internet-filter-review.toptenreviews.com/internet-pornography-statistics.html (accessed May 3, 2011).

7. Diary and Autobiography of John Adams, ed. L.H.Butterfield et. al. (Cambridge, Mass.: Belknap Press/Harvard University Press, 1962), 4:123.

8. Andrew Lloyd Weber, "Phantom of the Opera—Music of the Night lyrics" (Any Song Lyrics), http://www.anysonglyrics.com/lyrics/p/Phantom-Of-The-Opera/Music-of-the-Night-Lyrics.htm (accessed May 6, 2010).

9. Associated Press, "Lawsuit: 'Grand Theft Auto' Led Teen to Kill'" (Foxnews.com, February 16, 2005), http://www.foxnews.com/story/0,2933,147722,00.html (accessed May 6, 2010).

10. Tom Neven, "Teaching Kids to Kill," Plugged In, July 2006, p. 3.

11. Associated Press, "MySpace Teen Who Fled to Middle East Breaks Up with Arab Beau on 'Dr. Phil'" (Foxnews.com, November 27, 2007), http://www.foxnews.com/story/0,2933,313145,00.html (accessed May 6, 2010).

12. Proverbs 4:25

13. Matthew 11:15

14. Bob Smithouser, "Clearing a Channel for God's Still, Small Voice," Plugged In, August 2005, p. 12.

15. "MTV Is Rock Around the Clock," *Philadelphia Enquirer*, November 3, 1982, quoted in Joe Schimmel, "MTV" (Simi Valley, Cal.: Goodfight Ministries), http://www.goodfight.org/a_m_mtv_1.html (accessed June 28, 2010).

16. Proverbs 4:20

17. Job 27:3

18. Proverbs 12:10

19. James 3:8

20. Klayne I. Rasmussen, "Does Sarcasm Belong in Our Relationships?" (Meridianmagazine.com, 2006), http://www.meridianmagazine.com/familyconnections/060404sarcasm.html (accessed May 6, 2010).

21. Tertullian. Apologeticum (The Tertullian Project), 39:7, http://www.tertullian.org/anf/anf03/anf03-05.htm#39_7 (accessed May 6, 2010).

22. James 3:2

23. Matthew 15:11

24. Virginia Satir, BrainyQuote.com (Xplore Inc., 2010), http://www.brainyquote.com/quotes/quotes/v/virginiasa175185.html (accessed June 28, 2010).

25. Ecclesiastes 3:1, 5b

Chapter 7
The Outer Person—An Honorable Life

1. Fredrick L. Collins (TheQuotationsPage.com), http://www.quotationspage.com/quotes/frederick_l_collins/ (accessed June 28, 2010).

2. Ecclesiastes 11:8-9

3. Philippians 2:3

4. Thomson Reuters, "Forbes: America's Richest 400" (moneycentral.msn.com, September 23, 2005), http://moneycentral.msn.com/content/invest/forbes/p129955.asp (accessed June 28, 2010).

5. Nancy Gibbs, "The Good Samaritans" (time.com, December 19, 2005), http://www.time.com/time/magazine/article/0,9171,1142278-1,00.html (accessed June 28, 2010).

6. Song of Solomon 2:7, 3:5, 8:4

7. National Center for Missing and Exploited Children press release (missingkids.com, January 27, 2005), http://www.missingkids.com/missingkids/servlet/NewsEventServlet?LanguageCountry=en_US&PageId=1865 (accessed May 3, 2011).

8. 1 Timothy 5:1b, 2

9. Corrie ten Boom, *The Hiding Place* (Washington Depot, Conn.: Chosen Books, 1971), p. 31.

10. Katie Hintz-Zambrano, "Miss USA Contestants Wear Ultra Sexy Lingerie for Official Promo Photos" (stylelist.com, May10, 2010) http://www.stylelist.com/2010/05/10/miss-usa-lingerie-photos/ (accessed June 30, 2010).

11. 1 Timothy 5:1b, 2

12. Proverbs 6:25

13. Proverbs 5-7

14. Chad Eastham, *Guys Like Girls Who...* (Nashville, Tenn.: Thomas Nelson, 2008), pp. 26-42, http://books.google.com/books? id=QlUPwd8AUpIC&pg=PA29&lpg=PA29&dq=chad+eastham+gu ys+initiators&source=bl&ots=eo_AssXNdb&sig=RDZgJApRuaGG qcRDyThxZsmNfcw&hl=en&ei=7rgoTPHfJoH78Ab2o5nmDw&sa =X&oi=book_result&ct=result&resnum=1&ved=0CBIQ6AEwAA #v=onepage&q&f=false (accessed June 28, 2010).

15. The National Campaign to Prevent Teen Pregnancy, Parent Power: What Parents Need to Know and Do to Help Prevent Teen Pregnancy (Washington, DC: 2001), http://www.thenationalcampaign. org/resources/pdf/pubs/ParentPwr.pdf (accessed May 15, 2012).

16. The National Campaign to Prevent Teen Pregnancy, 14 and Younger: The Sexual Behavior of Young Adolescents (Washington, DC: 2003) p. 11, http://thenationalcampaign.org/resources/pdf/ pubs/14summary.pdf (accessed May 15, 2012).

17. Joy Lanzendorfer, "It's 10 PM, Do You Know? Kids Aren't Having Casual Sex, They're Having Oral Sex," (North Bay Bohemian, October 17-23, 2002), http://www.metroactive.com/papers/ sonoma/10.17.02/sex-0242.html (accessed May 15, 2012).

18. Pam Stenzel, in a speech at the Religious Education Conference, 2005. Quoted in Ellie Hidalgo, "Talking to Teens About Sex," (the-tidings.com, March 11, 2005) http://www.the-tidings. com/2005/0311/abstinence.htm (accessed July 21, 2010).

19. Fox News, "Missouri Woman Indicted in MySpace Bullying Case that Ended in Teen Suicide" (foxnews.com, May 15, 2008), http://www.foxnews.com/story/0,2933,356056,00.html (accessed June 28, 2010).

20. pureHOPE, "What Every Parent Needs to Know About ... Wireless Technology & Mobile Entertainment" (booklet), http://www.nationalcoalition.org/icareArticlesDetail.asp?id=144 (accessed July 22, 2010).

21. Gigi Stone, "'Sexting' Teens Can Go Too Far," (abcnews.go.com, March 13, 2009), http://abcnews.go.com/Technology/WorldNews/sexting-teens/story?id=6456834&page=1 (accessed July 21, 2010).

22. Amy Wallace, "Jamie Lee Curtis: True Thighs" (more.com, April 2009), http://www.more.com/2049/2464-jamie-lee-curtis-true-thighs (accessed July 21, 2010).

23. Gil Reavill, Smut: A Sex-Industry Insider (and Concerned Father) Says Enough is Enough (New York, NY: The Penguin Group, 2005). Quoted in Plugged In, November 2005, p. 10.

Chapter 8
Wisdom from Mentors

1. Romans 12:3b

Chapter 9
Authentic Parenting

1. Kristin A. Moore, Lina Guzman, Elizabeth Hair, Laura Lippman, and Sarah Garrett, "Parent-Teen Relationships and Interactions: Far More Positive Than Not," Publication #2004-25 (Washington, DC: ChildTrends.org, December 2004), http//:www.childtrends.org/files/parent_teen_RB.pdf) (accessed June 28, 2010).

2. The National Campaign to Prevent Teen Pregnancy, "10 Tips for Parents to Help their Children Avoid Teen Pregnancy." Quoted in "Families Matter" (Newark, Del.: University of Delaware Cooperative Extension, n.d.), http://ag.udel.edu/extension/fam/FM/issue/teen-pregnancy.htm (accessed Dec. 29, 2011).

Chapter 11
Surrounding Grace

1. Matthew 18:22

2. Luke 23:34

Chapter 12
Ages and Stages

1. 1 Corinthians 6:12

JENNIE BISHOP'S BOOKS

All Jennie Bishop's books are available online through www.purity-works.org or www.jenniebishop.com.

Children's picture books

The Princess and the Kiss (with or without audio CD), Warner Press
The Squire and the Scroll (with or without audio CD), Warner Press
The Garden Wall, Warner Press
The Crayon Kingdom, Warner Press
Jesus Must Be Really Special, Standard Publishing
The Princess and the Kiss: The Three Gifts of Christmas, Warner Press

For parents to use with children

Life Lessons from The Princess and the Kiss, Revive Our Hearts
Life Lessons from The Squire and the Scroll, Revive Our Hearts
Preschool Purity of Heart
I Want to Teach My Child About Manners, Standard Publishing

ABOUT PURITYWORKS

I n 2005, Randy and Jennie Bishop founded **PurityWorks®** as a not-for-profit organization devoted to assisting parents who asked, "How can I train my kids to be pure when I haven't made such good choices myself?" **Planned Purity®** is a methodology that uses a simple house diagram to explain how purity is defined and developed ideally in an individual's life.

PurityWorks exists **to equip, encourage and empower parents to create unique strategies for purity in each family.** This development naturally leads to each parent discovering how to be make their lives the best "training videos" in purity that their children can view.

The individual concepts introduced in Planned Purity training are familiar, but connected in a new way that provides an "Aha!" moment for parents trying to connect the dots. **Planned Purity transforms inaccurate definitions and understandings, giving parents new initiative** to make changes in family life that effectively build a household of purity.

Planned Purity has been presented for years in speaking engagements and seminars. **This book contains all the information usually presented in a live event for a parent to study and practice at home.** Reading *Planned Purity* can provide the impetus to begin a small group study, or groups and events for children and parents using Jennie Bishop's *The Princess and the Kiss, The Squire and the Scroll,* and the accompanying Life Lessons.

Please visit the PurityWorks web site at www.purityworks.org for more information, and to sign up for the monthly PurityWords newsletter with tips for purity in each issue. Through the web site you may also purchase materials by Jennie Bishop, inquire about speaking engagements, and have an opportunity to partner with us financially.

CPSIA information can be obtained at www.ICGtesting.com
Printed in the USA
LVOW121648010812

292532LV00009B/68/P